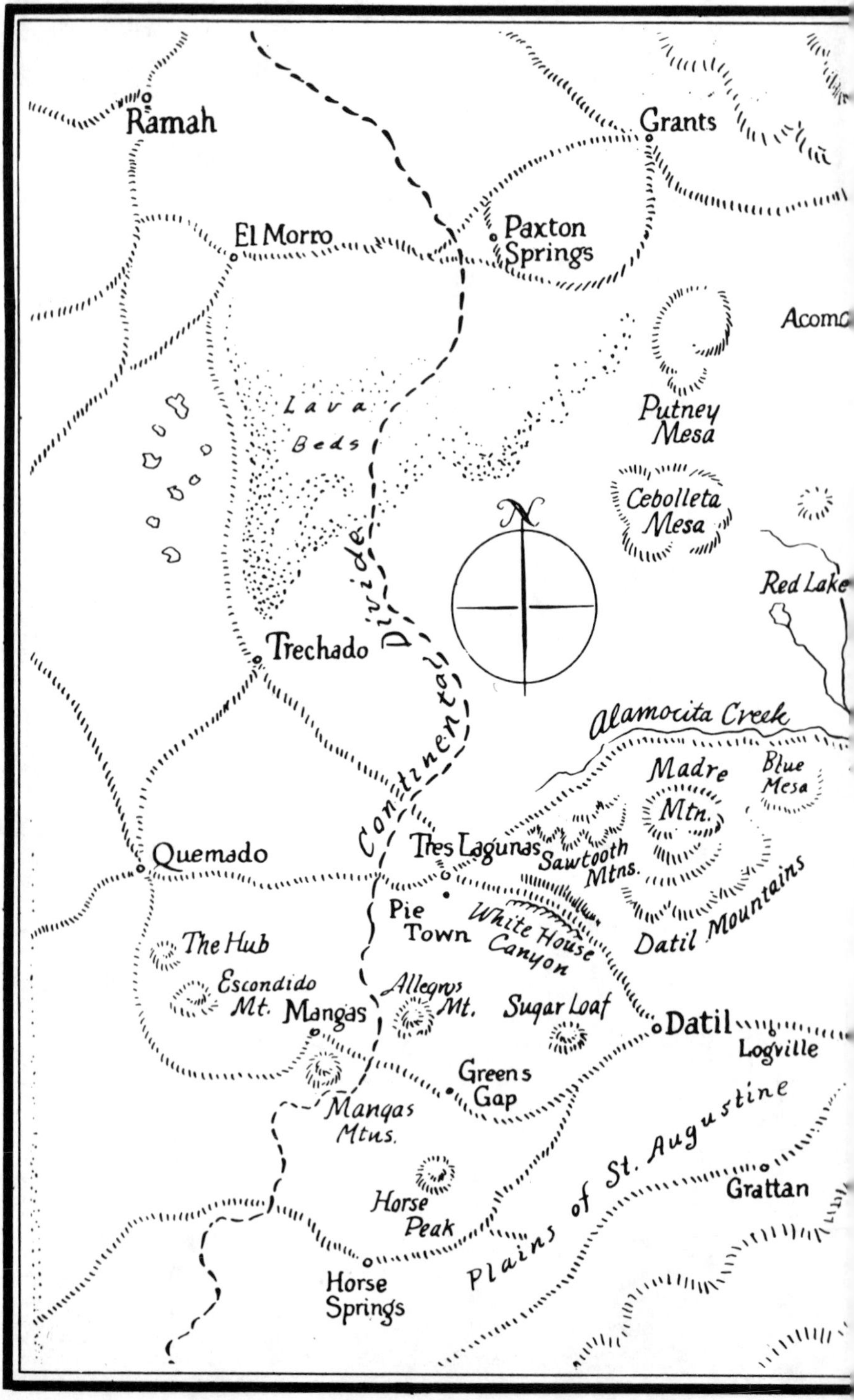

Ramah
Grants
El Morro
Paxton Springs
Acoma
Putney Mesa
Lava Beds
Cebolleta Mesa
N
Red Lake
Trechado
Continental Divide
Alamocita Creek
Madre Mtn.
Blue Mesa
Quemado
Tres Lagunas
Sawtooth Mtns.
Datil Mountains
Pie Town
White House Canyon
The Hub
Escondido Mt.
Mangas
Allegros Mt.
Sugar Loaf
Datil
Logville
Greens Gap
Mangas Mtns.
Plains of St. Augustine
Grattan
Horse Peak
Horse Springs

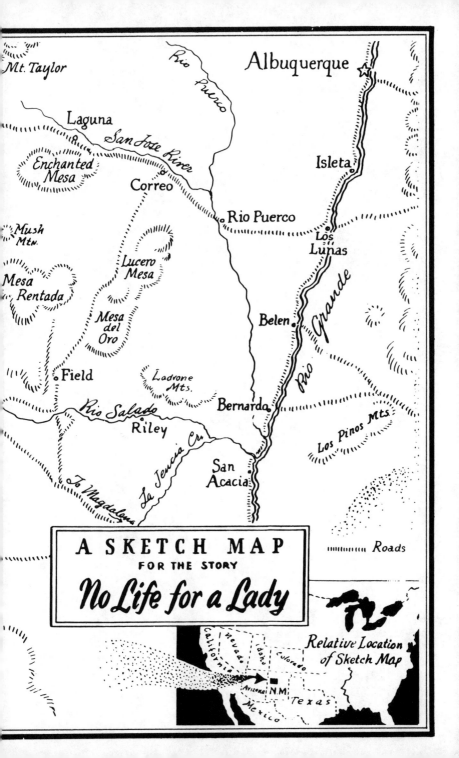

No Life for a Lady

BY AGNES MORLEY CLEAVELAND

ILLUSTRATIONS BY EDWARD BOREIN

University of Nebraska Press
Lincoln   London

First Bison Book printing: 1977

Most recent printing indicated by first digit below:
                                                9   10

Library of Congress Cataloging in Publication Data

Cleaveland, Agnes Morley, 1874–
   No life for a lady.

   Reprint of the ed. published by Houghton Mifflin,
Boston, in series: Life in America series.
   1.   Frontier and pioneer life—New Mexico.
2.   Ranch life—New Mexico.   3.   New Mexico—History.
4.   Cleaveland, Agnes Morley, 1874– 5.   Pioneers—
New Mexico—Biography.   I.   Title.   II.   Series: Life
in America series.
F801.C62   1977   978.9'04'0924 [B]   77–6825
ISBN 0–8032–5868–2

Reprinted by special arrangement with Houghton Mifflin
Company.
Manufactured in the United States of America

Dedicated to

All those Pioneer Women whose stories can never be adequately told but whose courage, endurance and determination to hold fast to their highest ideals contributed to the making of

AMERICA

Contents

IV. Ray the Cattle King

V. A New Era and an Old Ranch

NO LIFE FOR A LADY

While CLAY ALLISON
SHOT UP THE TOWN

Forty little girls in white dresses, each carrying a flag and wearing across her chest a ribbon inscribed with the name of a State of the Union, and eight other little girls, similarly clad except that each of their ribbons bore the name of a Territory, clambered down from the running-gear of a high-wheeled ore-wagon upon which tiers of planks had been fashioned into lengthwise seats.

Behind the wagon — the word 'float' had not come into general use — the rest of the parade was falling out of line, the uniformed men wiping their brows and drawing deep sighs of relief. The two-mile dust-choked walk to the cemetery in overpowering heat had been an ordeal.

There were no women among the marchers, nor was there thought in anyone's mind that a day would come when the 'gentler sex' would parade down the middle of a street brazenly inviting public gaze. No cause could have been thought of sufficient importance to justify such debasement of God's intentions concerning women.

The last little girl to descend from the bunting-covered ore-wagon wore across her ten-year-old chest a ribbon bearing the legend TERRITORY OF NEW MEXICO. She was trying to conceal the fact that she had been crying. A man in a battered Civil War uniform spoke kindly.

'You put no flowers on my father's grave,' she told him.

There followed a hurried consultation: the commander gave a crisp order. 'Re-form ranks. By some mistake the grave of our comrade-in-arms William Raymond Morley has been overlooked. The procession, except for the little girls, will return to the cemetery.'

It was the year 1884 in Las Vegas, New Mexico, and I was the little girl wearing the New Mexico banner. I had grabbed for it when the ribbons were distributed lest another claim the honor of representing New Mexico. My father had been accidentally shot the year before.

After this Decoration Day incident, my mother told me more of the family history.

When my father was seventeen, he marched 'with Sherman to the sea.' He was still wearing parts of his army uniform, for lack of better clothing, when at the close of the war he entered Iowa State University and there took a two-year course in Civil Engineering. There too he met Ada McPherson, who became my mother, a golden-haired sprightly girl with a musical talent which, added to her other carefully cultivated 'social graces,' made her something of a reigning belle. Moreover, the fact that her father, Judge Marcus McPherson, was a figure in Iowa politics, gave her standing in the eyes of her classmates. She was regarded, therefore, as slightly quixotic for noticing the uncouth soldier boy who milked the president's cow in part payment for his tuition. It was some time before her secret feeling of superiority was knocked out of her.

The railroad-construction era was just beginning, and my father recognized opportunity. He went to Denver, found himself a day too late to join a surveying party, and walked forty miles to overtake it. Impressed with his determination, the engineer in charge of the party hired him — but as axeman, the lowliest and hardest job in a surveying crew. Six weeks later my father was himself in charge of the party through sheer ability not only as an engineer but, of even greater importance, as a leader who could command loyal support and devotion from those with whom he worked.

In an incredibly short time, he was chief construction engineer of the Santa Fé Railroad, having accomplished some of the most outstanding feats of railroad engineering then known, the marvelously scenic Glorieta Pass in northern New Mexico, the La Veta Pass in Colorado, and the original Raton Pass connecting Colorado and New Mexico.

The Raton Pass made railroad history. In that day it was not considered possible that a railroad train could negotiate so steep a grade. But after it was an accomplished fact the president of the Santa Fé was quoted as saying, 'Morley builds railroads with one hand, fights Indians with the other, and lives on the bark of trees while doing it.' He might well have added, 'with a grin.'

His first reconnaissance over the Raton Mountains was made in company of 'Uncle' Dick Wooton, famous scout and trader who, in turn, had learned the route from expeditions made with Kit Carson.

The rising young railroad engineer returned to Iowa in 1872 to fetch his bride. My mother came to New Mexico on her wedding journey in a stagecoach under armed escort. Her destination was the little town of Cimarron in Colfax County in the extreme northeastern corner of the Territory.

It was presumed at the time that Cimarron would be a railroad center, and the little Mexican plaza on the banks of the Cimarron River had burst into joyous expectancy — only to be grimly disappointed when political and not topographical conditions decreed otherwise. During the political struggle over the routing of the new railroad — a struggle that became known as the 'Colfax County War' — my father had an interlude of retirement from railroad construction to become manager of the Maxwell Grant. This tract of a mere two million acres, title to which extended back to the old Spanish land grants, had originally been acquired by Lucien B. Maxwell, who, having started for California in the Gold Rush days of '49, paused in New Mexico and, like many another since his time, decided to stay.

He had built what was then considered a mansion, as, by comparison with its humbler neighbors, it indeed was. I remember it well, for I was born in the Maxwell House, and even after my family no longer occupied it, I returned in the years that immediately followed to make protracted visits with the family friends who did. Two-storied, wide-verandaed, with adobe walls nearly four feet thick, it formed one entire side of the town's cottonwood-shaded plaza. Its furnishings, however, were the real wonder. They had been freighted from Leavenworth, Kansas, and St. Louis, Missouri, by ox and mule team. There is extant some correspondence between Maxwell and 'Uncle' Dick Wooton in which the latter complains that he was inadequately paid for carting the furniture over the Raton Mountains. Considering the character of those mountains and of that furniture, 'Uncle' Dick might well have had some basis for his plaint.

I recall four large square pianos, massive beds and chairs, huge oil paintings in gilt frames. There was silver, and crystal, and fine china. One room was set aside as a museum where were gathered those oddments that rich men seem disposed to accumulate. There were hundreds of stuffed birds — rare species from remote corners of the world. My most vivid recollection, however, is of the two royal Indian tigers that guarded the foot of the grand staircase which led from the entrance hall. Many a time have I mounted one of those jungle beasts and galloped away to adventure'

My father's successor in the management of the Grant, an Englishman we called 'Lord' Sherwin, added to the already sumptuous furnishings of the Maxwell House and brought to it the most precious ornament of all, his sixteen-year-old daughter. Her suicide, due, so rumor had it, to a love-affair with a cowboy, which her father quite understandably took steps to circumvent, was my first acquaintance with the tragedy which lies ever close to romance. This ill-fated English girl became the heroine of my earliest dreams of romantic martyrdom. Of course this was after I was old enough to listen in on the conversations of my elders — with more comprehension than they suspected.

Along with the management of the Maxwell Land Grant, my father had taken over the editorship of the *Cimarron News and Press*, one of New Mexico's earliest English-language newspapers. In his editorial capacity he incurred the wrath of a certain political clique which, so he believed, were unrighteously exploiting the opportunities always present in a new country. Not content with exposing their machinations in his own paper, he and the Reverend F. J. Tolby, a crusading Methodist minister, wrote a series of articles about them for Dana of the New York *Sun*. The Reverend Tolby's tombstone bears the inscription, 'Assassinated Sept. 14. 1875.' Tradition in our family has it that my father had been marked for a similar fate a year earlier.

At any rate, acting presumably under orders from this group, Clay Allison at the head of a band of followers made a raid upon Cimarron on the night of June 26, 1874. And on that very night, I made an unexpected and disconcerting appearance upon this earthly scene. In later years my mother always said that my life-long vice of arriving places ahead of time had its beginning that June night when Clay Allison shot up the town.

'Shooting up the town' was ritual in the cattle country, but there were few who made as good a job of it as did Clay Allison, unless it were Billy the Kid himself, hero — or villain — of the then still smouldering Lincoln County war. (The one reason why Clay has never been so dramatic a figure as Billy in public imagi nation is that he voluntarily abandoned outlawry and became re spectable during the latter half of his life, dying prosaically from a fall off a wagon loaded with firewood.) My father, expecting Clay but not me, had retired to an already prepared hideout, from which he emerged to find Clay gone and the three-odd pounds of my militant self awaiting him.

Several months later Clay returned one night with his henchmen, dumped the printing press into the river, and upset the cases of type. When daylight came, my mother rushed over to view the wreckage. Unexpectedly, Clay himself strode into the wrecked printing office. He saw a young woman in early-morning dis-habille, her very long and very golden hair hanging about her shoulders. She was wringing her hands. When Clay appeared, she turned on him: 'Now see what you've done. You ought to be ashamed of yourself!'

I do not recall ever having seen Clay Allison, but I have talked many times with those who knew him and I reconstruct the picture as I imagine it. Tall, gaunt, with fine squint-lines at the corners of his eyes, he stands with his hat in his hand, his forehead above the sweat-band line very white, his skin below this line the color and texture of old rawhide. Out of this leathery countenance shine two hazel-brown eyes, steady and hard but not vicious, and now under my mother's scolding suffused with genuine embarrassment.

'Are you Mrs. Morley?' he stammered. 'Well, go buy yourself another printing press,' and out of his shirt he drew a wrist-thick roll of greenbacks, and thrust them into her hand. 'I don't fight women.'

He proved to be as good as his word. From then on his allegiance was transferred to my father's side of the feud. But this did not daunt the enemy for more than an instant. Deprived of Clay Allison's expert services, they were driven to a flank attack. They accused my mother of stealing a registered letter from the small and loosely run local post office, and had her indicted for robbing the mails. The charge was especially serious since they controlled the native law-enforcement agencies.

When Clay Allison heard of it his order went forth: 'Bring that woman to trial and not a man will come out of the courtroom alive.' With that, the independence of the local judiciary became academic. When my mother told me this story in 1884, the statute of limitations had not yet taken effect. 'I'm still under indictment,' she said.

I felt a glow of satisfaction. An outlaw in the family! 'Clay Allison must have been most as nice as Billy the Kid,' I said.

Mother looked thoughtful. 'I'm afraid it is time you were being sent away to school.'

And when I was sent, years later, I was sure that my indiscreet admiration for Billy the Kid had much to do with my exile.

It was while we were still living in Cimarron that there occurred the incident which is my earliest recollection.

A hot midday sun beats down upon the adobe walls of the old Maxwell House. I am sitting in the triangle of shade cast by one side of the deep doorway. In my two hands I hold a slice of bread and butter sprinkled with brown sugar.

There sounds a hoarse cry. Startled, I drop my slice of bread in the dust at the foot of the doorstep. Two men, one on foot, one on horseback, were coming toward me. When the man on foot reaches a point just in front of the doorway — he was evidently making for it as a refuge — the man on horseback, whose mount is all but striking the runner down, draws his six-shooter and shoots his quarry through the head.

I note the stiffness of the man's body as it pitches forward. It does not crumple, but falls as rigidly as a toppling statue.

The man on horseback puts his six-shooter back in his holster and dismounts, holding his snorting and rearing horse by a bridle rein. With a boot-toe under the prostrate man's shoulder the killer heaves his victim over onto his back and stands looking down into the dead face. I still remember the oath, the quick swing into the saddle, the cloud of dust which blots him from sight as he rides off in the direction from which he came.

I gaze upon two tragedies with equal distress — the dead man a few feet away from me and the slice of buttered and sugared bread in the dust at my feet. I see the flies which are already settling upon both.

The sun, as well as the flies, is on the dead man's upturned face. I go over to him and place his hat, which lies alongside, over that face, taking care not to step in the blood pool in which his head rests. At this instant the house door opens. I am snatched indoors. Then my father comes in. He takes me in his arms and holds me too tightly; my mother says, 'Rayme, I don't like this country.'

Years later, my mother told me that after I had been put in bed she and my father talked long into the night about the question of bringing up a family under conditions which made this day's happening possible. Toward dawn my father sighed and said: 'Well, Ada, we've put our hands to this plow. We can't turn around in the middle of the furrow. I've got to build the Santa Fé.'

It wasn't LOADED

It is difficult to evaluate one's own father, but there is extant enough historical data to establish the fact that his engineering ability amounted almost to genius. That he was universally respected is undisputed; that he was loved and honored by his friends with an intensity equaled only by the intensity of the fear and hatred on the part of his enemies is also undisputed. At his funeral, hundreds of his associates, strong and even rough men, sobbed aloud in uncontrollable grief. He had tremendous moral fervor together with a courage that verged upon foolhardiness. He feared neither man nor circumstance; but both had their triumph over him.

Around him there unfolded one of the most colorful sagas of the pioneer West. These are the historical facts of his most famous exploit, which came to be known as 'Morley's ride.'

A frenzied mining boom was in progress in the new town of Leadville, Colorado. The only possible route from Cañon City to Leadville was through the Royal Gorge, a breath-takingly beautiful crevasse which the Arkansas River has eaten three thousand feet down through the tightened rock barriers of western Colorado. Both the Santa Fé and the Denver and Rio Grande coveted a chance to serve this great new area of potential wealth, and sought to control the one approach, through which thousands were already flocking toilsomely.

Rights of way at that time rested upon the principle that possession is nine points of the law. The Denver and Rio Grande controlled the already existing rail approaches and telegraph lines into Cañon City, situated practically in the mouth of the gorge. Denver and Rio Grande officials planned the surprise move of taking a force of one hundred men, gathered in the neighboring towns of Pueblo and La Junta, into Cañon City by train in order to be first in the actual process of building a railroad through the gorge.

Santa Fé officials learned of the plan only when it seemed too late to forestall it. One thin shred of hope was all they could muster. If a man could get through ahead of the train and draft a corps of Cañon City people to begin actual construction, the day might be saved. The citizenry of Cañon City was known to sympathize with the Santa Fé.

The man to execute the coup must, of course, be one who could not only make the heart-breaking ride himself, but at the end of it explain his mission to an excited populace, and galvanize it into effective, well-organized, and, above all, instant action. My father was able to do both.

The ride itself was a negligible incident in comparison to getting a town's entire population out with picks and shovels on a moment's notice. That was the real achievement. But it was the ride which became the legend. Even Helen Hunt Jackson wrote a poem about it, a parody of the 'Charge of the Light Brigade,' in which it was Morley who 'volleyed and thundered.'

Bradley's *Story of the Santa Fé* has possibly the most dramatic account of the episode: 'Morley at once secured a good horse and started out at full gallop. It was a race of flesh and blood against a railroad and a desperate ride. Urging the animal to the limit of its endurance, Morley had arrived almost within sight of Cañon City when the animal fell dead from exhaustion. Leaping to his feet, the rider ran the rest of the way alone and safely reached the offices of the Cañon City and San Juan Company before the train of the Rio Grande laborers arrived.'

Another account, that of Cy Warman in his *Story of the Railroad*, has it that this historic ride was made with a team and buckboard.

Actually, it was made on King William, a well-bred coal-black horse with a white star in his forehead. And, for the sake of my father's memory and the family honor, I want to testify that with a forty-mile ride ahead of him my father did not start out at 'full gallop.' (It always enrages me to see that done in the movies.) He eased his horse along at a brisk trot until the animal warmed up, and then alternately trotted and galloped him as the character of the mountainous country permitted.

But he did beat the train!

The horse did not drop dead, either: on the contrary, King William lived to a ripe old age and died long after the untimely death of his master. Loyal friends of both horse and master saw to it that he was never ridden again, but spent his venerable years in the best horse heaven which devotion could provide — open pasture in summer, shelter and food in winter. All agree that he carried himself to the end with an air of conscious pride, as though

he understood his part in an adventure which has been the theme
for many story-tellers, both accurate and inaccurate.

Some people may think that these details are too trifling to be
insisted upon. But good horsemanship is not a trifle: my father's
dramatic ride was all the more notable because he finished a forty-
mile trip in record time without injury to his mount.

Tousle-headed, dust-caked, he rode into Cañon City, shouting,
'The Santa Fé is here!'

Hardware stores swung their doors open and issued implements
to all able-bodied men, who fell into line under my father's general-
ship.

Months of litigation and some physical violence, known as the
'Grand Cañon War,' ensued. The dispute was finally settled by the
purchase of the Santa Fé's rights by the Denver and Rio Grande.
My personal memory of it all is centered in one great moment:
when my father led me to the brink of the gorge and allowed me to
look over the rim. I have never forgotten my awe as I peered down
into that half-mile-deep crack in solid granite and saw a tiny silver
streak at its base, the Arkansas River, still going about its business
of cutting, cutting — not impatient, just inexorable.

With the settlement of the dispute over the railroad route, my
father went back to his first love, civil engineering. In 1879 we
left Cimarron, Mother and Father and my younger brother, William Raymond, Jr., and baby sister, Loraine, and went to live for
three years in Old Mexico while Father built the first Mexican
railroad connecting Guaymas with Nogales, Arizona.

All my personal recollections of my father are fragmentary and
uncorrelated. I remember riding with him on the cowcatcher of a
small locomotive on an inspection trip from one point of construction to another. I do not recall in just what territory it was, other
than that it was west of Albuquerque and probably on what was
then called the Atlantic and Pacific Railroad. The work train
may have been making twenty-five miles an hour, but twenty is

more probable. To me it was hurtling through space with a comet's speed. With my father's arms about me, making everything safe and right, the feel of iron and steel under me, an irresistible and deafening force thrusting us forward, I felt an exalted sense of dominion.

I recall the sternness of my mother's reproof when my father lifted me down from the cowcatcher on our return from our glorious jaunt: 'Rayme, you should not take such chances with the children. Suppose you *had* met a cow!' — a not too remote possibility in a country where there were perhaps a hundred cows for every human being.

I have only one other memory of my father alive. It is Nogales in the year 1882. The town is in gala array. Flags and bunting are everywhere. I remember my mother in her voluminous silk skirts (hoops had shrunk to a few wire strands suspended by tapes from the waist) and a little bonnet gay with flowers. There is an air of excitement about her, as well as about the throngs who move together in the direction of the railroad station.

Presently everybody is aboard. The locomotive is festooned from coalbin to mushroomed smokestack with red, white, and blue bunting. Little American flags whip in the breeze from every possible anchorage.

Slowly, with bells clanging and whistles shrieking, the train moves into the open country and stops. Everybody piles out. And there before us with its own cowcatcher but a few feet from ours is another bedecked locomotive at the head of a train of cars from which people are likewise descending. This train is also bunting-draped, but the colors are red, white, and green, Old Mexico's national colors.

I see my father, but scarcely recognize him. He is wearing a long frock coat and a high silk hat and he does not look quite natural nor wholly at ease. He is surrounded by other men, also wearing 'stovepipes' and carrying canes.

The ladies gather up their skirts daintily and everybody crowds together at the point where the two locomotives are all but touching. Workmen have already laid a polished mahogany railroad tie, and very self-conscious it seems among its plebeian fellows. One workman holds a small rubber-capped sledgehammer. Someone else holds a little rosewood box.

Men begin to make speeches. I remember only that my father's name occurred with great frequency, both in the speeches made in English and those made in Spanish. 'Don Señor Guillermo Raymondo' fell fervently from the lips of Mexican orators. My father makes a short speech, throughout which everybody laughs often, and I remember thinking that he began to look less uncomfortable.

Then the crowd stands back, and my mother steps forward. From the little rosewood box a gentleman takes a silver spike with an inlaid gold plate upon which are inscribed data appropriate to the occasion. The spike is placed in a hole already drilled in the mahogany tie to receive it; my mother strikes one ladylike blow, and the last spike in the Nogales to Guaymas road is driven. Then the two engines moved toward one another, and when the tips of their cowcatchers actually meet, a great shout goes up. The wife of a Mexican dignitary breaks a bottle of champagne over the junction.

Back in the special car attached to the Mexican train there are more speeches and the presentation of gifts, the spike and a gold watch to my father, a pair of ponderous and ornate gold bracelets to my mother, and, amid much laughter, a pair of small gold filigree earrings to me.

I recall the mixed emotions with which I received them. I didn't relish the idea of having my ears pierced! No other type of earring was known then. There were also gifts whose character I forget for Ray and Lora.

One of the Mexican gentlemen patted my head and asked me if

I still wanted my father to be a hack-driver so 'he would have lots of money,' a wish I had once uttered in the gentleman's presence when a hack-driver in the city of Hermosillo pulled a handful of coins from his pocket to make change. The gentleman spoke, and I answered, in Spanish, which came as readily as did my native tongue.

All the speeches made that day the road was finished were to the effect that this young American engineer had been launched upon a career of assured achievement and honor — for was he not already engaged to build a larger and more important line of railroad, the Mexican Central, with its terminus in Mexico City?

Three months later he lay dead of an accidental gunshot.

It was a jest among his associates that he was afraid of but one thing in the world — an unloaded gun. So when he asked that a rifle resting across the back of the driver's seat of a two-seated hack be removed 'because I don't like that thing pointing at me,' the driver laughed as he jerked the reins free from the gunstock around which they had become entangled. The explosion brought the firmament crashing down upon a little family's head.

'That's MY MOUNTAIN!'

WITH a sure instinct for future values, my father had invested here and there — in a hundred-and-sixty-acre tract in what is now downtown Denver; in some hundreds of acres in the area in Colfax County, where Eagle Nest Dam has since been built; in ranch properties in western Socorro County, holdings valued today at millions. But for all that ours is not one of the great family fortunes of America.

When my father died at less than thirty-eight years of age, these holdings passed into the hands of a young wife brought up, as was the tradition, to be dependent upon her menfolks. Alas, my mother had none.

Friends flocked to the wealthy young widow proffering advice, some from genuine loyalty and a desire to be helpful, others from self-interest and a hope of dipping into the all too widely flung estate. In the latter group was a persuasive and soft-spoken gentleman from below the Mason-Dixon line. His Southern drawl was pleasant to the ear, his bounding optimism was stimulating; his fondness for hard drinking and gambling was unsuspected. He loomed as a bulwark against others with whom Mother felt unable to cope. She married him. It was he who persuaded her to invest most of her available cash in a huge cattle ranch and stock it to the limit of its capacity.

Cattle-raising on a grand scale was the Great Adventure of the hour. Railroading had become a matter for experts, but anybody with sufficient cash could become a big rancher. My imaginative mother had about as much fitness for the rôle of cattle queen as could be expected from a young woman who had always leaned upon some 'natural protector,' but she had had her years of training in pioneer uncertainties, so she followed the new husband as confidently as she had her first.

It was under his escort that we traveled to our new home in what was then western Socorro County. It has since been divided, the western half becoming Catron County, but before the division it enjoyed the distinction of being the largest county in any State in the Union. It was approximately two hundred miles long and one hundred miles wide, and its population was roughly estimated at one person to ten square miles. The town of Socorro in the eastern half was the county seat; Magdalena, a little farther to the west, was the end of a spur railroad line, hence the cattle shipping center.

We arrived in Magdalena in February, 1886. The town sprawls in the sun at the foot of Lady Magdalena Mountain, a bare and defiant monolith in the midst of decently pine-clad sisters. Half-way up the mountain-side, Lady Magdalena herself gazes into blue sky resting upon far mountain peaks, her face turned away from the town. When one asks a stranger to look at Lady Magdalena for the first time, it is an even chance whether he will say, 'You mean that patch of shale up there? I can't see any face,' or 'Oh, I see her plainly; those bushes are her back hair.'

There is a legend that Lady Magdalena Mountain was a sanctu·ary respected by the Indians, where fugitives, whether deservedly or not, found refuge from pursuing enemies. The legend did not hold after the paleface came shooting his way into the land. Many a pursued man fell before his nemesis in the streets of Magdalena.

'Please give us a room that is not directly over the barroom,' my mother stipulated to the hotel-keeper the night we arrived. 'I'm afraid those bullets will come up through the floor.' It was years afterward before Magdalena gathered herself together and made it a misdemeanor to shoot within the town limits. But tough though Magdalena was in those days, it was all we were to know of civilization for a considerable length of time.

We set out again the next morning in a sheeted wagon pulled by four horses. Although it was midwinter, the sun was warm, and the air had that crystalline quality which puts a sparkle in your spirits as well as ozone in your lungs. It was sheer delight to wind gradually upward as the wagon road threaded its way through the timber, straggly piñon trees and their sleeker brethren the junipers, following a contour surveyed with utmost accuracy by the range cattle, which came and went on the easiest grades.

No sign of human habitation greeted us as we topped the divide west of town and gazed across at the blue bank of haze that blanketed the western sky — the Datil Mountains, our destination, forty miles away. Between us and the Datils the road unrolled in a long straight thread across the San Augustine Plains, an irregular ancient lake bed, fifty to seventy miles in cross distances. Rimmed by the Magdalenas, the San Mateos, the Datils, and the Gallinas, the plains form a vast saucer.

When our wagon reached the Little Sand, the shorter of two heart-breaking stretches, we all crawled out from under the white-sheeted bows; several hundred pounds of human flesh measured the difference between a maximum and an overload for the horses.

It was while we trudged behind the lurching wagon that an un forgettable sight burst upon us. Off to the left, where the San Mateos formed the southern rim of the plains, the dry earth appeared magically to have changed to tawny water, which rose and fell in long undulating swells. Even Hank, our teamster, presumably inured to any surprises that the country could produce, looked nonplused. For long minutes we all stood agape. The horses themselves turned their heads and pricked their ears sharply forward in wonderment.

The tawny flood, wave upon wave, flowed steadily toward us.

At last Hank found his voice. 'Well, I'll be hornswoggled,' he exploded, 'if it ain't antelopes! I've seen big herds of them before now, but I never before seen a whole township turned into antelope. I bet they's four thousand, mebbe more.'

The whole foreground seemed to be one mass of living creatures galloping flank against flank. They appeared not to have seen us and to be bent upon crossing the road at a point that would engulf and pound us into the sand under a myriad sharp-pointed hooves. Six-year-old Lora whimpered in fright, while the rest of us cast sidelong glances at the wagon with its meager promise of safety.

We had seen buffalo herds and knew their habit of pouring relentlessly toward a chosen goal, tramping down any obstacle in their path. There was the same suggestion of irresistible mass movement in this incredible herd of antelope.

Then the leaders saw us. On what waves of ether or of pure thought the command was carried to every individual in the horde, no man may yet say, but something magical happened. While we stared, the waves that had been rolling steadily onward appeared suddenly to break into foam against an invisible shoreline. Those thousands of antelope had turned with the precision of a well-drilled army battalion. Their feathery rumps, catching the sunlight, had changed the sea from dull saffron to gleaming white. Backward flowed the waves until in a few moments only a silver shimmer in the far distance told us that the antelope were still running.

Hank shook his head despairingly. 'Wonder how we can ever get shet of them,' he grumbled. 'They eat up too much range.'

He need not have worried. Two years later the blizzard of 1888 was to relieve him of his anxiety. When the snow melted, four months after it fell, the San Augustine Plains were again whitened, this time with the skeletons of those ill-fated creatures.

That night we stopped at Baldwin's, the stage station. It was an adobe house, with a two-story log structure at one end. Half a dozen doors opened from the long façade. The log end of the building was the store, the other the hotel.

Only ten miles remained before us when we started the next morning. A short way beyond Baldwin's we entered Datil Cañon; this, like the mountains, is named after a species of yucca (called 'date' by the Spaniards), which then grew profusely in the district but disappeared because cattle liked the fruit.

We used the word 'cañon' loosely to mean anything from a deep gorge to a valley flanked by mountain ranges. But though none of the flanking walls of Datil Cañon reach the perpendicular, they are nonetheless sufficiently steep and high to serve as enclosing walls, so it is a true cañon. My own definition was a place where an echo would come back to you from either direction. No echo, no cañon, to my mind. This, too, fitted Datil Cañon with reasonable accuracy. If one yelled loudly enough at almost any point between Baldwin's and the top of the divide, one would get a faint return echo. I speak from the standpoint of a thoroughgoing experimenter.

Lying in a generally north and south direction, Datil Cañon unevenly bisects the Datil Mountains. Leading into this main cañon are laterals like tributaries to a main river, separated from one another by timbered trachyte-porphyry ridges and ranges of boulder-strewn hills, mesas topped with rimrock, or steep mountains with shale-covered slopes. Between these endless ridges and small-scale mountain ranges lie friendly valleys carpeted with grama grass and rabbit brush.

The roads down the cañon were any level stretch over which a wagon could pass. When the ruts had become incipient arroyos and the high centers made traffic impossible, new wagon tracks had appeared beside the old until erosion claimed its own and a real arroyo forced an entirely new route.

Every now and then Hank would have to get down and pull aside the heavy pine bars that closed the gaps of the pole fences which crisscrossed the cañon. These fences marked the boundaries of the small homesteads which had recently been claimed.

The eastern slope of the cañon, which got the warm afternoon sun, was clothed with piñon and juniper; the western with pines, which seem to choose cooler spots. As the cañon narrowed toward its head, the pines took virtually complete possession even of the cañon floor.

At an elevation of eight thousand feet, a February day grows cold early; so we were delighted when Hank told us, 'It's just over the next rise.' The team strained against their collars for the last stretch: the ten-mile zigzag up from Baldwin's had been also a five-hundred-foot climb: now only one final short grade shut our new home from view.   Already we felt we were in our own dooryard.

Ray stood in the seat to be the first one to catch a glimpse of the house itself. Of course Lora and I wanted to stand there too, but it had been Ray's idea, and we were forced to concede his right to the privilege.

'There she is!' he whooped as the wagon topped the grade.

I have often wondered what passed through Mother's mind when it became possible without standing in the seat to see the little log house that squatted at the base of a mountain whose peak alone was washed in sunlight. Although she knew that this home was to be temporary, and that construction of the 'big house' would begin at once, she could scarcely have escaped a chill of spirit that was not due to the chill of the twilight, she who had had a private railroad car at her disposal, she who had driven the silver spike as 'first lady' of a ceremony upon which had been focused the eyes of two nations!

The house, which had been built by the original homesteader, was a low rectangle of logs, its flat roof covered with a foot of adobe sod from which occasional grass stalks stuck up stiffly. Behind the house, and flanking it, stood great pines, whose ranks climbed to the mountain-tops. Beyond, the cañon floor broke off abruptly and sheer hundred-foot-high cliffs, the dramatic Saw Tooth Group, became the northern face of the Datil Range.

We left the wagon road where it curved off through West Pass toward Quemado, the little Mexican plaza thirty-five miles farther on, and drove the last half-mile over trackless ground now frozen hard and ringing under the iron rims of the wagon wheels.

Mother was still silent when we drew up to the door, but we youngsters were not.

'That's *my* mountain!' I screamed, taking in a quarter arc of the horizon with a sweep of my arm. 'And that's my cañon, going alongside of it.'

Ray had beaten me to a first glimpse of the new home, but I

beat him to the idea of parceling out the landscape amongst ourselves.

'That's my mountain,' Ray echoed, waving toward another area
of piled-up mountain bulk, 'and that's my cañon on the other side
of it.'

'Don't forget your little sister.' This phrase fell from Mother's
lips with not quite its familiar ring, but we were too excited to be
concerned over the sound of Mother's voice.

'Lora can have West Pass,' I hastened to say. 'It's really the
prettiest scenery.'

'Lora ought to grab her own scenery,' Ray muttered as he prepared to help unload the wagon.

'You never give me time,' Lora called back over her shoulder
as, held fast by Mother's hand, she was led indoors before her small
bones could suffer any deeper chill. I followed.

At one end of the room into which we stepped was a crudely
built fireplace in which a piñon fire blazed. The few pieces of
furniture were makeshifts of rough lumber. A door led into another and larger room at one end of which stood a black iron cook-
stove, its pipe streaked with rust. A table flanked by long wooden
benches and a cupboard without doors, made of rough planks, were
the principal furnishings.

Ray staggered in under a bedroll. He flung his burden down
and addressed me: 'Say, you lazy thing, get out there and help
unload that wagon.' Though I did not know it then, Ray had
struck the pitch of my future career in the Datils.

The several men who were our first employees slept outside on
the ground in their heavy bedrolls, but we all ate together. An old
roundup cook prepared the food.

Mother was silent as we gathered for our first meal on this first
night of our new life. Well do I remember the talk that went about
that table. Joe Fowler had recently been the latest victim to hang
from Socorro's 'Death Alley' gallows tree, a big cottonwood.

Vigilantes had put an end to Joe's unrestrained career. We children listened with open-mouthed absorption to the details of the lynching while Mother imploringly signaled the new head of the family to change the subject.

He did. He switched it to Billy the Kid. This was the first but by no means the last time I sat in at an argument about whether Pat Garrett, sheriff or no sheriff, was justified in shooting, before giving Billy the Kid a chance to drop his butcher knife and reach for his gun. Or did Billy *have* a butcher knife?

Passions mounted as the discussion proceeded. Most of the group around our table contended that this twenty-one-year-old outlaw with a price on his head for killing twenty-one men — 'not including Indians and Mexicans' — had a right to his one shot in self-defense. The minority, on the defensive, held that it was time law and order were upheld 'if this country is ever goin' to grow.'

'I'm on Billy the Kid's side,' Ray squeezed in his declaration when there seemed a place for it.

'Me, too,' I hastened to his support.

'You children know nothing whatever about it,' Mother interrupted sharply; 'and Agnes, you know you should say "I, too"; and it's time for children to be in bed.'

We children were to sleep on the floor of the room in which we had dined; so Mother's remark brought to an end both meal and discussion.

When later Ray, Lora, and I were stretched out, each in his little bedroll, hard boards beneath us and fine dust from the dirt roof sifting down from between the cracks in the puncheon overhead, I called to Ray:

'How do you like this place?'

'Me? Why, I think it's *bully!* How do you like it?'

'I think it's bully, too.'

Poor tired little Lora was already asleep.

Did Mother think it was bully? Of course I never knew. My eleven and a half years were entirely too few to give me an understanding of grown-ups' problems. It was another year or two before Mother shared hers with me.

The next morning witnessed Mother's first gesture toward the homemaking which she was desperately resolved to achieve, but which was always to prove futile. She had Navajo blankets strung across the center of the larger room. Now at least the house had three rooms!

A fatherless SWISS FAMILY ROBINSON

IF YOUR home is in a cañon it won't be long before you climb
out to see what's on top. One day shortly after our arrival, Ray
and I climbed the mountain at whose base our log cabin sat, confident that from its top we should look out over the wide world.
We were disappointed. Another and higher mountain overshadowed the one we had so painfully scaled. We hadn't heart to
begin the conquest of another just then.

'And you'd have found still another mountain back of that one,'
Henry Davenport told us on our return home, footsore and weary.
Henry was supervising the building of the new house. 'I'll take
you up on the highest of 'em all some day when it's not so cold.
It's Sierra Madre and we'll have to go horseback most of the way.'

Sierra Madre proved to be not only Mother Mountain but pinnacle of enchantment. Rising baldly ten thousand feet into the
sky, its peak above our local timberline, it hovers over its brood of

lesser hills, the Datil Range. From its top we did indeed look out over the wide world according to the standards of our childish experience. A hundred miles to the north we could see Mount Taylor hazy in the distance; dark mysterious Putney Mesa was sharp in the middle foreground. Almost at our feet lay the sandy trough of the Alamosa Creek, cutting through its gray rimrock-topped mesas, countless numbers of which were the sites of prehistoric cities, so Henry Davenport told us, a fact we were later to verify for ourselves. To the east we saw the wide green valley of the Rio Grande, its eastern wall a lavender-blue smudge against the horizon; still more mountains. In closer focus lay the Magdalena Range, rimming the San Augustine Plains on the east; westward the two Rito Plains with Big Allegro and Little Allegro, in their isolation on the near sector of the flat miles sweeping about them.

'It's an awful big country.' Ray had no better words to express his enthrallment. I had no words at all. I was taking that scene into my heart and soul as *my country* for so long as I should live.

'Some day,' said Ray, 'I'm going to have been on top of every mountain I'm looking at now,' a vow he came so close to fulfilling that I am sure the recording angel will have checked it off the record marked OK.

'See' — Henry Davenport pointed north — 'there's the Alamosa this side of the malpais, and the North Plains; and a little east of that long dike — the Mexicans call it Trinchera — is you folks' Los Esteros Ranch. As a crow flies it's about fifteen-sixteen miles from here, and all the land between here and it is you folks' range. Of course your range goes in other directions, too.'

But it was not thus literally that I had taken that land into my possession. It did not matter to me whose it was in the sense that Henry Davenport was talking about. By my own standards it was mine. I knew what was mine when I saw it!

From where we stood we could see but little of the floor of Datil Cañon. There were too many of her children at Mother Mountain's feet for that, but we could trace its general course as it wound, a thin gash, through the piled-up mountains, a channel for that first trickle of human traffic that had begun to flow in little side rivulets from the tumultuous stream of men pressing toward the Golden Gate; rivulets that sometimes spread out too thinly and were to lose themselves in many a desert of our Southwest.

Although we could not see the actual homesteads that lay along the length of the cañon floor, we could check them off in our minds, all nine of them: Bill Goodlet, Frank Thomas, 'Old Man' Gumm, Jack Howard, Frank Stewart, Jim Baldwin, and so on down to the cañon's mouth. They had all come into the neighborhood a year or two ahead of us, and the manner of their coming was a tale Henry Davenport related to us on the ride home.

The first government survey of the region had been made but a few years previously, and every 'living water' had been promptly homesteaded in individual hundred-and-sixty-acre allotments, supplemented by another like allowance as a 'pre-emption' claim if one chose to fulfill the conditions. All this was contingent upon making no commitments to sell or transfer any claims before one had received final title. This condition was all too easily evaded. Most of the original influx of alleged homesteaders turned over their patents suspiciously soon after receiving them to one or two large holders of range land. The pole fences that had vaguely marked their homestead boundaries disappeared and the lands became part of the open range once more.

To the east of us a few genuine homesteaders who refused to

sell lived on scattered ranches in the heart of the V + T ranges.
But within a year or two Baldwin's became our nearest neighbor
to the south; there were scarcely any to the north, and none to the
west this side of Quemado.

Building our new house was itself an adventure. It began immediately after our arrival. The logs were felled on the near-by
mountain-sides and dragged by ox teams to the site in the cañon
bottom, itself eighty-three hundred feet above sea level.

Four expert axemen — superb craftsmen — had been brought
from Michigan logging camps to hew the logs. The original ten-
room house still stands, although, log by log, it has been moved to
another site and enlarged, serving now as a tourist 'motel.' Its
walls are true and plumb, with the axe marks scarcely visible; but
if the logs could talk, and still remember the days when they were
being snaked down the mountain by six yoke of oxen, poled by
cowpunchers who hated themselves for doing it, I shudder to
think what the ears of the present tourist might be subjected to.
I know that we children were kept as far as possible from the scene
while the oxen were being yoked to the running-gear of the heavy-
spoked wagons, preparatory to the day's work.

Bullwhackers are undoubtedly born and not made. At any rate,
they are not made of the same raw material that goes into the
making of a cowpuncher. How a house-building crew was recruited
from the lanky Texans who applied for jobs with the new cow outfit was ever a mystery.

The building of our house was the last job upon which oxen were
used in that section of the country. Missouri had begun to produce mules, and the bullwhacker was to give place to the mule-
skinner.

To this day, it is a mystery to me why we chose the least cheerful spot in Datil Cañon as a home site. The foundations were laid
about a quarter of a mile from the cabin. at the base of a preci-

pitous mountain which shut off the morning sun. The house sat at right angles to the mountain, facing down the cañon. It seemed to belong neither to the cañon nor to the mountain. One came upon it unexpectedly from any direction, and always with a slight gasp of surprise. Somehow a ten-room house just didn't belong there.

After a while, it became still more startling. The hand-hewn cedar shingles weathered to a soft gray, and since the boards that covered the ends of the logs, like the rest of the woodwork, doors, window frames, and veranda pillars, were white, the over-all effect was white, although the logs themselves were never painted. Soon the Mexican freighters between Magdalena and Quemado began to speak of 'Casa Blanca' as a landmark on their route; and in time we called it 'The White House.' Today the cañon appears on the maps as 'White House Cañon,' though the house is there no longer.

When the house was finally done, furnishing followed. First there came the library, begun by my great-grandparents, and added to subsequently by other generations of the family. Books came out to the ranch in wagonload lots. Walnut and rosewood furniture of the sixties and seventies arrived. There was the old Steinway in its rosewood case, and my mother's box of music. Itinerant piano-tuners appeared only at long intervals, and soon the piano got so badly out of tune that my mother's trained ear could not tolerate its dissonance.

One day before my mother hid the key to the piano, a party of uncouth-looking men stopped and asked for water and general trail directions. By what they did *not* volunteer, we knew that they were undoubtedly an outlaw band passing through the country.

As they were preparing to leave, one of them, who was in every way as rough-looking as his fellows, spied the piano through an open door.

'Madam,' he said, turning to my mother, 'with your permission I should like to put my hands upon that instrument just for a moment.' His voice had become that of an educated man. He strode to the piano, and then there burst from that long-silent box a flood of harmony filled with all the suffering-through-to-victory that makes music great. He played on and on. I remember the

enthralled look upon my mother's face and the respectful silence of his companions.

Finally, with a crashing chord that seemed to cry defiance to the world, he arose and thanked my mother.

'You cannot know what this has done for me,' he said. 'I had quite forgotten ——'

He did not finish his sentence, but bowed and walked out to where his horse stood with the others. Once he looked back as though to return, but, instead, squared himself in the saddle and, surrounded by his evil-savored companions, rode away.

But it was not merely the dissonance of the piano that accounted for its gradual disuse: more pressing but less aesthetic occupations soon engrossed my mother. Before we had been very long in the Datils she discovered how tragic had been the mistake of her second marriage. My stepfather vanished; and she who be·lieved more than anything else in education and culture found her·

self marooned with three young children on a desert island of cul-
tural barrenness, with no means of escape that would not sacrifice
her entire investment. We became a sort of Swiss Family Robinson without a Father Robinson to meet emergencies. She resumed
the name of Morley, and the ill-fated husband's appearance upon
the stage of our family life became a gradually receding reality.

Faced with the supervision of a well-stocked cattle range of a
good many thousand acres, she rode and did her indomitable best
to keep herself informed about what was happening to her livestock; but she was unable successfully to cope with the cattle-
rustlers who abounded and with the proclivities of open-range
cattle to wander. It is to the credit of some of the men she employed that there was salvaged from the threatened *débâcle* the
original ranches and a bit of 'steer-money' which gave each of us
children as much education as we individually cared to take, a
desultory sort of education in our earlier years, to be sure, and one
that had to be made up for with labor and pains later on. That she
survived the years that followed speaks volumes for her courage,
her stamina, and her self-sacrifice. It would have been so very easy
to sink under the all but overwhelming flood of hardships and disappointments that were hers.

For us children, however, the new life was from the beginning a
sort of glorified picnic.

We had been but a day or two on the place when a stranger appeared. He was something of a shock to all of us. He looked as
if he had been through some scathing ordeal, and his horse was an
even more pitiable sight — staggering, hollow-eyed, and breathing
with difficulty. In spite of the cold, he was sweat-caked, and as his
rider all but fell off him, it appeared that the horse would go down
too. I was standing close by, wide-eyed with interest mixed with
pity. The man turned to me.

'Here, little girl,' he said, 'will you ride this horse around a
few minutes so's he won't cool off too fast?' And without waiting

for an answer he picked me up and set me astride the horse. 'Just walk him about easy.'

No one asked the man any questions. He ate in silence. At the close of the meal, he spoke with complete matter-of-factness. 'I'll git a horse back to you if you'll let me have one — and how about trading hats with somebody?'

One of our less valuable horses was saddled for him, somebody gave him another hat, and he was in the saddle and gone, all within a few moments. 'The little girl can have that horse,' he called back, as he set out, a little too briskly for a man who wasn't afraid.

It was my first introduction to an outlaw. We were often to see others: western Socorro County, because of its wildness, was sanctuary to many a man 'on the dodge.' Mother's lips were set in a grim line, but I think she had already seen the futility of kicking against all the pricks, at least outwardly.

I was walking on clouds. I was a useful member of society. The horse never recovered sufficiently to be of any value, but the experience was momentous for me. I had earned the horse by not screaming in terror when a fearsome-looking stranger set me for the first time on a horse's back.

In addition to the outlaws, we had another uncertain neighbor — the Indian. If anyone imagines that the early settlers, by maintaining a proper attitude, could have lived in amity with the Indians, let him consider how little amity existed between the various Indian tribes themselves. From time immemorial, American Indians had lived by raiding, whether of the natural bounty of the land or the garnered resources of their neighbors. The net result at the end of thousands of years was that this continent, possessed perhaps of the greatest natural resources in the world, bore a population of less than a hundredth part of what exists upon it today, and this hundredth part lived precariously and in a state of perpetual terror. Ruthless and predatory Anglo-Saxons did not burst into a redman's Garden of Eden and wrest it from him. When all sentimentality about the fate of the American Indian has been cleared away, the bald fact stands out that today's American Indian enjoys this blessing at least; he need no longer fear his redskin brother's savage cruelties.

There were always rumors of Indian attacks, and frequent evidences that they had indeed attacked. On my first visit to the Los Esteros Ranch, our secondary headquarters over the Datil Divide, I was taken several miles 'up the crick' to see 'where the Injuns kilt them Mexicans.'

With the physical eye, there was little to see — just two grave-shaped mounds of loose rock with rough wooden crosses at their heads and beside them a litter of iron junk, rims of wide-tired wheels, hub casings, bolts, those parts of a wagon that would not burn. Most conspicuous of all was a twenty-foot length of chain, of irregular six- to ten-inch hand-forged links, with a large hook at one end. My companion, a girl slightly older than I, was a member of the household of Jim Broyles, our foreman, and knew more than I did of the life into which I had so recently come. She explained that the chain had been an extension of the wagon tongue to which the two forward spans of the six-ox team had been hitched. A suggestion of ashes still lay over the site, although the massacre had occurred a few years earlier.

This was what the physical eye saw. The mind's eye saw the sudden dash of yelling savages from the timber beside the dim wagon tracks that were the 'road,' tracks that in all probability recorded a previous trip of this same caravan carrying provisions to the few settlers farther down the creek; saw the swift, terrible slaughter of the surprised and helpless men; saw the oxen driven away to their own later slaughter, leaving behind them the remnants of what had been human bodies and a fire that blazed fearsomely — with no one to see. Now I was seeing it through eyes that should not have been looking upon such sights. We mounted our ponies and rode away in silence.

While we were still living in the cabin, the Indian menace suddenly became very real. The Apache warrior Geronimo was making one last despairingly futile gesture of defiance to the white invaders.

One afternoon, a courier dashed in on a lathered and dust-caked
horse.

'Geronimo is this side of Quemado!' he cried. 'Gimme a fresh
horse. I got to warn the folks in Nester Draw.'

Ten heavily armed men were at the time engaged in laying up
the logs for the new home. All out-of-door work was done heavily
armed, and it would have appeared on first glance that no safer
place could be found than behind those foot-thick logs guarded by
crack marksmen supplied with ammunition to withstand prolonged siege. But unfortunately the half-finished house stood at
the base of a steep mountain, and that mountain-side was strewn
with boulders ranging in size from a water bucket to a boxcar.

I've looked at that mountain-side many times since, and have
doubted that the Indians could have scored many direct hits had
they chosen rock-rolling as a means of attack, but the bare suggestion of it was too much for my imaginative mother. There seemed
such an inexhaustible supply of rocks! So, against the advice, even
the pleadings, of the men, she insisted upon taking her children and
going down to Baldwin's, which sat well out in the open.

There had been but three horses in the horse pasture and the
courier had taken one, so no mount was available for an escort to
accompany us. I well remember the disapproval in the faces of the
men as we set forth. But my mother was firm.

It was a ten-mile ride fraught with the ultimate of physical
and mental misery. Two on a horse is never comfortable, less
so when the pace is an unrelieved high trot, which was as fast as
we could force our ponies to go. Lora, riding behind mother, valiantly stifled her moans, and the robust nine-year-old Ray gouged
his fingers into my midriff as he clung to me, muttering child

profanity under his breath as he bounced up and down on the stiff saddle skirts which projected beyond the cantle.

At the end of what seemed at least a century, we arrived at Baldwin's, battered and bruised and so exhausted we had ceased to care whether our end was brought about by an Apache tomahawk or by one more jounce on a pony's back. Lora's legs were bleeding where the leather had rubbed them, Ray's were black and blue, but no more so than my own waistline, where he had clung to me with that amazing strength that was one day to carry him to the peak of the football world and rate him headlines in many a Sunday supplement.

But we had reached safety — we hoped. Other settlers had already come in from distant ranches, and the place was overflowing with terror-stricken families. The younger children occupied all the beds. The next older group, of which I was one, were put down on folded comforter pallets on the floor. The women, with white, strained faces, wandered restlessly about. It was while lying on my hard pallet, aching to the very marrow and unable to sleep because of the pain, that I overheard the discussion in the adjoining room where the men were making ready their guns and ammunition.

It was carried on in subdued tones, and, moreover, we children were supposed to be asleep. But if I had had no disposition to sleep up to this moment, which I had not, certainly there was none afterward. I heard old Jim Wheeler delegated to use his next to last cartridge to shoot me in the head in the event the Apaches' ammunition outlasted ours. The last was for himself. Another man was to perform a like service for Elva, Jim's only daughter, thus sparing the father this duty.

But the Apaches did not go our way, after all, and with daylight came news that they were far to the south, heading for the Mexican border, having left a trail of unspeakable carnage behind them.

Also with daylight came a new world to a child benumbed in spirit and in body, a world wherein life itself loomed as a blessing

so great that nothing again has ever seemed very important by
contrast. I rode back to the site of the new home a quite different
person from the one who had passed over that trail a few hours
before.

Then, too, I had a horse to myself. My mother and Lora had
been given a ride in a neighbor's buckboard, so Ray and I had not
to share one horse between us, but rode comfortably side by side.
I can still see his sturdy young body sitting erect in the man's
saddle, his feet in the leathers above the stirrups, riding with in-
born horsemanship. I can still hear his young braggadocio:

'I wisht the Apaches *had of* come. I'd of chopped their heads
squack off.'

Not long after that, something happened to prove that beyond
the boasting of a small boy lay a spirit which justified his cocki-
ness. He had become the possessor of two treasures which gave
him standing in the eyes of the community, a sleek black pony and
a long rawhide rope, which somebody had brought up from Old
Mexico. One night he staked his pony with the rawhide rope on a
patch of grass a full mile from the house. The next morning, on
another horse, he rode up the cañon to bring Negro back.

Hours passed, and he did not return. In fact, it was hours before he was missed. Ranch children betook themselves about their
own affairs and disappeared for long hours without the necessity
of reporting. Late in the afternoon a man was sent to search for
him. It was after dark before the two of them returned. I reconstruct Ray's report in his own language:

'When I got up to where I'd staked Negro he was gone. I
thought mebbe a coyote had chewed the rawhide rope in two, but
when I got up close I saw it had been untied from the stakepin.
Then I saw the tracks of barefooted ponies and right by the stakepin I saw moccasin tracks, so I knew Indians had stole him. I
cut sign and found they'd gone up Left-Hand Cañon, so I lit out
after 'em.

'The sign was pretty fresh. Some horse manure was still steamin'. They must have been hittin' the trail in the high places and goin' like the devil — all right, Mother, goin' like all git-out — for they had already got over the divide and down the other side of the mountain, and after that trailin' them was lots harder, because they wasn't goin' straight up a cañon like at first. But before I got plumb down to Trinchera Flat, I saw some smoke off to one side and some hobbled Indian ponies and I knew I'd caught up with 'em at last.'

If my mother was agitated at this picture of her only son, aged nine, riding alone into a camp of Indian horse-thieves, she concealed it with a technique she had been forced to adopt.

'Well, I rode into their camp, and there, sure 'nough, was Negro tied to a tree and five or six Indians all sittin' round a fire. They jumped up when they saw me and I said, "What you sons-of-guns mean by stealin' my horse?" — oh, all right, Mother, but that's what I said — and I said it loud and fierce, and then I went over to Negro and began to untie him, and one Indian came toward me like he was goin' to stop me, and I said even fiercer, "Don't you touch this horse, or I'll get all the cowboys in the county, and we'll follow you to the reservation and hang all of you." Seemed like one of them understood a little English and he talked to the others and they all talked and I just went ahead and took Negro and got on my other horse and lit out. I met Jim at the forks of the cañon comin' to look for me.'

As casual as that.

Great was the speculation as to what tribe these Indians belonged to. Ray was too young to recognize tribal differences; they were just Indians who had stolen his horse, and he'd gone and retrieved it. That he had done anything exceptional seemed not to have occurred to him, nor was there, in the attitude of the grown-ups, any disposition to make a hero of him.

'I didn't have time to come back and get help,' he explained.

'When I saw how hot I was on their trail I had to keep right after 'em. I'd not of got Negro back if I hadn't of.' In which he was very right.

Anybody's guess is as good as mine as to what went on in those Indians' minds. I offer it as an exhibit to offset the picture I have drawn of the Apaches. They may have been Navajos, or Zunis, or Lagunas, or Acomas, or Alamos, or any of half a dozen tribes located within roaming distance of our range.

That was the day, I think, when Ray himself put away a lot of childish things and took his place on the asset rather than the liability side of the family ledger.

And, before I leave the subject of adventures with Indians, I might note one of my own. First, the setting. The north face of the Datils breaks off sheer, in bluffs hundreds of feet high. At their feet lie the rough brakes of the Alamosa Creek watershed, gradually smoothing out into less broken country, with wooded patches pleasantly interspersed with small parks and swales and long gentle draws.

So many shades of green! The pine and spruce on the higher elevations, aspen a little lower down, piñons and juniper on the level stretches. So many brilliant hues of wildflowers on the valley floor! Lavender desert verbena, scarlet patches of Indian paintbrush, great blotches of yellow snakeweed. And above it a turquoise sky with white woolly thunderheads resting upon the mountain peaks.

I emerged from a juniper thicket into an open space; on my small buckskin pony I was a speck of humanity in a vast region of solitude. From the timber on the opposite side of the park a band of Indians rode out, in single file. Feathered and buckskin-clad, they came toward me with no break in the stride of their ponies. Although only a twelve-year-old, I was so enchanted with the pageant that it did not occur to me to be afraid.

Arriving at the spot where I waited — for I had stopped when the first Indian appeared — the leader of the band looked at me with an air of puzzlement and then circled his horse slowly around me. Each Indian that followed did the same: in a moment I was the center of a ring of horsemen who rode slowly around and around. Even though I had heard of this encircling maneuver as something Indians did before they attacked, it still did not occur to me to be frightened. I was as interested in the Indians as they were in me.

Finally I realized that the object of their interest was my blonde hair, which had come unbound and was hanging down my back in long wind-blown taffy-colored ripples; they were doing the equivalent of standing in line, that each might have his turn at a close-up view. After some moments of this silent riding in a circle, during which no word had been spoken on either side, the leader broke the ring and resumed the straight direction in which the group had originally been traveling, followed each in his place by the whole forty of them. I had even taken time to count them.

Almost fifty years after the event, I met an old and withered Indian garbed in a pair of faded Levi Strauss overalls and a frayed custom-made shirt, discarded by some white man. He could talk a little halting English. He asked me if I remembered meeting him and his band that day on Piñon Flat. I grabbed his hand and pumped it, to his mild embarrassment. Navajo dignity precludes such behavior. But I was so delighted to meet the old patriarch that I forgot my manners.

Then he told me that mine was the first woman's blonde hair any of them had ever seen and that it had fascinated them beyond words. He looked at my graying short-cropped thatch and shook his head disapprovingly.

To change the embarrassing subject I asked him how old he was. A faraway look settled in his dim eyes. His scrawny hands came up in a gesture of encircling a sphere the size of a grapefruit. 'When I boy, the moon thees beeg,' he said solemnly.

I could make my own calculations.

'Put a kid on a horse'

Riding the outlaw's horse was for me the beginning of an endless succession of rendering services to which I was unaccustomed but for which my small body was adequate.

When we first came, Magdalena was the nearest post office and of course our base of supplies. We might collect the mail every thirty days, when we traveled to town for provisions. For the rest of the month, any chance passer-by was apt to hand a letter to us if he didn't forget to deliver it. 'Any mail for the folks out west?' the west-bound traveler would ask the Magdalena post-master. We missed an occasional important letter, but on the whole the system was satisfactory. Someone was always going our way. Through Datil Cañon and past our door flowed all the traffic of the vast realm of cow-country to the west, for which Magdalena was still the base of supplies. In endless caravans wobbly-wheeled sheeted wagons went back and forth drawn by slow burros or skinny horses.

Several months after our arrival a weekly mail route was es-tablished from Magdalena to Baldwin's, which now became offi-cially 'Datil' by decree of the United States Post Office. If we hadn't done so before, we children certainly earned our bed and board then! In rain or shine, heat or cold, daylight or night-time, we made that twenty-mile round trip on horseback singly or in pairs every Monday of the world. With mail sacks flabby though never empty (for my mother was one of that species rapidly be-coming extinct — a letter-writer) going to the post office, and bulg-ing with mail coming back from it (we subscribed to innumerable papers and magazines), we children high-trotted back and forth, up and down that ten-mile stretch of Datil Cañon, for more times than I probably would believe if count had been kept.

With icicles six inches long hanging from my pony's nostrils, and with frostbitten feet, I have made the trip in sub-zero weather, or, in midsummer, I have ridden it with the sun blasting down with all the force of a glass furnace. I have ridden it on easy-gaited horses, on rough-gaited horses, horses that were gentle and horses that were not: I have ridden it when I wanted to and when I didn't, when my excited imagination had Indians following me, and when I knew that coyotes were.

'Put a kid on a horse' was the formula for sending messages. Between our several ranch establishments messages had to go back and forth continually; and we children carried them. Some-times we led a pack-horse loaded with supplies, or, if the size of the load did not justify an extra horse, our own saddles were hung with bulging sacks until we resembled juvenile mounted Santa Clauses.

It was while on one of our horseback errands that Ray, although still a very small boy, again showed his mettle. He had gone with some of the men over to Los Esteros to help gather steers for the fall market. Word came that a steer-buyer was in Magdalena offering the season's top price. Jim Broyles must be informed and his reply as to date of delivery be sent back to the steer-buyer.

I was immediately put on a horse to execute the first half of the errand. I made the fifteen-mile trip as fast as it could be made, and luckily found the outfit at headquarters. The foreman's oral answer was given to Ray. Much simpler than writing it, and anyway, Jim Broyles was a better cowhand than penman. Ray, in turn, was put on whatever horse could best be spared and told to 'split the breeze' for home, and, as it transpired, for the added fifty miles into Magdalena with scarcely a stop. This does not count the fifty-mile return trip.

I remained overnight with Mrs. Broyles at Los Esteros. The next day I started for home. The first half of the trail led through heavily timbered country, the characteristic piñon, cedar, and juniper of the lower levels. I had gone but a few miles when, in the trail ahead of me, I noticed tracks, a broad foot with toes spread as though the track-maker had never worn shoes. I remember wondering if it could be a Mexican sheepherder — pest of cattlemen. Then I saw that there was more than one track, and that Ray's horse's imprint often fell on top of the others.

Now, tracks of any sort were a puzzle to be solved, easily or after long, hard speculation. So for the next hour I devoted myself to trying to read the story of those tracks. I knew that I must be able to give an intelligent account of them when I reached home. It was part of the responsibility, upon return from a journey, to report upon everything that had been observed, and to do it minutely and reliably

When I arrived home on this occasion, I felt apologetic because I had not solved the riddle of those tracks. My mother rushed out to meet me with evidence of more concern than she usually showed. 'Goodness, I'm glad you're back. Did you see the grizzlies?'

What had happened was this: Ray, trotting briskly along that same trail in the late afternoon of the previous day, had suddenly come upon a large grizzly bear and two half-grown cubs, not fifty yards ahead of him. His horse had reared violently, while the shock of riding unexpectedly up to what is said to be the most dangerous wild animal known, a she-grizzly with cubs, had sent the blood spurting from Ray's nose in a veritable hemorrhage. My mother said that his shirt-front was so bloodstained that her first thought was that he had been stabbed.

The bear, it seemed, had been equally startled. She reared to her haunches and growled terrifyingly, but for some reason did not attack. Had she done so, Ray would have been doomed, because in thick underbrush a grizzly can overtake a horse, and Ray would undoubtedly have been raked off by the low branches. He said, however, that he and the bear both seemed petrified, and just stared at one another.

Finally, the bear came down on her four feet and began to walk leisurely along the trail ahead of him, her cubs at her heels. Here it was that Ray proved himself. He had an important message to deliver, grizzly bear or no grizzly bear. He followed those bears at a discreet distance for almost five miles, before they turned off the trail and he could make up for lost time by racing his horse the rest of the way home.

In later years, after considerable experience with grizzlies, he often said that he had instinctively done the only safe thing, in letting the bear have her own way and not attempting to ride around her. Of course, he could have returned to Los Esteros and confessed that he was afraid to go on alone in a grizzly-infested region with night coming on. But he wouldn't have been Ray had

he done it, nor if the shock had so unnerved him that he couldn't
start into Magdalena at two o'clock the next morning in order to
catch the steer-buyer before the train left.

Ignominy was my portion of the episode. I hadn't recognized a
bear track when I saw one, but rather had believed myself to be
following a sheepherder. Hence I could claim no credit for bravery.
Well, a bear track does look like a barefooted man's track. To be
afraid of the sheepherder did not occur to me.

The friends I was to make at school later always found it
hard to believe that we children went about alone with such
wild animals roaming around. But we never heard of a case of
unprovoked attack upon human beings by a wild animal. We
wandered as far from home as our enterprises called for. When in
camp, we spread our beds down wherever fancy or the absence of
cactus dictated, and slept the night through.

Once some of our twenty-miles-away neighbors, the three Bob
Wiley youngsters — the eldest aged eight — decided that they
wanted to go camping by themselves. Thinking that nightfall
would see them home, the parents consented. Night came, but no
youngsters, so Father Wiley went in search. He found them over
a mile from the house, sleeping sweetly in their blankets, and tiptoed away as a mother might from the nursery. It was three days
before a shortage of rations drove the young adventurers home.

Only once did Lora confess to having a bad night in camp.

'I kept hearing a man walking around and when I spoke to him
he wouldn't answer.'

'You *sure?*' she was pressed.

'Well, I could hear his spurs plain as anything!' she held her
ground.

What she had heard was the clink of chain hobbles on one of the
horses which grazed close to her bed. That was not the night, however, when she and Ray, both young for the business in hand,
hauled a load of grain from Magdalena. Camping in the timber at

the top of the divide out from town, they had heard coyotes. Ray, who was in charge, built a miniature brush corral around Lora's bed and lit a fire close by as protection for her. Then he climbed on top of the load of sacks of grain and slept in the hard trough between two of them. 'I had to keep the horses away from the grain,' he insisted. But Lora never ceased to accuse him of seeking the safer position — a point not too well taken, for both of them knew in their hearts that there was no real danger. Still, they were mere children, and coyotes do 'sound awful.'

Ray was once actor in an adult drama, but I am not entirely sure who was the hero. Anyway, Ray had gone with two of our cowboys to bring home a bunch of strays which had made their way back to their former range 'east of the river.' A thin trickle of water slipped down the lowest trough of the otherwise dry Rio Grande when they crossed over for a five- or six-day hunt for our ever-straying cattle. In those five or six days it rained prodigiously. Finding the cattle was given up as hopeless now that there were surface water-holes everywhere and cattle were no longer forced to come to the few all-year watering places.

On their way home the two men, with ten-year-old Ray in their charge, stopped at a little Mexican plaza a few miles back from the eastern edge of the river. An old Mexican couple on the outskirts of town gave them quarters for the night. Missouri Pete was determined to look up a little excitement: what are towns for, after all?

'If I didn't have the kid along,' Jim Broyles said regretfully, 'I'd sure go along and paint this here greaser joint red. But I done told his mother I'd look out for him.'

He sighed at the toll virtue was exacting, and pulled off his boots preparatory to rolling into bed beside Ray.

Toward dawn he was awakened by Missouri Pete hissing in his ear: 'Had a run-in with a Mexican. His shot missed me, but mine hit him. Don't know if it killed him or not, but the whole damn town is out after me.'

Jim Broyles, barely awake, nevertheless did some high-speed planning.

'Take my horse from the corral and drag it for the river. If you can't cross, hide in the willows 'til I find you. Double on your tracks as much as you got time for. I'll pretend we don't know you and that we just met up with you before coming into town, and that you've stole my horse. Damn lucky your horse ain't got the company brand on it.'

He paused. 'I'll have to judge by the turn things take what next. You know, it's the kid I got to look out for first. Don't forget that.'

Ray, who was awakened by now, remembered this conversation in minutest detail. Jim Broyles turned to him after Missouri Pete had vanished.

'Pretend to be asleep, kid,' he ordered, 'and don't forget that all the Spanish you know is "*No sabe.*"'

Moments later, a shouting mob of mounted Mexicans descended upon the place, to the utter terror of the old couple who had offered shelter to the gringo wayfarers. Every man carried a weapon of one sort or another, the leader a coiled rope in addition to his shotgun. The mob burst into the room where Ray and his protector lay feigning sleep. Naturally, there were no lights to be

switched on, the only illumination being a flickering candle held
aloft by the trembling master of the house.

'*Quien es?*' Jim Broyles asked, in the presumably last words
of Billy the Kid. Voluble Spanish filled the room. Missouri Pete
had shot a peace-loving citizen of the town, and hang the murderer
the victim's friends would, in instant revenge.

'And the other gringo wolf as well,' contributed a voice.

'And the wolf cub, for good measure!' shouted another.

It was one of those moments of unleashed frenzy which sweep
mobs into insane acts.

Jim Broyles faced the ring of baleful faces, doubly baleful in
the dancing shadows cast by the flickering candle.

'What yuh wastin' time for?' he yelled in their own tongue.
'Let's ketch him before he gits away!' He had assumed leadership
by sheer force of bravado. 'I never seen the cuss till he threw in
with us just before we hit town,' he went on, elbowing his way
through the crowd. 'My horse is in the corral. *Vamanos!*'

He was hauling Ray, who carried his boots in his hand, along
with him. The mob, Jim Broyles in the lead, surged out to the
corral. It was barely light enough to see the outlined forms of
two horses.

'*Caramba!*' yelled Jim Broyles. 'The —— —— ——' (Mexican
epithets, I am told, are quite as picturesque as our own) 'has stole
my horse, the best horse in the VV outfit. Give me that rope,
amigo!'

There were witnesses to the fact that Jim Broyles had indeed
ridden into town on a big bay branded VV and now missing.

'I'll hang the —— —— —— to the first tree when we ketch
him!' he thundered, reaching for the coil of rope. But the Mexican
who held it shook his head.

'We'll wait and see if you are playing a trick.' he snarled, 'and
if you are, we'll hang all three of you. Cubs that don't grow up
don't turn into killer wolves!'

Ray always said that he could barely hear above the chattering of his own teeth. Somehow he got into his boots and onto his horse. The other horsemen closed in around him and Jim Broyles as the mob headed for the timbered country between the plaza and the river in the direction in which Missouri Pete's tracks led.

Jim took one desperate chance. He spoke in swift undertone in English to Ray.

'Keep close to me, and when I say "Ride," you *ride!*'

A Mexican glowered at him, but it was evident that the man did not understand English. Few of those 'east of the river' Mexicans did in those days.

Jim Broyles was one of the best trailers in the country, and he was not long in proving it. 'But you'll have to let me ride in the lead if we are to make time,' he said, reasonably enough.

Missouri Pete had been clever at leaving a trail difficult to follow, and more than once Jim Broyles's pretense at losing it was convincingly plausible; every time he did so he jockeyed for a better position for himself and Ray.

Finally the river lay in sight a mile from the last of the piñon timber through which they were riding, and across a fairly open flat beyond which stretched a fringe of willows shielding the river's bank.

'*Ride!*' he commanded Ray from the corner of his mouth. Aloud he yelled, 'There he goes!'

He always insisted that when he gave that order he meant to indicate that he had picked up the lost trail, and had not seen Missouri Pete just ahead — that he was no less surprised to see him than was Missouri Pete himself when the racing pursuers broke through the intervening brush.

But if Jim Broyles was surprised, he kept his wits for the second time that day. He yelled after Pete:

'The river! And don't let us ketch you. for I'll help hang you if we do!'

The crazy race was on. Jim Broyles fired as he rode, his skill-fully placed shots kicking up the dust at Missouri Pete's horse's heels as fast as he could fire and reload. All three of the Americans were better mounted than the Mexicans and they steadily pulled away from their companions, whose shots in turn began coming disquietingly close to their own ponies' heels.

To the last day of his life Ray spoke with a sort of awed rever-ence when the subject of the accuracy of Jim Broyles's shooting on this occasion was mentioned.

'How shot after shot could come so close and yet not hit was unbelievable. Best markmanship I've ever seen,' he would say. 'Missouri Pete must have been doing some tall guessing.'

Jim Broyles, for his part, spoke modestly in reminiscence. 'Had to do it that way; didn't know myself if I was after him in earnest or not.'

The three reached the protecting willow fringe a couple of hundred yards ahead of the Mexicans. A moment later they were in the half-mile-wide stream, their horses swimming strongly.

'Grab your pony's tail, son,' he ordered, 'and keep as low in the water as you can.'

The two men likewise slid from their horses' backs and swam alongside the animals, holding a stirrup leather with one hand.

Bullets pinged on all sides of them, but the pursuers did not venture into the water. They knew that river!

'We were pretty badly waterlogged when our horses pulled us out on the opposite bank,' Ray usually concluded the tale, 'but really what bothered us was what we were going to tell Mother.'

'Tell her nothing' was the final verdict. This had been man's business. What women didn't know they couldn't worry about. It was many years before our trusting mother was told that once the unpredictable Rio Grande had saved the life of her son.

Children GREW UP

QUICKLY

We children were not at all unusual among the ranch children of our day. They had to behave like sensible adults on occasion, and they did.

Claude stands out in my recollection as a case in point. Riding down Datil Cañon one day, I saw him perched on a high, broad-topped gatepost, more than two miles from his home. He was at the age when children lose their front teeth, and I expected to see a dental hiatus when he greeted me; but Claude was not grinning. He stared at me with round, saucerlike eyes out of a face which suggested pallor, although, because of the usual small-boy smudges, I wasn't entirely sure of its hue. But I was sure that he was worried.

'What's the matter, Claude?' I asked, feeling that nothing short of a major disaster could change him from the puckish urchin I knew to this round-eyed and obviously distraught young man.

'I just seen a b'ar, right over thar on that hill, a sure-'nuff b'ar with a cub, and I clumb this post.'

'How long ago?' I asked.

'I dunno. I been sittin' up here quite a spell.'

'Where were you headed for?'

'Over to the edge of the plains. We got a milk cow runnin' over there and Paw told me to go 'n' hunt 'er up and see if she's goin' to have a calf anywheres soon and if she is to bring her home.'

I looked at Claude with new respect. It hadn't occurred to me before to regard him as an expert on bovine obstetrics.

'But I sort of hate to go lookin' for her afoot,' he went on; 'not with that thar b'ar headin' in the same direction ...' The point was well taken; Ray had been mounted when he met his mother bear. An irritated she-bear might well have been aware of the difference between a small boy afoot and one on horseback.

Claude climbed down from his pillar. 'I guess I'll go on home,' he decided. 'The last time I seen that thar cow I was dawgone sure she ain't ready to have airy calf yet.'

Later I had opportunity to ask him about the state of the cow's health.

'Aw, she's all right. I went over for her a coupla weeks after that b'ar scared me out and I got her home in time. 'Course, I had to bring her awful slow. She's got a purty bull calf.'

Then there was the incident of Lorny Adams and her burro. Lorny was an eerie, undersized little morsel of humanity, whom I remember best by her great black eyes set in a tiny face fringed with straight black hair. The only girl in a family of robust boys, with whom she could not hold her own in any pursuits, Lorny gave her unstinted devotion to a moth-eaten piebald burro who was companion, confidant, and comforter for all her childish problems. They must have been numberless in that riotous family of budding cowpunchers.

One of our periodic spring droughts had laid the country prostrate. Cattle died as the range gradually became sere and withered. The economic tragedy of having to haul high-priced grain seventy miles from Magdalena to keep alive even their few absolutely essential saddle-horses weighed heavily upon the Adams family. Feeding a useless burro was considered out of the question.

When the *morrals* were hung on the horses the burro would stand by nibbling at the improvised gunnysack feedbags, until kicked away by an exasperated pony or driven off by sticks and stones thrown by the pony's owner. It was more than Lorny could bear; so at feeding time she would lead her burro away from the ranch, searching out odd spots where a bit of herbage might be found in some nook or cranny, and because burros are hardy, the animal managed to exist, though his ribs became daily more conspicuous.

Then one day, in her search with her burro for food, she made a tremendous discovery. The big half-acre corral where herds were penned during roundup season was overgrown with that early succulent weed, lamb's-quarter. The corral bars had been left up and not a hoof had been within the enclosure for months. It was a burro's manna from heaven. It would last for a considerable length of time, possibly until the rains came; for already encouraging thunderheads had begun to form every afternoon and, some day, it would rain!

So to the distant corral Lorny and her burro repaired at feeding time, and only Lorny and the burro knew whither they went.

Then late one evening as they neared the corral, tragedy bore down upon them in the form of an approaching herd of several hundred head of range cattle driven by half a dozen shouting cowboys.

Lorny, astride her burro, saw one of the men dash ahead, lay down the corral bars, which of course she had always been careful to lay up, and gallop back to the herd. He apparently had not seen her.

Possibly the burro, too, sensed the emergency, for it took but slight urging for him to put on his full burro speed. Into the corral galloped Lorny, only a length ahead of the lead longhorn steers, who themselves had sniffed green feed.

The cowboys, of course, had seen her by this time and were doing their frantic but futile best to turn the herd.

There was time for the child to put but two of the poles in place before the herd was surging up to the opening. Climbing onto the lower bar, and precariously supported by the higher one, little Lorny turned into a young fury. She beat the foremost cattle in the face with her sunbonnet, screaming defiance. Providentially the bars held until horsemen could force their way through the crowding cattle to relieve the pressure upon them.

'You can't pen your old herd in this corral,' Lorny hurled defiance at the trail boss. 'This is my burro's pasture. It's all he's got to eat. Your old herd would tramp it all down in a minute, but it'll do my burro till it rains.'

The boss of the outfit who told me the story added the sequel:

'We was all plumb give out from standin' guard three nights already, tryin' to get that herd to town and shipped out of the country before they all died. We'd made a forced drive to get to this corral, so's we could pen the cattle and get ourselves a night's sleep, which we shore needed; but hell, what's a feller to do when a baby stands floppin' her bonnet in the face of a Texas longhorn and a-tellin' him to stay the hell outa her burro's feed lot?'

'What did you do?' I asked superfluously.

'Well, I sez, "Boys, it looks like we stand guard again tonight," and they all sez, "Looks like we do."'

An apologetic look came into his eyes.

'Funny,' he said, 'what a thing like that can do. That outfit was all bowed-up. Every man in it was wringy. You know how we all get in a dry spring tryin' to work pore cows? Well, I'd been prayin' all day — you know what I mean — that we'd reach that corral and let the men sleep off some of their tiredness and cussedness before real trouble broke out, but that night every man went out whistlin' to his turn at night guard, and even the cook acted almost human next mornin'.'

I am glad to add that it rained very soon thereafter.

Another story involved a small boy whose name I cannot recall. He lived over near the Muleshoe Ranch. A snowstorm descended upon the section and the youngster, unbeknownst to his family, set out horseback to look for his pet pony, which had been too long missing and for whose fate in the snow the boy was gravely concerned. He felt that he *must* find his pony, and find it he did, but only as a hollowed-out, skin-covered skeleton. Lightning had probably killed it, and then coyotes had eaten all the internal organs, leaving a clean and dried-out carcass covered with a hide too tough for the jackals to tear.

The little owner dismounted, sat down beside all that remained of a dear friend, and cried. The tears froze on his cheeks. As he sat there a sudden gale of blizzard proportions swept across the San Augustine Plains. The fury of the wind was so great that shelter, any shelter, was imperative.

'I knowed Billy'd want to help me if he could,' the boy said when he finally told the tale long afterward, 'so I just crawled inside him out of the wind and my other horse stood alongside all humped up. 'Course he had a saddle and saddle blanket on, which helped him. After a while it quit blowing so hard and I was getting so stiff and cold I knew I had to move around or I'd freeze, so I crawled out of Billy and took hold of Pete's tail and told him to go home and he did. He drug me through snowdrifts that'd 'a' been too deep for me, alone, and he never minded me pulling his tail. I wrapped some of it around my hands, and that helped keep them warm.'

Exhausted but alive, the child reached home. Yes, horses know!

But Daisy Field was without exception the most independent and self-possessed young person I ever knew. Her folks ran the Tres

Hermanos trading-post in the lower stretch of the Alamosa Creek region for the benefit of the few white cattlemen of the vicinity and the then orphaned tribe of the Alamo Indians, a lost Navajo tribe about whom it will be necessary to say a word before this tale is finished. No one was present to aid her mother when Daisy was born.

She was slightly less than four years old when I first made her acquaintance. Her parents and a small party, including myself, were on an exploring expedition to a gypsum cave in the foothills of the magnificent Ladrone Mountains. The cave had been discovered a few days previously by a sheepherder. Save for this Mexican, who had not gone very far into its many corridors and grottoes, we were in all probability the first human beings to penetrate its un- cannily beautiful stalagmite and stalactite miniature forests. Few have, to this day.

Of course, we had only tallow candles to light our precarious way. Daisy carried her own candle and asked odds of no one. Once or twice, finding herself left behind in inky darkness, she called to us, but never with any sign of fear.

We were some hundreds of feet along our way when we reached a small room whose only egress, other than the one by which we had entered, was an opening at the floor line, a mammoth rat-hole. A big dog might have wriggled through, but not a full-grown human being.

'I'll go in and see what's on the other side,' volunteered Daisy, and only a quick hand stopped her from executing the offer.

But the hole was enticing, and it was finally decided that I, being next in size to Daisy, would attempt to crawl through on my stomach, cautiously, and with two men hanging to my feet should the hole prove to lead nowhere but down.

I thrust my unlighted candle ahead of me and carried a few matches by their stick ends in my mouth. Then I began to wriggle. It was a tight squeeze, and I barely managed to get my shoulders

through and completely block the hole. Then I lighted my candle
— clumsily. On the instant my hair was ablaze. In the sudden
awful flare I saw a well of inky blackness falling away directly under
me and the candle I dropped went down, down, down. Frantically
I beat at my head, turned torch, with my bare hands and screamed.
Of course I kicked. This signal was understood. I was jerked back
through the jagged hole, torn and scratched and, needless to say,
badly singed, although fortunately not badly burned. I had, however, no eyebrows, eyelashes, or hair on the northeast quadrant of
my head, and as soon as everyone was assured that this was the
only damage, that cave re-echoed with its first human laughter.
Peal after peal rang out as one after another of the amateur explor-
ers held his candle to my face.

'You shore do look funny,' Daisy told me. 'I'm glad I didn't go
in there if I'd of come out lookin' like you.' If she'd have come out
at all!

That night, sitting by the campfire at the cave's mouth, Daisy
engaged me in serious conversation. By this time she had two
younger sisters and the subject of babies was of immediate interest.
I had just come home from my first year away at school and was
looked upon as an authority on all matters to do with 'back East.'

Gravely Daisy propounded her query:

'What does babies cost back East?'

'Well — er,' I floundered, 'I don't just know.'

'You can git 'em for nothin' in this country,' Daisy spoke orac-
ularly, 'but' — and she sighed — 'you can't git such good
ones.'

'I've got a picter of a baby angel,' she went on, producing from
her small packet of personal belongings a battered magazine.
Turning to a picture of Saint Cecilia at the organ, 'See them there
angels?' — Daisy pointed to the winged cherubs hovering above
Saint Cecilia. 'Well, them angels belongs to God. They works
for him. They hauls his wood, and when he gits through with

em he hobbles 'em so they can't run away to the Ladrones. God sure makes 'em work.'

The family's theology and its daily experiences were interwoven in her baby mind. She flipped a page to a picture of a crowd of people. 'God made all them, I s'pose. He's sure a hard worker Hisself, looks like.'

All of this is preliminary, however, to Daisy's act of real heroism. She was now about six and there were more babies — all girls — ultimately to the number of nine.

Naturally, 'store' toys were not the rule in the Field household. Daisy wanted a little red wagon which was depicted alluringly in Montgomery Ward's catalogue of enchantment. It cost two dollars, which was two dollars more than was allowed for such items in the family budget.

Daisy confided her longings to Johnny (Bowlegs) Payne, who was then a youngster cowhand for Father Field. Now, Bowlegs didn't have two dollars either, but feeling that he could probably negotiate an advance in wages or a loan and being quite sure of the improbability of needing to, he promised, with adolescent impishness, 'I tell you what, Daisy, the next time Eddie Becker comes along you jump on him and whip him good and I'll give you two dollars.'

Eddie Becker was a junior member of the Becker clan, merchants with widespread mercantile interests throughout New Mexico, and was accustomed to make trips with his father to the various small stores and trading-posts for which they were wholesale purveyors from their Belen headquarters. The Beckers were generally looked up to and respected — sole reason for Bowlegs's perverse suggestion. For surely the eight-year-old Eddie little deserved the fate that befell him the next time he and his father stepped from their buckboard in front of the Fields' trading-post.

Without warning, Daisy flew at him like a young termagant, clawing, kicking, and scratching until the heavy hand of Mother

Field dragged her off the dumbfounded Eddie before he had gathered enough of his wits together to fight back. Into whatever served as woodshed Mother Field led Daisy and there persuaded her, by the direct method of pioneer mothers, to mend her manners.

Daisy emerged slightly bruised in body, but exalted in spirit. She sought out Bowlegs. 'Well, I whupped him,' she said, wiping her eyes with the back of her hand. 'Give me my two dollars.' With a triumphant gleam in her eye she added, 'I'll haul them babies around now 'stead of carryin' 'em pick-a-back.'

It wasn't so long ago that I asked Bowlegs if he wasn't ashamed of himself. 'Well, yes and no,' he answered. 'Everybody's got to earn what he gets in this life, don't he?'

Animals WERE OUR
FRIENDS

Horses were an integral part of our lives. The day's activity began no more by putting on one's clothes than by 'getting up the horses.' It was routine to bring all the horses from the pasture into the home corral before breakfast, even though the day's plans were still unmade. Whatever those plans might turn out to be, they would involve horses.

And here again we children were useful cogs in the social machinery. It was we who were routed out of bed at dawn and sent to 'rustle the pasture.' The shoe leather I have worn out tramping over the brushy, rock-studded ridges of that home horse pasture would have shod half a dozen city youngsters in the same length of time.

Opinion was divided on the question of whether it was easier to find a horse wearing a bell or one without. Personally I held to the latter. My ears played tricks which my eyes did not. If I listened for a far-off tinkle of a horse-bell, I heard it from the moment I left home, and from several directions at once. But if I must rely upon

sharp vision, I could detect, as far as eye could reach, the rump
of a brown horse from a tree stump of the same shade behind
which he might be standing. Horses are very canny. If they
suspect they are wanted, they hide, as deliberately as children
playing hide-and-seek. They will stand motionless in a clump of
trees or behind a boulder, defying detection. Listening for a bell in
such circumstances is not only futile but distracting.

On the other hand, of course, horses aren't always motionless
when they are being hunted. They are hunted morning, noon, and
night, and they must move about to graze. So if your ears serve
you better than your eyes you'll line up with the opposition in the
discussions that still go on in the cow country.

But regardless of disputes in the matter of technic, everyone
would agree that nothing could go forward until the horses were
hunted — and found. In those early years of the open range,
when fences were few and everybody's livestock wandered at will,
hunting horses consumed a disproportionate amount of time.
Every ranchwoman has had to forego some sorely needed convenience in her living arrangements if there was not money to provide
both it and a wagonload of barbed wire to make horse-hunting
easier.

More projects had to be abandoned because the horses were not
found than would have developed two Wests had the projects gone
forward as scheduled. It was this utter dependence upon horses
who had ideas of their own that put an element of uncertainty into
every plan, and made orderly living impossible.

Not infrequently the errand for which a horse was used could
have been done with half the walking that was devoted to looking
for the horse, but one didn't do errands on foot. In fact, one must
never be seen afoot except in the business of looking for a horse.
I know that had I ever been surprised away from home afoot, I
should have invented a mythical lost horse rather than admit that
I had used my own legs for any purpose whatsoever other than to

look for a horse. As a matter of fact, 'hunting a horse' was a universal and invaluable, because always plausible, excuse for one's otherwise not easily explained presence or absence. It was a favorite alibi for prowling on another man's range. There were too many 'lost horse' hunters for my mother's business success.

Horses' personalities were even more vivid in our minds than the personalities of our human associates. The mounted stranger yielded first place in interest to the horse he bestrode. A year later we might have forgotten the color of the man's eyes, but never the set of the ears on his horse's head.

Had there been any local newspaper in Datil, the social items would have run somewhat thus:

> Owen Patterson got his mail at Baldwin's last Monday. He was riding a ring-tailed buckskin branded T L. Owen wants to match his pony against any one in the country whose owner has the notion it's fast.

> Bill Jones was seen riding down White Horse Cañon on his favorite cutting-horse, the sorrel with a gotch ear. The horse used to belong to August Kiehne.

Billy Swingle came over from the creek riding a pinto and leading a strawberry-roan pack-horse.

While we children did each have our own pet pony, as a sort of playmate, it was any available horse that must serve when we were on duty. The requirements were simply that the horse should not throw us off, or, if he did, that he would not run away and leave us stranded. Other than a reasonable hope — and this point was often strained — that we could stay on the horse at all, there were no standards set for our mounts. Horses of every temperament and every sort of habit, good or bad, provided there was expectation they would get us there and back, were considered 'safe.'

I recall a heated argument between two of our cowhands about whether I should ride one long-legged cayuse named Roadrunner. 'He ain't safe fer her,' argued one.

'What you mean, ain't safe?' retorted the other. 'If he throws her off he won't run away. She can ketch him again.' That was the criterion.

We couldn't choose easy gaits or amiable dispositions. Business pressed and we took whatever horseflesh was at hand. It is this which makes a rider — and bowlegs.

Johnny Payne explained how he came to deserve his nickname of 'Bowlegs': 'You see, I was never off a horse longer than two weeks at one time, and then I had the measles. I just kept on ridin' with all my other diseases.' He later became one of Ray's informal partners and one of the pair known as Towhead and Bowlegs. Ray's nickname was so well established that he once received a letter from a New York prankster addressed, 'Towhead, New Mexico.'

Ranch children played few games among themselves. Entertainment took the form of playing with animals. The pets which we acquired at various times ranged the gamut of animal life about us, both wild and the semi-domesticated range stock. One scene must have amused an onlooker, had there been one.

We had fenced in a quarter-mile square of cañon *vega* land for an overnight horse pasture. The easiest and quickest fence to build was one of pine logs laid end to end, their ends overlapping just enough to permit a short tie-chunk to be laid across the two tips. Then a second row of logs was put on top of those on the ground. Since the logs were eighteen inches to two feet in diameter, the top of the fence offered easy footing. There must have been a hundred thousand board feet of lumber in this fence, proving how highly we prized grass.

Of course we children raced around and around on top of this fence, and I have a vivid recollection of a procession that often made the rounds. Being the eldest, I led, then in order, Ray, Lora, Joe, a collie dog; Spotty, a young fawn; Smarty, a goat and foster-mother to the fawn; Bobby, the cat; Buffalo Bill, a rooster who, being our solitary barnyard fowl, turned to the rest of the menagerie for company and was received by them into full comradeship. Shuffling along in the rear came young Josh, a three-months-old black bear. On the ground alongside ran Pedro, the burro, and Bonita, the milk-pen calf, both apparently chagrined that they couldn't negotiate the fence-top. Occasionally Joe would step over onto the burro's back, to be followed by Buffalo Bill, who usually went where Joe did. The burro tolerated them, but never Josh.

In our extreme isolation all living things seemed to want to stick together. We did not try teaching these animals tricks, but we watched them develop their own. Old Mac, one of our horses, would turn a doorknob with his lips and thrust his head into the kitchen and whinny until given a biscuit. Block, another horse, watched Mac and then walked up and turned that doorknob himself. I shall never forget the astonishment when a bay head with a white blaze face appeared instead of the expected sorrel.

Block was a horse to be reckoned with. Because he had the habit of pacing when he shifted gaits on a long trip and wanted relief from the perpetual jog trot, he was disliked by the ranch hands, to whom pacing horses are anathema (they stumble), and was turned over to me if I thought I could ride him — a matter of doubt in the cowboys' minds, for Block was given to 'swallerin' his head' upon slight provocation. This turn of fate suited Block perfectly. He disliked men as much as they disliked him, but liked women and children.

I looked out the window one day to see a four-year-old girl astride him, whooping gleefully. What made the apparition startling was the fact that Block was lying down, presumably to enjoy a mid-morning siesta. Instead, he was patiently serving as stooge for the young lady's first attempt at solo horsemanship.

It was this same young person who shortly thereafter essayed her first real ride unattended. A few moments later she appeared, slightly disheveled.

'What happened?'

'Well,' she said, with elaborate nonchalance, 'old Block shied at a board.'

'Yes, then what?'

'Then I got on him again.'

We did not do violence to pride by insisting on a complete explanation.

She found it easy to dismount — she simply came down his foreleg like a fireman down a brass pole. But to remount sometimes offered difficulties. Nevertheless, she asked help of no one.

One night at supper she sat in her high chair, unusually thoughtful. Finally she burst out: 'I've got it! I'll tie a rope around Block's neck and lead him to the fence and then I'll tie the other end of the rope to the fence. And then I'll get a box and climb on him and then I'll untie the rope from around his neck. That'll fix it.'

Ranch youngsters were given to facing their own problems. We learned, less from our elders, than from our own mistakes, usually because we undertook more than we could manage.

One summer morning Milt Craig, his elder sister Lulu, and I — all of us in our early teens — set out from the INM Ranch on the Alamosa with the Datils as our destination — normally a trip of twenty-five miles. We decided to try the Red Cañon Trail — a route which only experts in trail-following attempted. Milt had ridden races at the State Fair in Albuquerque when he was eight, and was accounted the best jockey of the lot. He considered himself also an expert in trail-following, but the Red Cañon Trail proved his undoing. There were countless cañons all looking amazingly alike, and of course there were cattle trails leading up all of them.

At a critical point, Milt led us up a left-hand fork instead of a right-hand one and we were promptly and hopelessly lost in the steepest, jaggedest, brushiest country in ten states. This fateful choice occurred early in the morning. At sundown we were on top of a high peak overlooking the San Augustine Plains at a point closer to Magdalena than to Datil. It was midnight when we reached Datil, having covered something like sixty miles without food. We did not suffer for lack of water. It rained the last seven hours.

The next time I traveled the Red Cañon route under competent escort, there was a sign cut into the white trunk of a huge cottonwood which stood at the critical forks. Crude as was the lettering, it must have taken some zealot a half-day to carve it. It read, 'Take rite hnd trale or you be damn sorry of it.'

Milt denies authorship to this day, but I am unconvinced.

Ray AND I FIGHT IT OUT

THE rivalry between Ray and myself in those first years was keen. His masculine strength was pitted against my two years' advantage in age and corresponding stature. Lora, a frail child, was never a competitor in the tests of bravado which Ray and I felt called upon to set each other. I held a slight edge over him until the day we fought over who should remove the ticks from the calf's ears.

I discovered the wood ticks in the milk-pen calf's ears and set about removing them with a bent wire. Ray insisted that I hold the calf and let him perform the operation. I countered with the claim that by right of discovery I should have the morbid satisfaction of digging out the ticks and he should hold the calf. The dispute quickly reached the violent stage and we grappled. I succeeded in getting my arms around his neck from behind and

holding his head tight against my chest with the idea of cutting off his wind, while I used my feet further to enforce my point of view. It was a tactic that had proved successful before. But this time there was a difference. Before I knew what had happened I was on my back and Ray was sitting on my chest. 'Give up?' he asked — a quite superfluous question under the circumstances — and then with characteristic magnanimity he added, 'All right, I'll let you take the ticks out of one ear.' After that I never challenged him on his own ground of sheer physical strength, but confined myself to taking him on in matters of skill or cleverness, where I was often no more successful.

If he reported some feat of which a small boy might be proud, I was given to saying, 'Oh, I could have done *that*.' I was, unquestionably, extremely offensive in my determination to deflate his masculine ego. Until the day he scored his second triumph.

He had been on a trip to the Los Esteros Ranch with a pack-horse laden with supplies. The pack had slipped en route and it had taken all of his eleven-year-old prowess to get it back in place. ('I could have done *that*' — from me.) There had been a small cloudburst and the flood water in several arroyos had made fording precarious. ('I could have done *that*.') He had found nobody at home when he arrived at Los Esteros so he'd been compelled to unload the pack unaided, tired as he was. ('I could have done *that*.') Had I been less smug, I would have noted a sort of cat-having-eaten-the-canary gleam in Ray's eyes about this time, but my thirteen-year-old self-sufficiency blinded me to the danger signal. 'I thought I'd go on down to the Box Bar's because the boys had taken all the beds [bedrolls] at Los Esteros, but I found the Alamosa Creek was up too high to cross and it looked like I'd have to lay out all night.' He waited for my refrain and I wasn't smart enough to avoid the trap. 'I could have done *that*,' I chanted. Ray hurried on, 'Just then I saw a Mexican sheep camp and I went over to it and slept all night with a dirty Mexican sheep-herder.' He paused, and then in perfect mimicry: 'I could have done *that*.'

Amid the loud guffaws of a tableful of listeners, I fled, my ears red and my spirit crushed.

Ray was dangerous with fists or with tongue, when occasion warranted.

Betting the other he was afraid to get on some horse of dubious character was our favorite sport. When Ray was gray of head and had to have spectacles to read, he confessed to me for the first time that he had ridden many a horse because he feared, should he hesitate, I would get on it with what, he assured me, was my infuriating air of conscious superiority. Once when he made such a bet with me and I took him up on it, quaking in my soul, the horse balked. He stood in ominous stiff-legged immobility, ears a little back, nostrils dilated.

'I'll make him move!' Ray yelled, reaching for a length of board.

'Don't you hit him!' I yelled back. 'He'll rear up.'

'He'll come down again,' Ray assured me, as he brought the board down on the horse's rump.

Rear up he did and come down he did — over backward — and only the Providence which guards growing children prevented me from being caught beneath him.

We didn't tell the grown-ups. A miss was as good as a mile.

Why we weren't maimed far more frequently than we were seems, in retrospect, miraculous. When I catch myself admonishing my granddaughter to 'be careful,' I sometimes remember how Ray, Lora, and I risked our young necks, usually with horses, and how frequently we were pushed to stoicism to conceal injuries from the grown-ups. Once in particular I recall that a horse bucked Ray into a woodpile, but it was almost a week before our mother discovered evidences of a very real injury, so skillful had been his concealment of it, aided and abetted by Lora and me, whose turn, we knew, might come next.

Grown-ups were apt to be unreasonable about such things. They might do something arbitrary and damaging to prestige, such as forbidding one to ride that particular horse again.

By the time he was twelve, Ray was the acknowledged head of our family expeditions. There was an occasion when Mother decided to go with us on the trip to town for provisions.

Ray by right mounted to the driver's seat and gathered up the lines. Mother sat beside him, while Lora and I made ourselves as comfortable as possible on the wagon bed. Considering that this was not a 'spring wagon,' but one whose seat alone was mounted on springs and whose bed rested directly on the running-gear, the 'comfortable as possible' resolved itself into no comfort at all, beyond that afforded by a few pieces of bedding and the big tarpaulin for covering the load on our return. We dispensed with the wagon bows whenever possible because their broad expanse of canvas made harder pulling for the team.

Mother had not yet become inured to camping out, so we had left home before daybreak and planned to make the whole journey into Magdalena in one day. The return trip even with a load could be made back to Baldwin's. With an extra day's rest in town, so Mother reasoned, the horses would suffer no greater hardship under this arrangement — a consideration that was always present when she was planning.

It was a torturing all-day grind across the plains, and Ray magnanimously let me drive a part of the way while his bones were jolted out of their sockets in the wagon bed. We made the journey tolerable by hopping in and out over the tail end of the wagon, running along behind until we tired, and then scrambling back in. There are always ways to ease hardship if one is young enough and supple enough.

It had been cloudless when we set out, but by late afternoon the sky became blue-black and eventually rain came down in sheets. Water ran in the wagon-wheel ruts, and before long it was evident that we could go no farther. Fortunately we had reached the edge of the timber, thirteen miles from town, the im-memorial camp-ground for freighters. We pulled into a clump of trees which broke the direct force of the rain, though they suggested more protection than they actually offered.

We were wet, shivering, and miserable. Ray assumed command. He felled a dead piñon tree and set fire to it. Even in rain a resinous dry piñon will burn after it gets well started. Lora and Mother nursed the fire along by hovering over it, until it blazed too lustily for that. Ray and I unhitched and staked out the team.

'My idea,' said Ray, 'is to pitch a sort of camp on the warm ground where this fire has been. We can tie one end of a rope to this tree and the other to that tree,' indicating two between which the fire was burning, 'and stretch the tarp over the rope like a tent. Then we can all crawl under and keep dry.'

Keeping dry on any terms was what we were thinking about. When Ray decided the fire had burned long enough to have dried the ground beneath it, he ordered us to rake off the burning brands. It took all hands to pull away the dead piñon's main trunk by its unburnt end. Lora, with juniper branches, swept away the last vestiges of sparks and ashes while the rest of us rigged the improvised tent over the bonfire's recent site.

It was agreeably warm under the tarp, and we ate the remainder of our lunch in high spirits. Then we spread our few quilts on the warm earth and lay down to sleep in sardine pattern: Ray on one outer edge, then Mother, beside her Lora, and myself on the other outer edge. I dropped off to sleep to the accompaniment of a pleasant patter of rain on the canvas.

It was not long before Lora's restlessness disturbed me. I hunched over and dozed again. Lora's restlessness increased, and I spoke testily to her: 'For heaven's sake, can't you lie still?'

'I'm hot,' Lora wailed. 'I'm sweating.'

Wide-awake now, we all agreed that it *was* pretty warm, but of course it wouldn't last very long. So I exchanged places with Lora to allow her to cool off on the outer edge. A few more winks of sleep and I was again disturbed, this time by Mother. She was sitting up. 'It is pretty warm,' she said.

Ray mumbled irritably, 'Can't you wimmin let a fellow sleep?'

'Well, *you* get over here on the inside,' Mother commanded, 'and let me have a cooler spot.'

She and Ray exchanged places and I dozed again.

'I'm cold!' Lora's plaint aroused me. 'Agnes keeps pushing me out under the tarp.'

Lora and I again exchanged places.

'You're shoving me, Mother!' It was Ray's voice which waked me this time.

'I'm just trying to keep under the tarp,' Mother told him.

'Well, if you've cooled off, let's trade places again.' We suited the action to the word.

All night long we kept up this leap-frog game, alternately sweating and cooling off suddenly and much too effectively. By morning our nerves were frazzled, but mercifully the rain had stopped.

When we had harnessed the team and were leaving our camp-ground, the imprint of our community bed was sending up a faint steam where the dripping branches above sent down occasional drops of moisture.

'That was certainly a perfect Turkish bath you rigged up,' Mother told Ray, probably not meaning to be as critical as she sounded. I was less disposed to be charitable.

'Ray never asks advice,' I complained; 'he always thinks he knows just what to do.'

'I s'pose you'd of known exactly how long to let the fire burn,' he snapped back. 'I s'pose you think I should of asked *your* advice!'

'Stop quarreling, children,' Mother broke in. 'My only hope is that Lora won't catch pneumonia.'

She seemed to know that neither Ray nor I would, and that anxiety on that score was superfluous.

Aunt Laura TAKES A HAND

Wʜᴇɴ I was thirteen, my mother went to Denver for several months of medical attention. With some idea that our manners needed rehabilitation, she sent for Great-Aunt Laura to stay with us while she was away. Aunt Laura, my Grandmother McPherson's elder sister, regarded a New Mexico cattle ranch as an invention of Lucifer for demoralizing the young.

Forebodings assailed the three of us when we overheard her remark, even before the creak of the buggy wheels which were taking our mother away had died, 'Six months isn't much time for undoing my niece's mistakes of a lifetime with her children, but I'll do my best.'

There ensued for us heretofore free souls a period of bondage comparable to a jail sentence at hard labor. We had never known routine nor discipline as Aunt Laura conceived them. Our rebelliousness was coupled with sheer amazement that anyone could regard certain trifles as being as important as Aunt Laura seemed to regard them.

The first test of opposing viewpoints came when Ray wanted both sugar and syrup on his dish of dried-apple sauce. That was his idea of seasoning. It was not Aunt Laura's. The contest ended with Ray being led from the table by one ear. But he was not vanquished. He repaired to the corral and spent a joyous hour riding the milk-pen calves.

It was skill thus acquired which later made him undefeated champion in many a local rodeo, for a half-grown calf is one of the most difficult of all animals alive to stay on top of, if it doesn't want you to! Unless it be a cantankerous burro. The hides of both are loose upon their frames and give the impression that everything is sliding out from under. I know. I've ridden both.

To anchor himself, Ray would grab the calf's tail in one hand and an ear in the other and 'let 'er buck.' Even little Lora became proficient in the art of 'calf-bustin'.' And it was some time before Aunt Laura discovered what was going on. But she did.

Now, in spinster Aunt Laura's mind this was no proper occupation for children and decidedly not good for the calves. Much better that children should be gathering chips for the kitchen stove or splitting kindling. She forbade us to go near the calf pen. Ray promptly disobeyed this order, to his way of thinking altogether unreasonable. He had an old saddle, so small it was called the 'chicken saddle,' and he wanted to use it. With Lora's help he succeeded in cinching this saddle anything but securely upon the largest calf, a six-months-old bull.

Lora's task was to hold the end of the lariat and not let the calf get away while Ray mounted. They had worried the animal to a spot out of sight of the house, and Lora's further duty was to see that it didn't get within range of the kitchen window, Aunt

Laura's observation post. Ray succeeded in getting on. Then the calf assumed command.

Bucking and bawling, down past the house it came, with Ray swaying drunkenly in the saddle, which slid from rump to withers with every leap the calf made. At the end of the rope, dragged along just a little too fast for her short spindly legs, lunged Lora.

Aunt Laura heard the commotion and was on the scene as promptly as her longer but no less spindly legs could get her there.

'Give me that rope,' she commanded, and jerked it from Lora's hands.

Promptly the calf ran two circles around Aunt Laura before she got her bearings, and the next instant she, Ray, and the calf were a writhing heap on the ground, all beautifully tangled up in the lariat. Ray extricated himself first and betook himself away from there, Lora racing at his heels. Aunt Laura's difficulties had just begun.

It was unquestionably her duty to get that calf back into its pen. The saddle had turned completely and was now suspended from the calf's belly — to his utter disgust, which he proclaimed by increased bellowing and sunfishing.

Aunt Laura jerked on the rope. 'Come along now,' she commanded. And the calf did — right past her to the rope's end with a speed which for the second time yanked her off her feet.

She could, of course, have avoided this by letting go the rope. But she came of an unyielding strain. She got up and again spoke peremptorily to that calf. 'Behave yourself,' she ordered, as one expecting obedience, 'and come along.'

This time the calf came entirely through the saddle. But he didn't come along in the direction Aunt Laura had in mind.

Realizing her dilemma I ran to help her, but she ordered me away. This was a test of mastery, not to be vitiated by outside interference. I saw the heads of Ray and Lora sticking out from behind the trunk of a pine tree and knew that for the sake of

Aunt Laura's future status I should hope for her triumph. The calf, with a bellow of derision, rushed past her once again, this time pulling the rope completely through her hands, leaving two deep rope burns. Nevertheless capture it, and put it back where it belonged, she finally did.

Ray and Lora were slated for punishment; but capture must precede execution. They vanished for the rest of the day. In the end, they went to bed supperless but impenitent. The next day they called me before their drumhead court.

'Are you with us or against us?' they wanted to know. 'We saw you try to help her.'

I tried to explain that Mother had put us on our honor to be 'good children' during her absence and that ——

'Cheese the goody-goody stuff,' Ray cut me short. 'Mother never thought she'd act like she's doin'.'

But, because I have an abortive conscience which functions just enough to keep me in perpetual trouble, I refused to join the rebellion — and paid for my self-righteousness.

When it came time to go for the milch cows neither Ray nor Lora was to be found, and although the duty of bringing in the cows at night had not been assigned me when Aunt Laura made a schedule of our respective duties the first day she took command, it devolved upon me to go after them now.

Two of the cows wore bells of distinctive tone. It was only the sound of the bells that made finding them halfway easy in the rough, timbered two-thousand-acre cow pasture.

I had not gone far when I located the sound of one of the bells as coming from the top of a steep rocky ridge to my right. Laboriously I climbed the ridge, to find no cow and to hear the other bell in a wooded patch on my left. But again no cow and again the unmistakable sound of cowbells, now here, now there. Finally, quite exhausted and no little baffled, I sat down to rest and consider.

Almost immediately the mystery was made clear. Across an

opening in the timber a hundred yards away I spied the figure of
Ray running in a bent-over posture holding the clapper of old
Bess's bell — strapped about his waist!

Rage lent wings to my feet. I overtook him in the sandy bottom
of an arroyo, into which he had leaped and which had narrowed
unexpectedly to nothing before he could clamber out of it. To his
honor be it said he didn't use the cowbell as a weapon of defense,
relying rather upon his superior strength to offset my superior size
and years. It was a fairly even battle until Lora leaped from the
arroyo bank with Old Pied's bell around her waist and entered the
fray. Outnumbered, I was thoroughly trounced, humiliated, and
momentarily chastened. It was pointed out to me that my fra-
ternizing with the enemy was an act of treason and that, unless
I saw the light, I would be given the status of a scab and might
expect even harsher punishment.

But that troublesome half-pint conscience began to stir again,
and before we reached home I had issued a declaration of independence. Mother had told us to obey Aunt Laura, had said she
would get well sooner if she had our promise to do so. Therefore, I
told Ray and Lora to count me out of the rebellion.

A sense of conscious virtue buoyed me up as we entered Aunt
Laura's presence. I walked with confidence bred of knowing I was
right. Aunt Laura looked at the three of us with a cold glitter in
her eye. We were, of course, dirty, disheveled, and bruised, myself
beyond the others.

'Been fightin', have you?' she accused, with complete prescience.
'Well, my patience with you young uns has come to an end. Your
mother has a lot to answer for the way she's raised you.'

And with that she gave me a clop alongside the head with her
rope-burned open palm that sent me spinning. Then she reached
for Lora, but wasn't quick enough. Ray had already fled. So I
alone suffered for the sin of having tried to support her against
her enemies.

Next day Ray was missing, as was also his pony and saddle. I fully enjoyed Aunt Laura's anxiety, which I didn't in the least share. I thought he had gone to Los Esteros. He had.

When Mother returned Aunt Laura told her we were three hopeless young sinners. We were called to the judgment seat. When our self-defense floundered and was on the verge of completely bogging down, Ray, the resourceful, took matters in hand.

'You see, it's like this, Mother, we *had* to do it.' He hurried on, undeterred by the challenge in Mother's expression. 'You remember the preacher that was here, the one in the God-wagon you invited to stay as long as he liked?'

Mother's expression changed to one of uneasiness and the sternness in her voice was not quite so convincing.

'Raymond! What do you mean by "God-wagon"?'

'Why, you remember,' said Ray, 'he had "Heaven or Hell: Which?" painted on one side of his wagon, and "Eternity: Where will you spend it?" on the other, and he fed his horses so much of our grain they like to foundered, and he took two pieces of pie when there was just enough to go 'round and he cheated at mumblepeg and ——'

Mother interrupted.

'What has all this to do with the report I get from Aunt Laura about your own naughty behavior?'

She seemed eager to change the subject, for the person in the God-wagon had been a shock to her. His credentials as a man of the cloth had consisted solely of the two questions painted on the high sides of his wagon, and our credulous mother had asked for no more before offering him her unlimited hospitality. That he could have stolen the wagon and team did not occur to her. We children had decided among ourselves that he had done so. I am not sure that our mother did not come to agree before the day when, still trying to be tactful on the off chance that she was mistaken, she nevertheless pointedly suggested to her guest that his welcome was beginning to wear thin. His horses had gained considerable weight on our corn, hauled from Magdalena and costing two dollars per hundred at that point, and the reverend, if such he was, himself was showing signs of responding to nourishment, if not of terminating his visit.

Ray, conscious of Mother's preoccupation, pressed his advantage.

'You remember the Sunday you made everybody come in the parlor and have the preacher preach to us?'

Mother undoubtedly did, but she seemed less than enthusiastic about acknowledging it. She continued to look at Ray uncertainly.

'Well,' said he, 'the preacher told us how he had been a sinner and how he had been saved. He said everybody was sinners and had to be saved. Agnes, Lora, and me, we want to be saved.'

This was one time Mother did not correct his grammar: she was probably too busy thinking up her own line of defense.

'Of course' — Ray's own voice had taken on a tinge of the preacher's unctuousness — 'if you don't sin you ain't a sinner, so Agnes, Lora, and me, we thought we better sin or maybe we wouldn't be saved.'

I could have slapped him, but Mother, under the adult's handicap of responsibility for the child's theological education, dared not be so direct, nor so right.

'We'll talk about it later,' she said weakly.

Of course we never did. She gave us the presents she had brought but had withheld up till now on Aunt Laura's advice.

Mine was a small pen, with mother-of-pearl handle and gold point, a feminine counterpart of the larger pen Father some years previously had given to his good friend, the then governor of New Mexico. In acknowledging the little token of friendship, the governor had written that he would use it in his work upon a book he was writing, a book whose scenes lay amidst turmoil — political, racial, and social — not much more violent but far removed from those into which his own official duties had plunged him. The letter was signed **Lew** Wallace, and the unfinished book was *Ben Hur*.

Aside from some satisfying philosophy, inspired by the incident of Aunt Laura's boxing my thirteen-year-old ears, I owe her much else. She taught me to sew, to knit, to have some knowledge of the rudiments of household arts. I can now understand her horror at the spectacle of children of her own blood growing up young heathen without discipline or schooling, for until now we had had hardly any formal education. To be sure, we read all the books in our library that were suitable for us and many that were not. I read Washington Irving and Cooper and Bryant only because I wanted to. How well I remember sobbing over Little Nell's death in the cold of an early dawn after I had read all night until the kerosene in the lamp was gone! Aunt Laura would have sent me to bed promptly at nine o'clock. My mother didn't. It is not for me to say which was the wiser. Though we seemed to Aunt Laura undisciplined, actually we had grown up in a discipline imposed by circumstances, far harsher than any she could have imagined.

Take, for example, an incident that occurred when I was somewhere in my teens. Word reached us that one of our cowhands had lost one of his string of saddle-horses, and was greatly in need of a replacement.

At this time each man attending the roundup had from eight to fourteen horses in his string, depending upon available grass, the only feed to be had. Each horse was ridden half a day one day a week, if the range were poor, oftener if there was a good season and grass abundant. This had been a poor season and loss of a single horse was a matter of concern. So it fell to me to deliver another horse to replace the one which had strayed.

Directions were to meet the trail herd at noon at White Lake on the following Wednesday. White Lake is a *galeche* bed at the lower point of the saucer that is the San Augustine Plains. Rainwater stands there until it evaporates, gradually forming a thickish white liquid of which the cowboys who drank it, as drink it they sometimes must, were accustomed to say, 'A feller needs sand-paper to git the water he don't swallow out of his mouth.'

To reach White Lake by noon I must start at daylight. We had no alarm clock; they were not very common then, and I relied upon waking myself up at the chosen time, a trick at which I was fairly proficient.

On this occasion I woke suddenly and was aghast to find how light it was. Blaming myself for having overslept, I hurried to the corral, saddled my horse, and gathered up the lead rope of the horse I was to deliver. I remember reading the lettering on the paper wrapping of a tin can that lay on the ground. I could easily have read a newspaper. I rode several miles before I realized that the sun hadn't come up and that it wasn't daylight at all, but one of those incredible New Mexico moonlight nights that rival mid-day brilliance. I had no idea what time it was, whether ten o'clock at night or four in the morning.

It turned out to be closer to the former hour, for when I was well out on the plains there was still no promise of sunrise. So much the better, I decided, for at least it was cool. Then suddenly I was in doubt. The horse I was leading snorted and jerked vio-lently at his rope. I looked around, to see the largest pack of coyotes I had ever seen following me not ten yards behind. Of course I knew, with my reason, that coyotes do not attack people on horse-back. But there were so many of them!

They began to howl. The noise drilled into my nerves with the force of a dental bit seeking the sensitive spot. Neither of the horses seemed to like it any better than I did. The led horse jerked at his rope with every fresh burst of sound until my arm ached from the strain of it.

I won't dwell upon all the misery of that night. But those

coyotes followed me hour after hour, even after the sun finally came up, by which time I was within sight of White Lake.

White Lake at last — but no trail herd there. I strained my eyes looking for a haze over the surface of the plain that would be the dust kicked up by hundreds of hooves. Nothing! Just that great plain, and silence which seemed to reverberate even more deafeningly than the coyote demon chorus which still punctured it at intervals. One coyote can sound like a host. That coyote band sounded like the wailing of all the tormented in hell. The ghastly sound went trailing off to the rimming mountains in wave after wave.

I dared not dismount. It probably would have been safe to do so, but I could not bring myself to test the truth of the theory that the coyote is a cowardly beast. There was something unnerving in the persistence with which that band kept at my heels.

By now, thirst began to bother me. There was, as was usual for the greater part of the year, no water in White Lake, the late summer rains having not yet begun, and even had there been water, it could but have added to my torment since I dared not leave the safety of my horse's back.

It was as far back to the ranch as forward into town, and the horse I was delivering would be needed for the outfit's return trip home. So I decided to go on and wait for the outfit in Magdalena.

When the coyotes finally dropped behind, exhaustion settled into every fiber of my body. Fifty miles is a long segment of the earth's great circle when one is traversing it on horseback, leading another horse which does not travel freely alongside, and a band of coyotes is behaving like a pursuing bunch of timber wolves. Those last ten miles seemed like a hundred.

Ultimately I rode into the Magdalena livery stable. I remember seeing a man get up from a chair in which he had been sitting tilted back against the outside wall and start toward me.

A half-hour later I opened my eyes to see the livery stable man and his wife bending over me and telling me that I was all right.

'I was to have met the trail herd at White Lake,' I explained; 'we had word they'd be there Wednesday noon. Isn't this Wednesday?'

'Sure it's Wednesday; say, Allie, is this Wednesday?' the livery man bawled to his wife.

'How do I know?' she retorted. 'Days are all alike to me in this country.'

It turned out to be Wednesday. The hitch was that the trail boss thought it was Tuesday, a fairly serious miscalculation with five hundred head of cattle to be delivered at the stockyards on a set date. He insisted, however, that he had the date of the month correctly in his mind, if not the day of the week.

Clock and calendar both having failed, I paid out of my hide. I sometimes think of it when I fume because a delayed telephone call makes me lose twenty minutes.

I learn THE PLIGHT OF
THE EDUCATED INDIAN

THE fatal day in the fall of my fourteenth year, when sentence of banishment was finally imposed upon me and I was put on the 2 A.M. train at Socorro with a pass in my hand and a Philadelphia school as my destination, saw the pendulum of my fate take one of its violent swings. Ray and Lora suffered a comparable fate in due time. The idea was to launch us upon a career as far as possible removed from that upon which we were then embarked. We were to learn at first hand something of the plight of the educated Indian.

The immediate cause of my departure was that a shock-headed young Swede had given me a bottle of perfume, the first masculine attention to have come my way other than being ordered about. I could tell that, for some reason obscure to me, the incident troubled my mother.

Of course, my uncensored reading hadn't left my mind wholly

virgin to the implication of a very personal gift! I had discovered *Jane Eyre* among the family books, and *John Halifax, Gentleman,* not to mention *Vanity Fair.* So I knew that Romance had found me at last and felt that the moment must be memorialized. I poured out the perfumery, for I couldn't bring myself to feel that the young Swede had hit upon my tastes very well, but the bottle I liked, and resolved to dedicate it to a worthy use. What worthier than repository for a poem?

Certainly I remember the poem, but just as certainly I will not dishonor it by dragging it out to be laughed at now. It had nothing whatever to do with the young Swede, my mother to the contrary notwithstanding!

I wrote the two eight-line stanzas in a careful, precise hand, and put the sheet of paper in the bottle, and sealed it with its pressed-glass stopper. Then I rode to the spot where I had met the Indians who were so interested in my hair. Under a tree, which stood a little apart from all the other trees, I buried my bottled poem.

I hope it is there yet, nestled in the safe embrace of the clinging earth, guarded by the silent mountains, sung to by the whispering trees, all undisturbed by the eerie howl of coyotes, or the agonizingly human cry of mountain lions! I left with it something precious and satisfying, the more so that nobody knew anything about it. It was a sort of I-who-am-about-to-die-salute-you.

In Philadelphia I was entered in a Quaker school where, as I look back upon it, there must have been a large measure of understanding. I recall that the first theme I chose for a composition was 'A Wild Horse Hunt,' and the principal, beloved Quakeress Annie Shoemaker, patted my head and said kindly: 'Thee expresses thyself well, my child. Be careful that thee does not let thy imagination run away with thee.'

Through a series of introductions I became before long a member of the household of the Reverend Charles Gordon Ames, then pastor of a Philadelphia Unitarian Church. The Ames household was the center of a group of friends of which Edward Everett Hale was an intimate. They were kind to me beyond belief, and even in the necessary corrections of my speech I was usually not humiliated. The one exception was when I had been telling something of my New Mexico life and had said with entire truthfulness, 'There was an awful row.' Mrs. Ames smiled indulgently, but said, 'Agnes dear, do you think "row" is exactly the word? Wouldn't "dispute" be better?' Meekly I said that I supposed it would. Today, I think "row" the better word, remembering the circumstances. Mrs. Ames was thinking of the King's English; I was thinking of two armed men arguing over a brand.

In response to kindly queries about my 'news from home,' I read aloud to these friends three letters from my family which came to me during the first months of my banishment.

Dear Daughter:

Some 'kin folks' of the Hammers family have come to make an indefinite visit. How that many people can live in those two small cabins is a mystery. One of the 'kin' is a small girl about Lora's age who seemed like a bright little thing so I thought it would be nice to bring her here for a week and let Lora have a little companion. The poor child gets so lonesome at times. She just can't keep up with Ray. So the next time Ray and Lora rode to Baldwin's for the mail they brought little Lovey home with them on Malo Noche behind Lora. He is still as fat as a butterball. Lovey is the child's real name. I asked her mother about it and she explained, 'Well, I warn't goin' ter let my child lug ary name like mine around through life so I give her a nice girl name.' I asked the mother what her own name was and she said something that sounded like 'Canstee' and turned out to be Kans T, an abbreviation of Kansas Territory. Her own mother, she said, was born in Kansas before it became a state and was always so homesick that when her child was born she named the baby Kansas Territory, and it became 'Kans T.' Anyway, little Lovey arrived at our house wrapped in a quilt and came in walking pigeon-toed and 'all spraddled out' as she put it. I asked her why she didn't walk with her feet together and received this reply, 'Cause I'm froze in this shape. That horse is so blank-blank fat.'

I began to wonder if I'd made a mistake in choosing a companion for dear little Lora.

I asked her how her family was and she said, 'Well, Paw's sort of puny. He kicked the stove because the blank-blank fire wouldn't burn and broke his toe.' I reproved her for using profanity and she replied, 'Well, I'm tough, and when I grow up I'm goin' ter be tougher.'

When I put the two little girls to bed in Lora's room Lovey looked around and said, 'This is a damn big room for two people no bigger'n me and Lora.' I made up my mind then and there to send her home next day.

In the morning I was awakened by 'whooping and hollering' and went into the girls' room to find Lovey astride the round-topped Saratoga trunk with the trunk straps run through a handle for bridle reins. She was on her way to the roundup. Lora offered her her dolls to play with which interested her for a short while because she had never seen a 'store' doll. She took as many of them as she could hold and got back on the trunk and began 'prisin' it up' and using language that I couldn't have Lora hearing, so I told Lovey she was going home.

'Oh, no, I ain't,' she told me. 'You said I was to stay a week and you're a damned liar if you make me go, when I only been here one night.' That was a poser, so I told her if she'd stop swearing and be a little lady I'd let her stay. She promised, but pretty soon she was 'cussin' out' Rollo for falling off the horse and I took the doll away from her and said, 'Lovey, you cannot use such language in my home.' 'Well,' she said, 'that's my kind of language and if you don't like it I guess I got to go. If you'll give me my pick of the dolls and a dollar I'll go home.'

I sent her with Lora's best doll and that silver dollar that has been in the sewing machine drawer so long, back to Kans T by Orrin. He told her mother she'd gotten homesick. 'I reckon she takes after her grandmaw,' Kans T said. 'Her grandmaw was allus homesick.'

I remembered the dollar in the machine drawer. So little use did we have for money that this silver dollar had taken on the quality of one of the spools of thread. We paid our bills in town twice a year when we sold the steers.

And from Ray:

Dear Agnes:

I bet you wish you had of been here last night. We had the most exciting time. In the middle of the night a row broke out on the front porch that sounded like all the dogs and cats and coyotes in the world in a fight. You never heard anything like it in your life and right in the middle of it Queenie's pup smashed right through Lora's bedroom window, glass and all. Because of the cold night the window was only open a little way at the top so the pup had to go through the glass to get into the room. Then Lora began to screach her head off and Mother and I came running to see what all the row was about. We looked out the window and saw Queenie fighting a big mountain lion right on the porch. It was moonlight and the snow made it lighter and we could see plain as anything. Mother lit a lamp and that scared the mountain lion and it ran and jumped up in the big pine tree by the house and all we could see was its tail hanging down and swinging back and forth.

I got the rifle, the one the railroad men gave father, with the gold plate in the stock telling about it, and ran upstairs so I could get a better view of the lion. It was still in the tree but not in very plain sight and I opened the window and shot at it. I must of hit it for it jumped out of the tree and when it ran up the side of the mountain it looked to me like it limped. I shot at it some more and I'm sure I must of hit it.

Now is the sad part. Queenie was dead when we went out to see if she was hurt and the pup had one ear chewed off besides being cut where he went through the glass window. There was blood all over Lora's bedroom floor, but we think the pup will live but he will always have his left ear a crop.

We think the lion must have tried to get the pup and Queenie must of jumped on the lion.

It was sure an exciting time. I bet you are sorry you missed it.

Some months later Lora wrote:

Dear Agnes:

I got two things to write about. One was a skunk dance. Maybe you don't know skunks dances, well they do just like folks. Mother called me to come look and I got out of bed and wrapped a blanket around me and sat on the porch and watched them in the moonlight. They was having a squar dance and their tails was all bushed out and it was sure pritty. They sort of pranced back and forth towards each other and sort of bowed. There must of been eight or ten of them. I bet you didn't know that skunks dances.

And I bet you didn't know that rattlesnakes swallow little rattlesnakes, either. Two men was here arguin' about it and one said rattlesnakes doesn't do it but I saw one do it so if anyone tries to argue with me I know better.

Ray and I was hunting horses and we sat down on a big rock and pretty soon we heard a funny sort of noise, kind of like a hiss and we looked around and there was a rattlesnake and there was five baby rattlesnakes and the mother rattlesnake opened her mouth and the little rattlesnakes ran right down her throt. If you don't believe it you just ask Ray and if anybody argus with me I'll tell them they don't know what they are talking about.

This pronouncement on Lora's part has kept her in a state of heated debate for fifty years, inasmuch as the question whether or not rattlesnake mothers swallow their young in times of danger still rages.

I still remember the expressions on faces when I had finished reading these letters aloud.

While I was struggling with the *Rudiments of Latin Grammar*

(I had never looked inside of an English grammar) in staid old Philadelphia and using the 'plain language' of my schoolmates, more than occasional intimations came to me that all was not going as well financially as might be at home.

It has been stated that money acquired by any method other than having stored it up penny by penny oneself, lasts three years on an average. To my mother's credit it must be said that she exceeded this average, but by the time I was old enough to be admitted to the business side of the ranch drama, the family was no longer on a 'keep-the-change' basis. Nevertheless, I was told in my mother's letters not to worry, that we children would get our education 'somehow.'

Although I distinctly felt that in Philadelphia there was an awful lot of overemphasis on nonessentials, the severity of the discipline which circumstances had forced upon me on the ranch equipped me for the discipline of the schoolroom. I overheard one of my teachers say to a colleague, 'If the educational system could begin with a few years on a New Mexico cattle ranch, I think children might make better progress in school' — testimony that I wanted to learn. I wanted to be equipped to go home and keep the books for the family's business. Instinctively I knew that they were sadly in need of keeping. By the time I was so equipped, however, not even a Philadelphia lawyer, much less a Philadelphia schoolgirl, could have found much head or tail to them. But we continued to get along 'somehow.'

Impatiently I awaited the summer vacation, when I could go back to the ranch and 'make a hand,' thereby saving the wages of a man. One day that summer, as Ray and I sat on a sunny hillside resting from a long and fruitless search for the saddle-horses, we faced the fact that our mother was tragically miscast as a range boss.

'Y'know,' said Ray, chucking a stone down the mountain-side, 'cow business is man's business. Women oughten to be doin' it.'

'Is *that* so?' I retorted sarcastically, in instant defense of my own status.

'I'm talkin' about grown-up women, not kids,' Ray assured me. 'I don't think Mother was ever cut out for a rancher. Y'know she thought that crumpled-horn cow that came in to water yesterday was the same one that came in the day before, and they didn't even have the same horn crumpled and they don't look any more alike than — than' — Ray cast about for an appropriate simile — 'than you look like Lora. Nobody will ever get along in the cow business who can't recognize their own stock.'

He screwed up his face in genuine distress. 'Mother writes too darn many letters,' he went on. 'What does Susan B. Anthony know about the cow business? And all the others she writes to. Y'know, while she's writing letters, our stock's disappearing. I haven't seen some of that last bunch we bought from over across the river for a long time now.'

'Jim Broyles —— ' I began.

'Jim can't handle it' — Ray was wiser than his years. 'Jim don't *own* the cattle.'

What Ray didn't know was that nobody could have successfully handled the stock business as it was conducted in western New Mexico in that era unless he adopted the accepted technique, which was to steal back from one's neighbor as many cattle as he stole from you. The more successful of our business competitors

were those who 'swung a long loop' and got more than their pro-
portional share of the 'longears,' calves as yet unbranded but old
enough to wean. It was only after fences began to appear and
boundaries between respective ranges were at least vaguely established that respect for the other fellow's property supplanted,
however slightly, the general belief that to the hardest-riding belonged the spoils.

Ray and I on our hillside were confronting an almost insoluble
problem. But of course Mother, with her background, her temperament, and her belief in the standards of the day regarding 'gentle-
women,' was, of all people, least qualified to enter into competition
with cattle rustlers. Ray and I, in the confident ignorance of youth,
suffered no such handicaps. 'Y'know,' Ray concluded, as we prepared to resume our search for the horses, 'our family's motto is
a darn good one: "If a fellow bites you, bite him back again."'
A fairly reasonable translation of the admonition on the Morley
escutcheon, '*S'ils te mordent, mords-les.*'

Ray and I resolved to live up to it. We spent a good deal of
time 'burning brands,' current phrase for redesigning them, but we
did this on paper to a far greater extent than on flesh. Our competitors had less paper than we. Our own brand, V on the left
shoulder and V on the left hip, showed up as double cross keys
($\mathcal{X}$) on many an animal too far from home.

Anyway, Ray and I, in our own minds, did begin to take over
the management of the ranch. Lora was still too young to be
regarded as a partner. Mother, seemingly grateful for any reed,
however broken, upon which to lean, gradually let us do it — when
we weren't away at school.

Letter-writing was the one slender thread which connected her
to the life she had turned her back upon at the invitation of the
soft-spoken gentleman who had disastrously failed her. Now she
clung desperately to the fringes of that life. Many 'movements'
were in their infancy: 'Emancipation of Women,' 'Temperance,'

'Prevention of Cruelty to Children' and its humbler brother, 'Prevention of Cruelty to Animals.' Mother took a keen interest in them all. Some of her fervid correspondents would have been confused by the apparent gulf between Mother's professions and her practices, at least in the matter of cruelty to children, for certainly the conditions of our daily lives were far from models of that sheltering care to which the young are presumed to have a right. Not that we actually suffered — far from it — but we were frequently very hungry and more frequently very tired, and we slept upon hard pallets upon the ground at least half the time.

But Mother saw things in their general bearings. Children as a class must not be treated cruelly, animals as a class must be protected, alcohol was a menace to the human race — so Mother wrote letters which resulted in the organization of New Mexico's first W.C.T.U., its first Society for the Prevention of Cruelty to Animals. The social order concerned her more than the immediate domestic trifles.

It is true that the immediate trifles were beyond her capacity to deal with, but the broader issues were not. Her contribution to the world in which she lived was no small one. It was at a very great personal sacrifice that she saw to it that her children went to school, even when we would vastly have preferred to stay right where we were.

EDWARD BOREIN

Cows WERE OUR UNIVERSE

The cattle business in those days was conducted on horseback. Any rider who knew what to do was on a parity with any other rider who knew what to do, so, as soon as we children had mastered the art of sitting on a horse with some assurance, our value to the business became out of all proportion to our age. The art of horse-sitting is acquired rapidly if one keeps at it from daylight till dark day after day, so we quickly learned to ride by the simple process of riding.

Mounted on a horse, we were useful in direct proportion to our powers of observation and our ability to interpret what we saw,

faculties, of course, which are sharpened by interest. Our interest
was boundless. Cattle became the circumference of our universe
and their behavior absorbed our entire waking hours.

First it was necessary to know where our cattle were, an extremely difficult thing in a country without fences. The most that
we could hope to do was to make an intelligent guess. In general,
they tended to range within a few hours' walking distance of one
of the various springs, and to stay for considerable periods of time
in that district.

Of course, range feed near the watering places is quickly eaten
out and trampled off, so that the distance between food and
water steadily increases. This is especially true if there is over-
stocking, and ten miles was not a prohibitive distance for a cow
to walk to and from water. It was this long walk which kept them
lean in dry years.

While cattle will drink every day if convenient or possible, and
be the better for it, they can, nevertheless, thrive reasonably well
on every other day's quenching of thirst. And I don't like to think
how many days I've known them to go waterless in drought
seasons.

'There's lots of cattle watering at the Davenport Spring' was a
valuable bit of information, and one a bright-eyed child could
relay as well as an adult. If the report were to the effect that it
was the same bunch that had previously been watering somewhere
else, the report was doubly valuable, and mounted in proportion
to the detailed information about each and every animal.

Were there unbranded calves in the bunch old enough to live,
however precariously, if forcibly weaned, hence potential 'sleepers'? Then no time must be lost in branding them.

You, dear reader, don't know what a sleeper is? I can scarcely
believe that such ignorance exists, but I will patiently explain.

A sleeper was a calf which had been earmarked but not branded.
Every owner had his individual earmark as well as brand. If an

animal was earmarked, the presumption was that it was also branded, both operations being normally performed at the same time. The reason for earmarking is that an earmark can be seen at a greater distance than a brand. The oval of a calf's ears can be cut into an almost endless set of designs, underslopes, crops, swallow forks, ginglebobs, half crops, upper and under slits, and so forth. With two ears to enlarge the possible combinations, it is not difficult to work out one's exclusive earmark. Our own was underslope both ears so that our cattle's ears looked like little supplementary horns.

A sleeper, so it is hoped by the one who has 'sleepered' it, will be seen from afar and be presumed to be also branded and its rightful owner will ride on without closer inspection. But the ears will have been only slightly reshaped — just enough to be deceptive. Then, when the opportunity arises, the calf will be taken from its mother and kept in hiding until Nature has completed the weaning process. Its ears are then worked over into its new owner's earmark and it bears the new owner's brand and — so what can the owner do about it?

Spotting sleepers was one of the valuable contributions we children were able to make to our business, for sleepers were common in those days.

To locate a maverick, a calf that had been entirely overlooked and had weaned itself before being either earmarked or branded, was like finding a gold nugget, and we raced home with the news with no less excitement. Sometimes one of us would try to keep the bunch in which the maverick had been discovered within sight while the other carried the news home, or if we thought we could, we'd try to drive the bunch into the nearest available corral. This was not always possible because any bunch with a maverick in it was apt to be pretty wild, having encountered no human beings for a long time.

Another invaluable report would be that of finding a cow 'bogged down.' Rain puddles sometimes became death traps of sticky mire unless the victims were rescued in time. So 'pulling bog' was a routine of the rainy season, and it was of course a tremendous time-saver for the adult wrecking crew to have the bogged-down cow located beforehand. The time came, considerably later — after I abandoned side-saddle, however — when Ray and I pulled them out ourselves, an achievement made possible by the fact that here again the horse did the actual work.

I reconstruct a typical 'bog-pulling' scene. Ray wades into the bog and loops his saddle rope around the cow's horns and claws her feet as free as possible from the mud, sometimes an extremely difficult operation if she is lying with her legs tucked under her. If he finds himself in danger of bogging down himself, he lies across the cow while loosening her hooves from the mire. Then I wrap the other end of the saddle rope around the horn of my saddle and give the signal to my horse. He digs his toes into the ground and strains forward while I lean far to one side to avoid being cut in two with the rope. We pull the cow's head a little back over her shoulders to avoid the strain of a direct pull

on her neck. Ray meantime has her tail wrapped around his hands and is heaving mightily at the rear. Sometimes she comes and sometimes she doesn't — in the latter case, we shoot her. If she comes, things happen rapidly. Once on her feet with solid ground under them, the cow almost invariably decides that her rescuers are the cause of her woes and proceeds to square accounts by charging at whomsoever is closest at hand.

Fortunately for the rescuer, the cow is apt to be a little dazed and wobbly, and dodging her is only a matter of agility. As Ray grew older, he didn't dodge. In the tone one uses to a naughty child he'd say, 'Now, now, sister, none of that!' and seize the angry cow by the horns. A quick twist of the head and down she'd go, unless she decided to behave without this discipline.

The time we rescued a cow from Paddle Cross Lake was probably the most famous instance of this kind of lively work. Paddle Cross Lake was queer, to begin with. For nine months of the year it was no lake but merely a depression — a reddish clay saucer — in the line of natural drainage. After the rainy season began, if it did, Paddle Cross Lake filled with a viscous terra-cotta liquid which cattle appeared to think was water and drank freely with no ill effects. I've drunk it myself as a last resort.

On the day in question we arrived at Paddle Cross with a small bunch of range cattle, a long dry drive. The herd rushed into the lake, some of them belly-deep. At first, no one noticed that one cow had gone in beyond her depth and was firmly mired in the sticky mud which was the lake's floor. Only her nose protruded, letting her breathe. As soon as she was observed, two of the men rode their horses into the lake to rescue her, but the horses began to sink in the ooze and the men dared not ride close to the distressed cow.

For both humanitarian and financial reasons (cattle were high that year) every effort must be made to save the animal. So shedding as much impedimenta as a mixed audience permitted, specifically chaps, boots, spurs, jumper, and hat, Gene dived from his horse and swam to the cow with a rope which he looped over her horns.

Bill, similarly stripped for action, except that he refused to remove his outsize black hat, still sat his horse at a safe distance from the bogging-down point. He took a couple loops of the lariat around his saddle-horn and held the cow's head above water, while Gene strove to claw the cow's feet loose from the mud.

Cowboys are not experts in water, and anyway, the enterprise demanded more of ingenuity than of good diving form. Gene would disappear and emerge by crawling out on the cow. Finally he sent an SOS and Bill swam to assist him, leaving the well-trained pony to keep the rope tight. The comedy of the next few minutes sent the audience into literal hysterics. Bill wouldn't dive because he wouldn't take his hat off, but he would lend a hand to Gene, when the latter came up sputtering after having clawed another hoof loose.

Both were steadying themselves by holding to the cow, who suddenly set up a pathetic mooing, signal that she had given up. Thereafter she refused to help herself at all, even when she was freed from the mud and began to float. Had she been a wind-filled bag she couldn't have been less purposeful or effective in contributing to her own rescue. She flopped on her side and rolled her eyes.

Gene got hold of her tail and tried to twist it, with not much success, due to his own unstable position. Bill was valiantly holding her nose out of the water and yelling for Gene to push. Gene pushed and the cow spun around. Bill, his big black hat still on his head, spun with her. The cow was now tail end to shore, and pulling seemed a better technic. This was resorted to, with equally indifferent success, until the horse took a hand. He decided to go to shore himself and went, towing the cow after him, Gene and Bill in splashing pursuit, for by now the cavalcade had got into sufficiently shallow water to offer dubious footing to all concerned, including the cow, had she chosen to avail herself of it, which she didn't. She still floated, wholly oblivious to the language being directed at her.

Only when her sides scraped bottom did she appear to decide that she was still on earth and show signs of returning life — with a vengeance. Scrambling to her feet, she lowered her head, calculated the distance to a nicety, and chased Bill and Gene back into the lake, as far as the rope, still tied to the saddle-horn, would permit.

Help now came from the audience, in the form of shouted instructions, principally, 'Take off your hat,' 'It's your hat she doesn't like.' Maybe it was, for she kept a baleful eye upon it while Gene cautiously deployed around and reached the horse — and it was all over. A man, even one dripping Paddle Cross mire from head to heels, on a well-trained horse is master of such a situation. The cow was unceremoniously yanked about face, the

rope jiggled off her horns, and she was escorted back to the herd at a clip which would seem to belie her determination to end it all only a few moments before.

Bill waded out, triumphantly wearing his hat.

As youngsters we learned to recognize the individuals among the cattle as though they had been people, and we watched for their coming with the same interest we would have had in the arrival of personal friends. We apportioned the herds among ourselves, each claiming as his own anywhere from a hundred head upward, as the numbers who came in to water varied. And we knew our own dry cows or long yearlings or three-year-old steers or maturing heifers as city children know their schoolmates.

How well I remember them coming in to the home watering troughs, in the later afternoon, coming with a rush the last few hundred yards, bellowing and flipping their tails, drinking until their sides bulged to barrel-like contours, then standing about in stupid relaxation or licking the salt blocks which all good cowmen supply in abundance.

Twice a year roundups were held (we called them 'works'), in the spring to brand the new calf crop, and in the fall to segregate the cattle which were to be sent either to Kansas or Nebraska to be corn-fattened for market later, or directly to the slaughterhouses in Chicago.

It was always occasion for deep heartache when we children saw our friends set forth on their last journey, but it was part of life and we had to face it. The one phase of life, however, which I refused to face directly was the branding itself. However much of an accessory to the crime I may have been in the matter of rounding up or even roping the calf, when it came to the actual applying of a hot iron to sentient flesh, I couldn't do it.

However, I hasten to add that cruel as it sounds, the calves certainly did not suffer to the same extent, emotionally or physically, that a human being would have done. They usually scrambled to their feet, whisked their tails, and galloped off with no evidences of shock or even acute discomfort. A skillful man with the branding iron knew exactly when the hair had been burned away and the flesh merely seared enough to prevent the hair from growing again. I like to think the bawling was more from fright than from suffering.

Another useful function which we children were able to perform and which added to our sense of our own importance was 'riding fence line' along the few fences with which we began and the many which came later. To hop off one's horse, with a boot-top bag full of fence staples — which everybody called 'steeples' — and nail a sagging wire back in place satisfied something real in the matter of feeling useful.

When Ray was not yet fourteen, he was the equal of the average cowpuncher. The ascending scale in open-range cattle business is from horse wrangler at the lowest rung to range boss at the highest. Between them lie cook, riders, fence-line riders (after there were fences), run-of-the-mill waddies. Ray ran the whole gamut before he was through.

Perhaps our decision at the ages of twelve to fourteen to sixteen that we were valuable in the scheme of things was not so preposterous after all. It was only in the bookkeeping end of running the ranch, the end that spelt success or failure, that we were completely inadequate.

When this summer ended, I went reluctantly back to school. Ray, too, was banished for the first time, to Chester Military Academy in Chester, Pennsylvania.

Gray Dick

CONCERNED as I was in my Philadelphia schoolroom with the doings of early English kings, I did not have time to worry greatly about the ranch; but I should have worried more than ever, for the crash I had been fearing since Ray and I first began to share responsibility had come at last.

When Father died, he left a will executed before the birth of any of his children. To assure all protection possible to the girl he was bringing into a land of violence and sudden death, he had bequeathed everything to his young wife. Perhaps he did not know that after he had children this will became invalid; that unless one leaves something, no matter how trifling, to a child, the will can be set aside by a court whose business it is to protect the helpless. Perhaps he intended to make another will and his untimely death cut him off before he could carry out his intention. In any event, invalid though the existing will was, it was probated. Mother, relying as always upon some trusted male adviser, promptly gave a power of attorney, and Father's estate passed to all practical purposes into alien control.

No one seems to have realized what had happened until some years later a relative of Mother's who had succeeded to Grandfather McPherson's law practice in Iowa called attention to the elementary fact of law that the unborn cannot be disinherited.

Father's property was situated principally in the Territory of New Mexico, but one tract of land lay within the boundaries of the then little town of Denver, Colorado. Suit was brought in the Colorado courts to set aside the will and recover the children's share of the estate of which Mother's action had dispossessed us.

Setting aside the will was promptly achieved, the court taking no time at all in the matter. Twenty years, however, were required to settle all the claims involved, and the 'Denver lawsuit,' as we called it, became a vexation of spirit, though in the end the sole source of family income.

In the meantime, of course, Mother had sunk a large part of her available money in the ranch. Around Easter time of that year, word came to me in Philadelphia that we were penniless. I went back to New Mexico, feeling that the lives of the early English kings were placid compared to mine. I found Mother distraught. An attachment had been levied upon part of our cattle and all our horses, she told me. The income from the Denver lawsuit was coming in too slowly to stave off immediate disaster.

While we were trying without success to think of solutions, a letter arrived from the guardian who had been appointed by the Denver court, an old friend and business associate of my father's, who lived in another part of New Mexico. He invited me to come and stay at his home. With some idea that he might work out a plan, I decided to accept the invitation.

I knew my guardian's home well. We had gone there directly from my father's funeral. It was the beginning of Holy Week and the Penitentes were 'out,' as we phrased it. Even my anxiety over the ranch was for a moment forgotten in the prospect of seeing Penitentes in action.

Their rites proved to be as emotionally upsetting as it is their purpose to be, I suppose, even to unwelcome spectators. Our visiting party was on horseback, of course, and my own mount, a cream-colored pony, was soon flecked with blood that spurted from self-lashed human backs as the yucca plant cat-o'-nine-tails tore through raw flesh. I had no business to be so close. But I wanted to see what expression a man's face would wear as he meted out his own torture. I could not see: the faces were too bloody. I stayed too long; I found myself surrounded by an angry mob of armed men — not the flagellants, but other members of the Hermanos de Luz Order. For a moment it seemed that neither my youth nor my sex would save me. These Penitentes were not putting on a sensational exhibition for such as I. They were putting to a fiery test what they held to be eternal truths. No profane curiosity-seeker should vitiate that test! When the mob, muttering fiercely but obeying one who seemed to speak with authority, finally opened its ranks and let me pass, I had the impression of coming up out of hell.

The next night, in spite of the fact that my recklessness had aroused the temper of the celebrants, we intruded into the even more sacred *tinieblas* ceremony. The Hermano mayor, chief of the order, was bribed to admit us. Juan de Dios (I have substituted a name) appeared very ill at ease, and warned us that he could not be blamed for anything that might happen. For his thirty pieces of silver he led the four of us after nightfall through a little rear door of the church and settled us in a cramped space behind the altar, locked the door and put the key in his pocket — a precaution we observed with apprehension.

The church was a thick-walled adobe building, with high narrow windows, blanketed now with bright-colored Navajo rugs. Its single room was about seventy-five feet long and a third as wide.

There were no seats; save for the altar at one end and the font at the other, there were no articles of furniture whatsoever. But it was overflowing with people. Men, women, and children sat huddled together on the floor, packed together as closely as it was possible for them to squeeze, men on one side, women on the other, and there were almost as many dogs as children. The presence of these shocked me until I discovered later the reason for it.

In the center of the room, however, was a hollow space of possibly ten by twenty feet, and from it a narrow lane led to the front door between the crowded celebrants.

From our dark recess behind the altar we could peer surreptitiously into the dimly lighted body of the church. Candles in brackets along the walls were the only illumination. Their flames did not flicker, for no breath of outside air came through those curtained windows.

The air was already heavy when we entered, and even before the ceremony began I had begun to entertain doubts of my ability to stick it out, only to remember that I was locked in.

Juan de Dios's voice was now raised in a prayer of supplication for divine blessing upon the ceremony about to start. It was a short prayer and at its close a candle was blown out. Juan de Dios prayed again and a second candle was blown out. He prayed on and on, the room slowly growing darker. At last only two lighted candles remained.

Restlessness among the people had been increasing — I became aware of a child's whimper and occasionally a dog's stifled whine. Then Juan de Dios was praying for the Americanos. He did not add the word 'present,' but we knew that was what he meant. He supplicated the Almighty to see that no harm should come to us — an ill-deserved request, under the circumstances, I could not help feeling. His prayer added nothing to my peace of mind.

Only one candle now remained. Juan de Dios was silent. The whole congregation was silent, as though holding its breath. A

sudden stream of fresh air cut through the fetid atmosphere like a
clean blade. The front door had opened and down that narrow
aisle came a ghastly procession walking in single file — the flagellants. Their once white trousers, brown and stiff with dried blood,
their hair matted with it, they staggered as they came, carrying
their yucca whips over their shoulders. The door behind them
closed, shutting out all air, sanity, and hope. Juan de Dios's voice,
hysterical now, was lifted in a final prayer for the souls of all the
dead, and the last candle went out.

The congregation held its breath for one second longer. The
blackness and the silence were as one. Then came the explosion
with all the force of the rending of the heavens after the Crucifixion,
which the ritual symbolized. It came as a child's shrill terrified
scream, swallowed up in an instant chaos of noise that cannot be
described. Women's shrieks, the hoarse moaning of men, the howling of dogs, and, to this awful medley of vocal sounds, a mechanical
accompaniment of noise-producing devices. Chains rattled, empty
bottles were blown into producing a sound peculiarly weird, empty
barrels were beaten, and, riding high above it all, the thin nerve-
tingling wail of the Penitente *pito* or flute, and the harsh clatter of
their wooden rattles. But it was the now-and-then distinguishable
scream of a child — I had seen babes in arms before the blackness
blotted everything out — that gave the final touch of horror to the
bedlam. That gripped me even more, I think, than the knowledge
that in the center of this mass hysteria stood that little group of
self-tormentors — the whippers, in their last agony of penance.

It went on and on, the air becoming more and more foul, until one
dreaded the next breath. Juan de Dios had known what he was
doing when he took that key.

I was told that it lasted an hour: time was swallowed up in doubt
whether another ten seconds could be endured. But the hour did
pass and the sudden silence that came at its end was even more
nerve-shattering. At what signal did the children cease their wild

screaming, the dogs their howling? The mystery of that is as great in my mind today as it was then.

A candle was lighted in the far end of the church and with its dim flicker a hoarse whisper sounded in our ears. 'Out of here *pronto.*' Juan de Dios was turning the key in the lock. Never was sound so welcome. Our little party of heretics stumbled into the life-giving air, leaving behind us the long slow process of relighting those in-terminable candles one by one. That human body or soul could endure it longer speaks for the toughness of their fiber.

Why this deliberate self-hypnotism? They say to frighten away the evil spirits who might be hovering about the holy preparations for celebrating the breaking of the Easter morn.

I saw it break, but it was upon a world still unreal and fantastic.

These two adventures did not help me think clearly or calmly about my anxieties. Nor did my guardian have any suggestions that would work out. I went home in dread to face poverty.

To me, poverty was a hideous word. It carried no suggestion of hard work, simple food, or coarse clothing. I had known these things and had not found them bad. But I had also read typical stories of the day about 'poor widows.' To my inexperienced imagi-nation a poor widow always supported herself by taking in washing, and sent her children to an orphan asylum. The mental picture of Lora in an ugly calico dress, of Ray — Ray of the dauntless spirit — marching in a line of sad-eyed small boys, of my lady mother at a washtub, was staggering.

The disaster as it turned out was very different from my imagin-ings, though it had its painful moments. I found that a sheriff had already taken our remuda into custody, and was using it to gather our cattle for his 'sheriff's sale.' My only consolation was that the young chap he had deputized to bring in our horses had decently refrained from taking Gray Dick, my favorite white pony, who, he knew, had been presented to me as a sort of good-will bonus when we had bought the original horse herd.

Therefore it was no mild shock to me to discover that the sheriff's deputy, a man I had never liked because of his cruelty to horses, had insisted that Gray Dick was to be included and had taken him from our home pasture without a by-your-leave.

Ray and I promptly borrowed two horses and set out to bring him back.

We rode into the camp where the roundup, our cattle and horses, was being held. Then I saw red. A hundred yards from where a

dozen men were at their midday meal grazed our remuda, fifty to sixty saddle horses, every one of them a personal friend One horse, however, was not grazing. It was Gray Dick. He stood with his head down, his white shoulders blood-spattered from cruel roweling in a horse's most sensitive spot, his forelegs hobbled together much too tightly, and as a final badge of ignominy, an oversize cowbell on a wide strap around his neck. He had been overridden, spurred and beaten, and left for me to see when I should ride by, as it was rightly assumed that I would, on my way to the post office.

Subsequent happenings made local history. I rode into the center of the group of men and confronted the deputy sheriff.

'I've come to take my horse,' I said, as steadily as I could.

'Can't have him,' was the reply.

I wheeled my horse and made a dash toward the remuda. It promptly stampeded — right through camp. Men dived under the chuck-wagon, went up trees, sought any safety offered.

Hobbled as he was, Gray Dick could not keep up with the other stampeding animals. I was racing toward him when I dropped a bridle rein. We always rode with divided reins, and this one was a long, inch-wide ribbon of leather. My mount stepped on it and jerked himself into a complete somersault. A dozen men swore ever afterward that I, too, turned a complete somersault in midair and 'lit a-runnin' like a cat.' I think they must be right, for I do not remember picking myself up from the ground. I recall only that I spoke to Gray Dick, and that he turned and whinnied, that silent whinny of recognition and confidence. Then I was taking off his hobbles. When I straightened up, I saw my enemy approaching, looking mean and determined. I unbuckled the bell-strap from Gray Dick's neck and held it by one end, the bell dangling at the other.

'One step closer and I'll brain you with this bell,' I told the advancing officer of the law. It was a nasty weapon that I swung, and he eyed it uncertainly.

'Stop right where you are,' I told him, beginning to feel a sense of mastery, 'or I'll split your skull wide open.' He muttered something about resisting an officer, but stopped.

'Bring me a bridle, somebody.' I was issuing orders exultantly now. Ray pulled the bridle from his own horse and handed it to me. Twelve men ever afterward swore also that I leaped upon Gray Dick's back with a single bound — sideways, of course — and that I hit him a wallop with my hat. This last touch, I know, was a fabrication, so probably I did not mount him in a single bound either. Anyway, I left camp on a high run, headed for the Wheeler Ranch, about a mile away. Then I heard pounding hoof-beats behind me. As if in an effort to escape his late tormentor, Gray Dick extended himself to a flashing gray streak, belly close to the ground, nostrils wide, hooves drumming a swift tattoo on the hard trail.

Why I did not crash over his head and into the fence when he stopped at the ranch corral, I cannot say. I slipped from his back and whirled to have it out with the officer who, I supposed, had followed me. I was looking about for some substitute for my bell when I came to my senses and realized it was Ed Wheeler and not the law who had been pursuing me. Ed set his own horse back on its haunches and spoke breathlessly. 'Shall I kill him, Mis' Agnes?' he wanted to know. 'I'll shore do it if you say so. I don't want to take no tricks thet belongs to you, but I'd shore admire to kill him.'

I thanked Ed for his friendly offer, but told him I guessed I had played the trump already.

'Thet's what we all reckoned,' he went on. 'There was half a dozen guns drawed on him waitin' to see if you missed yore shot with thet ar bell, but o' course we didn't want to spoil your play.'

Again I thanked him. He had treated me as an equal. They all had, and that was the important thing. The villain in the little melodrama never lived it down. In all my dealings with Western men, his was the only unchivalrous action I ever encountered.

Later, Gray Dick was found dead from no ascertainable cause. By this time I was away at school again. The news reached me in a letter from a neighbor. Accompanying it was a nosegay made of white horsehair looped intricately on wire spirals. The dear lady had wrought it lovingly and painstakingly from Gray Dick's tail. I bawled like a baby when I saw it.

The ruin I had expected never quite came. Money dribbled in from Denver, the ranch did not have to be sold, some of the cattle and horses were salvaged, and life went on, not smoothly, but certainly not with the drabness I had feared.

Twelve PUPILS:
FROM SIX TO SIX-SHOOTER

THOSE of our neighbors who could not give their children even the disjointed sort of private education which we were given during our early childhood did nevertheless make sporadic efforts to organize schools. There was, naturally, no public-school system which embraced the remote districts. Even in more thickly settled communities the schools were sometimes in charge of Mexican teachers, whose command of English was so limited that the major part of their teaching was conducted in their native tongue. I recall the tearful report of one little girl who had been reprimanded for spelling *choose* c-h-o-o-s-e.

'The teacher said it should be s-h-o-e-s, and I don't know yet which word she was trying to have me spell.'

That summer of my sixteenth year, our Datil community decided to have a school. Here at hand was I, a teacher well qualified
to take charge, for hadn't I been away at school for two consecu-
tive terms? What more could be asked? A diploma, a teacher's
certificate? Wholly superfluous. These parents wanted their
children to read, write, and 'figger,' and if the teacher could do
these things she could 'learn' the children to do them, too.

So I answered the call of duty and a school was set up in a log
cabin on the Ole Zaccarison place, a conveniently central point.
It entailed a daily fourteen-mile horseback trip for teacher, seven
miles each way, but three miles each way was the greatest distance any of the pupils had to walk.

The student body of twelve ranged from little Early Wheeler
and Owen Dean, both under six, to Gus Wheeler, who topped me
in age by a few months and in stature by almost a foot. Gus
furnished the school with its major problem in discipline. Naturally he didn't want to do what the younger ones did and the
younger ones did want to do what Gus did, notably spend recess
in target practice with Gus's forty-five, which he wore to school
and was with difficulty persuaded to lay aside in the schoolroom.

'I never go without my gun,' Gus told me. 'No tellin' when I
might need it.'

'You won't need it during school hours,' I tried to reassure him,
but he was unconvinced. 'I needed it at the other school I went to,'
he came back at me. 'When the teacher tried to make me do
something I didn't want to, I shot up through the roof and scairt
the liver out of him. He quit teachin' before very long.'

'You won't scare the liver out of me by shooting through the
roof,' I promised him. He looked at me with a calculating eye.

'You can't make me do nothin' I don't want to,' he said.

'Oh, can't I?' and I lunged at him. I struck him in the pit of the
stomach. He crumpled with the impact and surprise of it.

'That wasn't fair,' I told him when he had regained his breath, 'but you didn't play fair eitner. Suppose we call it quits.'

'Quits it is,' he grinned sheepishly, looking around to reassure himself that none of the younger children had been witness to his downfall. Fortunately for him, they were all collected at the sheep corrals, where lambing was in progress. From this absorbing spectacle they were with difficulty called back by the clamor of the school bell.

All but little Owen Dean. He came racing in a few minutes late, gasping in uncontrolled excitement, 'A-lamb-with-six-legs, a-lamb-with-six-legs, shore 'nuf, it's got six legs!'

Nobody waited for school to be dismissed. We all made for the sheep corral. Owen had reported correctly. A newborn lamb with six legs lay at its mother's feet, breathing its last.

Ultimately I got the school reassembled, schoolroom morale considerably shaken.

'We will now have our lesson in geography,' I announced in my very best pedagogical manner. 'Lawrence, will you tell me what a volcano is?'

Lawrence was bright. I always expected the right answer from Lawrence.

'It's when a mountain busts.'

I marked him 100, and put the next question to fourteen-year-old Elva.

'Elva, will you define an island?'

Elva shook her head in defeat. I coached her along.

'Why, Elva, didn't you ever see some land in the middle of a lake or river?'

'How could I,' Elva shot back, 'when I ain't never seen no lake nor river?'

The geography lesson finished, we proceeded to the lesson in physiology. The textbook had been supplied by my mother. It dealt principally with the effects of alcohol and nicotine on the human system. 'One drop of nicotine on the end of a cat's tongue ——'

I asked young Joe how about it.

''Tain't so,' he informed me promptly. 'When my Aunt Minnie chaws terbaccer, she swallers it. If it killed cats it'd kill Aunt Minnie. I don't believe all that book says.'

I felt it my duty to uphold the prestige of the printed word.

'Aw, shucks' — Gus decided to get into this — 'my grandpaw he couldn't spell "cat" and he lived to be most a hundred. Reckon if he could git along without book learnin' I can too.'

'Not while you're in this school,' I reminded him, 'and you better sit up straighter in your seat.'

Gus hauled in his long legs and made a pretense of sitting up straighter.

Feeling a bit routed in the field of physiology, I decided to move to surer ground, and asked my assembled pupils how many could tell me the name of the Father of our Country. There was a reassuring general response, 'George Washington,' but fourteen-year-old Joe looked blank. 'George Washington?' he repeated dubiously. 'He must have left this here country before us'ns all come. Where'd he come from — Texas? And what made him leave here?'

'Our country' had no boundaries beyond New Mexico and Texas in Joe's mind, and one's reasons for leaving either place were always full of interesting possibilities.

Friday afternoon arrived, and with it the parents for the 'exercises,' recitations which the children had been laboriously memorizing during the week.

To Gus had been assigned one of our immortal national poems. There was a question what he would do about it. He had placed on record his objections to 'speakin' a piece' for the beaming parents. Totally out of character that, for gun-toting Gus — but I had been firm.

I called upon him after the others had, each in turn, stumbled or raced through their 'pieces.'

'Now, Gus,' I said brightly.

Gus slumped down onto his shoulder-blades, his legs protruding from under the bench in front of him.

'We're waiting, Gus,' I said, hoping that I sounded more assured than I felt.

A tense silence was broken by Claude's hoarse whisper to his seat mate, 'Betch'her he won't do it.'

Gus shot him a mean look, sprang to his feet, and was off: 'Life-is-real-life-is-earnest-and-the-grave-is-not-its-goal-dust-thou-art-to-dust-returneth-was-not-spoken-of-the-soul' — the words rattled out, with the inflexionless rapidity of a machine gun. Three verses and Gus sat down, far down in his seat, his legs again protruding from under the forward bench.

'First teacher ever I done *that* fer,' he growled defiantly.

'Thank you, Gus,' I told him, and his reply was a glower that brought his carrot-topped brow into closer communion with his freckled, sun-blistered cheeks.

I was to meet Gus two years later, in the hotel in Magdalena, on another of those regular returns home for the summer.

'Been to school this year?' I asked him.

He leaned back against the clerk's desk, his legs in their characteristic out-in-front position, his freckled face split by a wide grin.

'Ain't never goin' t' school nary 'nother day till you come back an' teach me,' he announced in a voice that carried well out into the street.

The guffaws that met this ultimatum made me blush.

'Your education is evidently finished,' I told him as I retreated with what dignity I could command.

The closing of the school term came about with tragic suddenness. My pony was pawed to death before our horrified eyes by a vicious stallion who broke through the fence to attack him. Gus offered to shoot the stallion, but not in time to save Malo Noche, and no use to do it afterward.

The parents were kind in their expressions of appreciation for my services. I collected twenty-three dozen eggs in material reward.

Cowpuncher ON A

SIDESADDLE

My BRIEF experience as a schoolteacher over, I went back to 'making a hand.' Although I rode sidesaddle like a lady, the double standard did not exist on the ranch. Up to the point of my actual physical limitations, I worked side by side with the men, receiving the same praise or same censure for like undertakings. I can still hear Bowlegs scoffing at me because a 'longear' got away from me in the brush. What kind of brush rider was I that I couldn't keep close enough to a yearling to see which way it went?

Just to show what my failure consisted of, I may say that riding through the brush, or, as we called it, 'breaking brush,' is a specialized kind of cowpuncher horsemanship, just as 'hopping prairie-dog holes' is another. New Mexico cowboys hooted derisively at cowboys from the plains of Texas who hesitated to ride full tilt at a clump of trees whose branches interlaced to form a veritable hedge. Texas-bred horses had the same inhibitions. On the other hand, our cowhands who had been over to the Staked Plains came back with tales of how their hair had turned white at the way Texas 'peelers' ran over prairie-dog towns where there seemed to be no solid ground between the dog holes. Both seem incredibly dangerous.

'Brush-breaking' derives its name from the peculiar brittleness of the timber in the high dry altitude of the Southwest. One can ride at full speed into a piñon tree and the chances are that the momentum will develop force enough to smack off even good-sized branches. 'If you can't dodge 'em, stick your chest out and break 'em,' is the rule for brush-riding. And sometimes when your chest is stuck out, your horse is leaping a fallen log and doing it with a twisting motion to escape crashing headlong into the trunk of another tree which had not been visible.

I have, in my presumably saner years, ridden slowly through country where I remembered having torn at top speed in pursuit of some cow critter who had the advantage of less height than that of my horse and me combined, and have told myself that nobody ever did run a horse through that labyrinth of dead and living brush.

Some credit is, of course, due to the rider's fearlessness and skill, but more should go to the horse. Cowponies, like human beings, become specialists. There were brush horses, cutting horses, roping horses, and show-off horses. Whenever possible, every cowpuncher had one show-off horse, a high-stepper, which he rode 'up and down the road,' meaning wherever there might be an audience. Especially a feminine audience. 'Watch Shorty spur that old stick he's on in the off shoulder, 'cause there's a lady present,' was whispered to me more than once by some envious cowboy who was not at the moment engaged in showing off, himself. Possibly we ladies showed off a bit too.

Most of our real work was done in silence. Tenderfeet always complained, with justification: 'Nobody tells me anything. How am I to know what to do?' Kibitzing was our greatest social sin. A stranger could be with a cow outfit for days without knowing who was boss. Nobody shouted orders around a cow outfit. The boss merely picked up his bridle and started for the corral. Sometime during the process of saddling he managed to convey to the other riders that the drive would take in such and such territory and that so and so could work the *rincon* or west pass or piñon flat. And the men rode off in silence, each knowing what to do and needing all his resources to do it.

'Chasing cattle' was a phrase the uninitiated often used. Well, we 'chased' them as little as possible. The object was, of course, to see that they went where we wanted them to go, and often this entailed racing with them until the horseman got in the lead and could turn them back. But chasing is hardly the word. We were given to saying disgustedly, 'That tenderfoot "chased" the steer clear out of the country; seemed to think he had his horse down to a run, but he was never out of a high lope.'

Strange how often newcomers thought their horse was running when he wasn't. The horse knew it, too, and didn't put on that extra ounce of steam which distinguishes a running horse from a galloping one.

The classic *faux pas* of all was for two tenderfeet to take after the same animal and 'make a lane,' which is to say, to get one on either side of the quarry and ride just fast enough to keep it between them.

On such occasions someone would be sure to bellow: 'That's right! Make a lane!' and then dash out and really head off the animal.

I never made lanes, and I knew when to keep out of the way. In fact, after fifty years, I vaingloriously affirm that I enjoyed a local reputation in the one field where reputations most counted — that of good horsemanship. To prove it, I cherished for years a

clipping from *Mine and Lariat,* an early weekly paper which flourished briskly but briefly in Magdalena. It informed our local reading public that 'Miss Agnes of the Datils and Three-Fingered Pete are the best riders in the county.'

Even though I didn't rope and brand and do the harder and harsher part of the cow business, there was usually some place where I could function profitably. The time I 'represented' when Bud Jones came through with his trail herd was more or less typical of the sort of duty I might be called upon to perform.

When large herds passed through the country, it was impossible, of course, to avoid 'picking up' cattle of other owners across whose range the herd was traveling. So it was customary to allow such self-invited visitors to remain until the entire herd had reached the last confines of their owner's presumed range, and then ask the owner himself to ride through, inspect every brand, and cut the herd. This was a courtesy never to be omitted.

When a big herd was to be cut, owners or their representatives often numbered a score or more. 'Working the herd' was the pinnacle of cow-work. It was here that a degree of expertness came

into play that never ceased to amaze me, accustomed as I was to it. Only men and horses who were masters of their craft were permitted in a herd. The man must recognize the brands, earmarks, and fleshmarks instantly and unerringly, and the horse, once the cow to be taken out was indicated, must work his quarry to the edge of the herd, then 'push' it out, the rider assisting only at this critical moment by a yell or slap of his quirt or bridle reins upon leather chaps.

Another rider is waiting to 'push' the animal on into a smaller group of 'cuts' or culls, which are being held at some little distance away. It requires the best horsemanship to prevent the first few cattle in the smaller herd, called the 'cut,' from rushing back into the fancied protection of the larger group, so that to be assigned to 'hold the cut' is to be awarded one's cowpunching diploma.

On the day Bud Jones brought his herd across our range, Ray was unable to inspect it in the interests of our outfit and I was sent to 'represent.' I reported to Mr. Jones. By his side, on a wiry cowpony with a knowing eye, sat his ten-year-old son Jimmy, an exact replica of his father in every detail of accouterment — boots, chaps, spurs, sombrero — all cut to size. The other cowboys, perhaps twelve or fifteen, gathered around, less to receive their orders than to hear Jimmy and me receive ours.

'W-a-ll,' drawled Bud Jones, a twinkle in his eye, 'I reckon we'll let Jimmy here and Miss Agnes hold the cut right over bv that patch of timber.'

The twinkle passed from eye to eye among the cowboys. 'Over by that patch of timber' was no place to hold a cut, and a girl on a sidesaddle and a ten-year-old boy the least reasonable of all possible choices for attempting it.

Should I refuse and stand forever discredited for having violated the code which allows no one to refuse an order from the boss, or submit to playing the lead in a Roman holiday for a bunch of gleeful cow-waddies? Jimmy was already headed for his proper post, midway between the rim of the herd and the timber patch. I followed, inwardly raging.

The first animal to be worked out of the herd, by the elder Jones himself, was a rangy two-year-old steer. Here was gross violation of proper procedure, which called for a seasoned old cow, preferably one with a calf, as the unit which would most probably stand quietly until joined by enough others to give the bunch a feeling of solidarity.

'What the hell?' growled Jimmy, but he bent over his pony's neck and took in behind the steer. I got around between it and the timber-patch just in time to keep the animal from dashing through it and on and on to liberty. Next came a long yearling. Any cowman will see instantly what was up.

One by one the cowboys drove out for us to hold the snakiest, orneriest, most fractious critters they could find — just to see us ride. Well, I couldn't see myself ride, but I could see Jimmy when I had time to look. He would lie along his pony's neck in a flank-to-flank race with some cow brute until his horse got a nose-length ahead, then he'd lean over and slap the animal in the face with a length of rope and both would turn in their tracks with such sudden reversal of speed that it seemed incredible anything not anchored tight to the horse could stay on it. It was horsemanship of the first order.

In due course the cut grew until it was large enough to satisfy the new arrivals and everything quieted down.

Then Jimmy dashed around from his side and sat his horse back on its haunches in front of me.

'By God, girl, you ride all right,' he told me.

I was deeply flattered. Jimmy's was expert judgment. He flung a leg over his saddle-horn and, thus relaxed, did me the honor of settling down for a chat. He opened up with small talk. Eyeing a large rent in my riding skirt he remarked, 'A feller needs chaps in this here brush to keep from gittin' his clo's tore off.'

I agreed, and he went on: 'But chaps won't keep you from gittin' yore face tore off. I like to lost my face a coupla times lately.' Then, the small talk disposed of, he got down to business.

'You carry a gun?' he wanted to know.

Not to lose standing in his eyes, I replied a little vaguely but truthfully, 'Oh, sometimes.'

Jimmy did not, I think, look back over his shoulder, but his manner suggested it.

'What size?'

'Thirty-two,' I told him. 'It doesn't kick so hard.'

This time he did look back. 'How about tradin' for a few thirty-two cat'r'dges?'

I looked for the first time at the row of cartridges in his belt. They were forty-fives. His pistol was a thirty-two.

I shook my head. 'I'm short on thirty-twos,' I said equivocally.

Jimmy sighed in disgust. 'Don't seem like the's any thirty-twos in the country. I been tryin' to git some, but it don't seem like anybody's got any.'

Not for a ten-year-old, we hadn't. Not even for one who made a hand in a cow outfit.

His father told me later that his one nagging fear was that sooner or later Jimmy would get his thirty-twos. 'And then no tellin' what!'

I didn't suggest that Jimmy might be forbidden to wear a gun of any caliber. I knew that Father Jones would shrink from any such form of cruelty to children.

Satan DIDN'T LIKE
PARASOLS

Every Monday we rode to Datil for the mail; less regularly but almost as often we went to collect our heavy supplies, which, before the days of parcel post, came by express or freight to Magdalena. It usually took three days in a Studebaker or Bain wagon to bring them the rest of the way home.

We often made the trip between Magdalena and Datil with the stage-driver. When stranded at either end of the route, one was always delighted to have the opportunity to ride for ten or twelve hours in a one-seated hack with mailbags piled high behind.

I once tried to tabulate the different modes by which I have journeyed across the San Augustine Plains. There were various trips behind a trail herd; there were innumerable journeys in freight wagons; there was the one time by burro (three days); there was once sitting in the tail end of the wagon doggedly trying to master the technique of our universal musical instrument, the harmonica, or mouth-organ as we called it. I arrived in Magdalena with swollen lips but triumphant spirit. I could blow 'Home, Sweet Home,' and several bars of 'Where Is My Wandering Boy

Tonight?' In time I became expert enough to relieve the fiddler and let the dance go on.

I even traveled in the high two-wheeled cart that belonged to Montague Stevens. He was a young Englishman who lived still farther to the west than we, and more than a hundred miles from town. When he did not make his necessary trips on horseback, he usually made them in a light cart for the sake of speed over rough country.

I shall never forget one such trip. I had returned from school for the summer vacation. The to-be-expected miscalculation had taken place and there was nobody in town from the ranch to meet me. But, providentially, Montague Stevens happened to be there. With his invariable courtliness he offered to drive me to the Datils. His cart was drawn by a long-legged black horse appropriately named Satan. Satan's physical stamina was commensurate with his strength of character. A hundred-mile trip two days previously had produced no perceptible softening of his disposition.

Young Montague Stevens helped me into the high seat and took his place beside me. 'Steady, Satan,' he admonished, handling the reins with inordinate skill, in view of the fact that only recently he had lost his left arm in a hunting accident.

We took the first ten-mile climb to the top of the divide at a leisurely pace: then Satan was urged to a faster clip. It was a hot day and the sun beat down unmercifully on the wide plain. I was wearing a small 'civilized' hat instead of the insulating Stetson which awaited me at home, and I suffered from both heat and glare.

'Why don't you raise your parasol?' my companion asked. Yes, I really carried a parasol when I masqueraded as a young lady. I thanked him for his thoughtfulness, but cast an appraising eye at Satan's ears — sure barometer of a horse's temper. I found little to reassure me.

Montague Stevens interpreted my hesitancy correctly. 'Oh,

I can handle him,' he assured me, and, lest he misconstrue refusal
as doubt of it, I cautiously raised my figured silk parasol.

It was something entirely new and utterly distasteful in Satan's
experience. With no warning whatsoever, he turned at right
angles and headed for the Gallina Mountains instead of the Datils,
those premonitory ears flattened back, the bit between his teeth,
his long legs spurning tufted hillock and gopher holes. I let go
the parasol and it floated away, to be an object of suspicion to the
coyotes and range cattle so long as a shred of purple pansy on gray
silk clung to its ribs.

With consummate skill tightening his hold on the reins, Montague Stevens smiled around at me. 'He won't keep it up long,'
he admonished. 'Hold on.' But it seemed long to me before the
futility of his performance penetrated Satan's obsessed mind.
The Gallinas were probably too far off and, anyway, that detest-
able contraption that had risen up behind him was no longer there,
so Satan finally permitted himself to be turned back toward the
road. When again we were headed for the Datils, young Stevens
apologized for his horse's behavior by explaining that ever since
a bear cub which he had captured and was carrying home in the
cart had leaped upon Satan's haunches, the horse had been unduly
sensitive to what went on behind him.

We made the rest of the forty miles without incident, Satan
arriving with less evidence of fatigue than my shaken bones
reported.

Crossing the plains on horseback, I once came upon a surprising
tableau at the exact halfway point between the Datils and town.
An assortment of household furniture was arranged in orderly
fashion at the side of a freight wagon whose team had been un-
harnessed and was grazing near-by. A brass bedstead, a mirrored
dresser, a rocking-chair, and other items of the luxurious life were
set out as a woman might be expected to arrange them. But it was
not a woman who sat in the most luxurious chair, one that we called

an Ottoman rocker. Instead I was taken aback by the sight of
the huge and burly form of a masculine neighbor, one given to
conviviality. He was rocking and beaming. A jug sat on the
golden-oak 'parlor' table beside him.

'This is the life,' he announced. 'I done sold my steers in Kansas
City for a dollar a head more'n I calculated, so I'm bringin' a
surprise home to the wife. I'm settin' here practicin' the use of
sich elegant furniture. Have one?'

I declined with thanks and rode on, leaving him to his foretaste
of living for the first time in his life in a house with 'store furniture.'

Ray, of course, had an adventure to match mine. His story was
that, driving to town behind a fast-stepping team, he had come
up behind a sort of miniature covered wagon, a low-wheeled,
canvas-topped affair which was moving at a snail's pace. The
road at this point was such that he could not easily give entire
right of way to the vehicle ahead, and moreover the code was for
it to pull over and share the road. This was one code for which
Ray was a stickler. He yelled at the unseen driver, with no effect
whatsoever. He yelled louder and more profanely. Still nothing
happened. Exasperated, he whipped up his team, swung out of
the road, and came alongside. Leaning out, he let go an educational
blast calculated to mend the ways of any uneducated user of the
public thoroughfare.

'Then,' said Ray, 'I almost fell out of my own seat. Sitting in
the other seat was a black bear and beside him a monkey. A burro
team was hitched to the wagon.'

I smiled derisively.

'Don't believe it if you don't want to' — Ray sounded injured —
'but it's the God's truth. When I came alongside, the burros
stopped. I was still pinching myself to see if I was dreaming, when
a man poked his head over the bear's shoulder and said "Whatta
da mat?" He turned out to be a dago with a traveling animal show.
He told me he always slept on long straight roads.'

High tribute to the safety of our highways!

Then there was the incident — for tragedy was always near at hand — of the steer herd which stampeded one dark night and thundered over the site of an abandoned and uncovered well, hand dug before it was realized that only machine drills could ever penetrate to water five hundred to a thousand feet below. I always looked in the opposite direction when I passed that ghastly monument to man's carelessness.

Frontier CHIVALRY

As a class, certainly, the men of our frontier were chivalrous in their attitude toward women. It may be that when people live in a less highly organized state of society, and everybody is under the same pressure of external circumstances in order to keep alive, the sex issue of itself recedes. Or, it may be that evilly-disposed men were less likely to go unhanged. Women, because of their very scarcity, were undoubtedly more valued and their own men correspondingly more fierce in their protection. Anyway, the crimes with which my youth was conversant seem to me to have been cleaner crimes than the sex horrors of today. Gun fights between men, or even horse-stealing, carried with them something of sportsmanship, which, while not making them praiseworthy, at least removed them from the realm of rank cowardice.

In all the years of my youth I never knew a case of assault, and the frequently heard statement that a 'good' woman was always safe seems to have been historically true. Only once did I feel even vaguely ill at ease when I found myself alone with any man, stranger or not. Even on this one occasion my emotion was less fear than cold wrath.

It was shortly after Gray Dick was taken. I had stationed myself for several weeks at one of the outlying camps to take care of our remaining horses in the big pasture which had been built there. (We always 'built pasture' rather than fences. Incidentally, the fences often cost more than the land.)

One afternoon a trail herd with half a dozen men in charge passed my cabin. The men all came in for a drink of water and, of course, discovered that as frequently happened I was alone and had been alone for several weeks. The boss-owner of the small outfit inquired about leasing the pasture to let his cattle 'rest up and put on a little weight.' When I refused, he took his outfit on, but in half an hour he was back, alone, and in the house before I realized it, doors being seldom closed and never locked.

Assuming that he had come back to discuss the lease matter again, I motioned him to a chair and sat down myself on a cot across the room. It was only a moment before he came over and sat down beside me.

I was saying, 'I'm sure we don't want to lease the pasture; we need it for our own horses,' when he reached over and ran his cupped hand down the length of my braided hair. And *that* was in the category of forbidden things. There was not that easy attitude toward the laying on of hands that exists today. Instinct, however, on this occasion warned me that there were explosive possibilities in a wrong move, and that my rôle must be casualness.

'Yore hair'd make a dandy cinch,' he said, with banal attempt at humor.

'Wouldn't it?' Ostensibly I fell in with the jest, and with a laugh arose and crossed over to a side table, upon which lay my own small thirty-two. I thrust it into my belt and returned to my place beside him. 'No,' I said, 'I'm sure we don't want to lease the pasture.'

The man looked at me, his eyes slightly narrowed, and then he rose to his feet with an assumption of casualness equal to my own. 'Good afternoon to you,' he said. 'I never let no woman take a shot at me' — and was gone.

This was the closest approach to having to 'fight for my honor' that ever confronted me in the hundreds of instances when I was alone with men, singly or in groups.

One incident in particular shows to what lengths most men, even of the roughest sort, carried chivalry; I used it once in a published story with a story-teller's license, but I want to relate it here without the hampering requirement of 'a beginning, a body, and an ending.'

One Monday in late summer when I went for the mail, my mount was Chico, a young mustang of boundless endurance and bad disposition. The mail was later than usual and Chico became restive from standing for hours at a hitching-rack. When the stage finally arrived, well after dark, it brought with it the county sheriff. I was trying to tie my mail-sack to the saddle-strings and having trouble with the snorting and pawing Chico when the sheriff came out to help me.

'Going up the cañon alone?' he said. I thought I detected an odd quality in his voice. 'Hadn't you better wait till daylight?'

I assured him that I could not, that I had often made the trip alone after nightfall, and what was there to be afraid of, anyhow?

'Mebbe yore right,' he conceded, I thought reluctantly, and

held Chico's bit while I mounted. For once I did 'start off at full gallop.' I couldn't help myself. Chico had had enough of that hitching-rack and he was going home. It was several miles before I got him quieted down to an impatient high trot.

We had just topped the brow of a hill, where the trail skirted around the fenced cañon bottom, when Chico snorted violently and stopped. In the trail just ahead, clearly outlined in the bright starlight of that high altitude, was another horseman. He, too, had stopped precipitately. I could hold Chico still but for a second. We came almost horse nose to horse nose before the man spoke.

'Good evening, miss?' with a sort of inquiring inflection on the 'miss.'

'Yes,' I said. 'Good evening.'

'Nice evening,' the man said, to which I echoed, 'Nice evening.'

He drew his horse out of the trail and waited for me to pass, Chico still champing his bits and pulling on the bridle reins.

An hour later the man lay dead, with the sheriff's bullet in his heart. He had made the mistake of trying to steal a fresh mount for himself from Baldwin's horse pasture instead of taking mine. A fresh mount was all he had needed to get himself and the gold which weighed down his saddlebags over the border into Mexico and safety. He threw away his chance, and his life with it, to protect a young girl from a bad fright.

Impersonal circumstances, however, were quite indifferent to such codes of honor: they took their toll without regard for chivalry.

Once, when I had stopped to 'noon' on a trip to town and my team was feeding, I climbed back into the high seat of the wagon and picked up a book. I did not hear the silent footfall of a horse and was startled when one of the team snorted. I looked up to see a horseman beside the wagon. He was a Mexican, swarthy and begrimed. He looked at me curiously.

'You all alone?' he asked in his own tongue. I told him I was.

I could read puzzlement in his face. Mexican girls did not go about alone, even in our country.

'Why you all alone?' he persisted.

'Have to,' I told him.

This seemed to puzzle him all the more. He sat looking at me intently.

'You not afraid?' he asked finally.

'No.'

'Why you not afraid?'

I reached under the edge of the Navajo blanket that covered the seat and pulled out my little thirty-two.

He nodded approvingly.

'*Bueno*,' he said, and rode on.

Another time I was alone at the ranch when Lon, a neighboring cowboy, came in and stayed for an early supper. During the meal a bat flew in at the open door and repeatedly circled close above my head. Now, bats *will* tangle in long hair.

When this bat's claw-tipped wings had repeatedly all but brushed the top of my head, I got up from the table and put on my Stetson.

'Why, Miss Agnes!' Lon exclaimed in pained surprise. 'This is the first time I ever seen you *scared*.'

'If that bat ever got tangled in my hair,' I explained, 'you'd have to cut my hair out in little chunks to get the bat out.'

A look of horror came over his face.

'Oh, I'd never do it, Miss Agnes,' he said, in the tone of one rebuking sacrilege. 'I'd cut the *bat* out in little chunks.'

After he had helped me wash dishes, we sat awhile by the open fireplace. He smoked in silence a moment and then said: 'Sitting here like this reminds me of the story of Johnny Gollymike. Ever hear tell of him?'

I looked at my visitor askance. 'Johnny Gollymike!'

'Y'see,' said Lon, with elaborate innocence, 'Johnny Gollymike

was sorta like you. Not scared of nothin' — that is, *almost* nothin'.
So some fellers told him they bet he was scared of ha'nts. Johnny
said he wasn't, neither. Well, the' was a ha'nted house near-by and
Johnny said as how he'd go stay in it all night all by hisself. He
went to the house and built him up a fire in the fireplace, and when
it was just twelve o'clock, the time the ha'nt allus come, Johnny
rolled hisself a cigareet. He looked around, and thar a-settin'
on the bench beside him was the ha'nt, a-rollin' hisself a cigareet,
too.

"'Nice smoke you and me's havin' together," says the ha'nt,
and Johnny Gollymike went away from there. He took out like
a jackrabbit with a coyote after him. When he was plumb give
out, he set down on a log a-blowin' like a windbroke horse, and
there a-settin' alongside him on the log was the ha'nt, a-blowin'
like a wind-broke ha'nt horse, too.

"'Nice footrace you 'n' me had," sez the ha'nt.

"'It sure was," says Johnny, "but pardner, it wasn't nothin'
to the one we're goin' to have right now.'"

While I was deciding whether or not this was the place to laugh,
Lon picked up his hat.

'Well, I guess I better be gettin' along like Johnny Gollymike.'
Chivalrous exit from a *tête-à-tête*, that!

I'll call this one Tod — good a name as any.

All summer long, Tod had hunted his peripatetic but wholly
mythical horses in our end of Datil Cañon. He was also regular
about being at the post office on Mondays ready to ride home
with me. He came bringing gifts, usually a quarter of beef, in a
sack carried on the saddle in front of him. Saddletrees were not
then the present-day short, squatty affairs with swell forks, but
were long enough in the seat to accommodate many kinds of
things besides the rider, including babies, as many a ranch woman
can testify.

But during all of this summer when Tod rode with me we talked of — well, I suppose it was horses. Maybe we mentioned cows, but it was horses about which most conversation revolved.

Finally, the last Monday before I must go back to school arrived. Tod rode home with me as he had done every Monday of the summer. But now he did not have anything to say. Once he slapped my pony's neck with the ends of his own bridle reins as if giving release to some unspoken feeling, but other than that we rode side by side in complete silence. I think I was afraid to start a conversation lest it take a turn which I dreaded.

At last we were in sight of the house. I remember that the last afterglow of the sun lay on its bleaching shingles, giving them a silvery sheen. Tod drew his horse to a stop.

'Miss Agnes,' he said, 'yo're leavin' tomorrow. No tellin' what things'll be like when you come back, so I just got to tell you I got mighty fond of you this summer.'

There it was. My face must have shown dismay, but before I could choose words that I hoped would be kind, Tod had gathered in his bridle reins.

'It's all right, Miss Agnes,' he said simply. 'Don't fret yoreself about me. I'll git over it.'

Gallant gentleman, I salute you! I remember you long after I have forgotten others who swore to high heaven they'd never get over it, and promptly did.

I did not go back to my Philadelphia school which I had left at Easter time, so confident of returning soon — Philadelphia seemed much too far away: and since we had friends in Ann Arbor I finished high school there.

But at Ann Arbor as at Philadelphia life had very little reality for me. I worked hard, but everything except the ranch was unimportant to me. The next summer found me joyfully getting off at the Magdalena railroad station.

In sickness AND IN
HEALTH

I HAVE often been asked, 'What did you do when you got sick —
with no doctor?'

My memory is that we didn't often get sick, and that for minor
ailments we youngsters lay on the ground. I don't know how the
superstition that lying on the ground was a cure became rooted in
our youthful minds. I can see Ray, whose malady was without
doubt digestive, lying face down in the sharp shadow of the trunk
of a tall pine tree. As the shadow moved, Ray moved with it, all
the sunlight hours. Offers of help or sympathy were met with a
brief 'Let me alone. I'll be all right by the time the sun goes
down.' And he was.

Then there was supreme faith in the curative properties of
Oregon graperoot, a scrubby variety of which grew on our shaded
mountain-sides. Its bitter quininish taste suggested potency to
cure any ill.

Perhaps the supreme instance of home remedy was the case

history of Piute Charley. He appeared one day at our place, as sick a man as ever bestrode a horse, one arm in a very dirty improvised sling. An aged Mexican and his wife lived in one of our several ranch cabins and they assisted in getting the visitor, practically a stranger, onto a couch.

'I done run away from that horspital in town,' he said. 'That sawbones was fixin' to cut my arm off.'

His words came with difficulty, but he went on with his tale, unapologetically.

'You see, I got drunk and lay out all night in the snow and froze one hand which I'd lost the glove of, and my hand all swole up and turned black and then my whole arm swole and I went into town to see a doc, and he said gangrene had done set in and I'd have to have my arm cut off to save my life. I don't want my arm cut off' — his tone pleaded indulgence for his unreasonableness — 'so I just went away from that horspital and got on my horse and rode out here. Thought mebbe you'd know something that would cure my arm 'thout cuttin' it off.'

Staggering proposition that was!

The old Mexican woman came to my rescue. 'I know something,' she said in her native tongue. 'I'll show you.'

Humbly I set about following her instructions. They were minute and ritualistic. We got a large onion and peeled off the outer leaves. Then taking a few of the inner succulent leaves we put them on live coals raked from the fireplace; when they were toasted to a degree of tenderness we put a pinch of Duke's Mixture (no other brand, I was assured, must be used) into each leaf, spread these leaves on a cloth, and applied them warm.

It was a long, harrowing three-weeks course of treatment. Onion, tobacco, and gangrene is a combination calculated to make a trained nurse shudder, much less an amateur. But every three hours day and night either I or the old Mexican woman toasted onion leaves, sprinkled them with Duke's Mixture, and bound them around the most repellent piece of human flesh I have ever looked at.

I dared not stop the treatment nor vary the formula. To have done so would have been to assume responsibility, and that was unthinkable! The patient at the risk of his life had run away from responsible medical help. I could not, either physically or morally, have forced him back to it. The old Mexican woman had stepped into the rôle from which the medical man had been cast out, and the responsibility was hers. Mine was meticulously to obey orders

Duke's Mixture and onion leaves proved too much for gangrene. Or was it faith? Anyway, the man recovered, and when he rode away he rewarded me with a 'I shore do thank you. I thought as how you could keep me from gittin' my arm cut off.'

I never saw him again.

Shortly afterward, I was alone, this time at our headquarters ranch. A haggard-looking man on a haggard-looking horse stopped at the door. I thought his face changed when he saw me and I know that my porcupine bristles raised. It was my friend who wouldn't let no woman take no shot at him.

He jerked off his hat, less in salute than to show two red marks, not unlike cat scratches, close to the hairline of his forehead. His voice shook when he spoke.

'A hybie-phobie skunk bit me.' His tone said: 'I am doomed to die of hydrophobia.'

My heart sank. There was no Mexican woman this time to offer an infallible remedy. Moreover, a neighbor had died of hydrophobia from the effects of a mad coyote's bite, and the shock of hearing the details had not completely left me. It was in a state close to panic that I waited for what the man would say next.

'They say that there's a madstone in Socorro!' he said. 'If I can git to it in time! I've been on this one horse twenty hours already. He can't make it on into town.'

Vast indeed was my relief. I bade him dismount and lie down, while I cared for his horse and found him a fresh one. He drank a cup of coffee and fell over as one dead on the couch, while I rustled the pasture and saddled a new horse for him. He was sleeping so soundly and with such complete relaxation in every line of face and body that it seemed cruel to awaken him a couple of hours later, but I dared not postpone his reaching his madstone.

'I feel some better already,' he assured me by way of thanks as he rode off. Two days later he reappeared. His manner was debonair. 'Ever see a madstone?'

I told him I had not. I have seen one since, though, so I know what it looks like. It is a growth which forms in the stomach of a deer, probably a pathological condition, because the deer, so it is said, turns white. The growth is round, about the size of an orange, and grayish in color. When sawn in two, it presents row upon row of a cellular structure not unlike ends of small hollow tubes.

My friend described its operation. I vouch only for his words, not for his veracity.

'Old Man Gleason what owns the madstone,' he said, 'soaked it in milk and then stuck it on my wound. Pretty soon it began to pull and it kept on pullin' and I could feel the hybie-phobie pizen bein' pulled right out. And then it fell off of itself and Old Man Gleason washed it out in the milk and that milk turned green and he put it back on and it done the same thing over again tell it quit turnin' the milk green.'

The fame of this instance of preventing hydrophobia added naturally to the prestige of our local madstone and to the certainty in the public mind that there were hydrophobia skunks about. But that, too, was a matter for naturalists to debate. I never saw a skunk that looked any more dangerous to me than a skunk's popular reputation might warrant!

Neither my friend nor I gave any sign that we had met before.

Then there was the time Ray and Bowlegs stopped one cold night at Bob Wiley's camp and found Bob short of bedding. 'Just bought a Navajo blanket from an Indian,' Bob said, producing a beautiful Navajo rug. 'It might be some help.'

It wasn't much, for a Navajo blanket, in spite of being all wool, is too stiff and too heavy for warmth. 'Just as well try to keep warm with a set of chain harness,' we used to say. But Ray and Bowlegs shivered under the blanket until daylight — and then they shivered worse, for in burst a very irate young Navajo. Spying the blanket, he seized it.

'That no-'count cousin of mine,' he stormed in Spanish, 'stole this blanket and sold it 'stead of burying it with my father who died on it. That cousin of mine he ben off to white man's school and thinks he's smart.' Then, as a postscript, 'My father he die with *viruelas*.'

Viruelas, amigo, is smallpox.

Ray and Bowlegs went into seclusion in a remote horse camp and waited to come down with smallpox. Each day they carefully inspected each other for symptoms, the actual eruption being the only symptom they knew.

'I think I see a *viruela* behind your ear,' or, 'Here's a shore 'nough smallpox pimple on the back of your neck,' were their cheerful exchanges of pleasantries — while they waited.

They decided that after nine days they could again mingle with their kind. It grew very monotonous ticking off the days: 1, 2, 3, 4, 5, 6, 7, 8, 9 — and one for the margin of safety.

Their prolonged absence had begun to worry us, when eventually they rode into the ranch. Looking hale and hearty, they explained:

'We just been keepin' out of sight to see if we had the smallpox or not.'

They were little more than youngsters, and we wondered what might have happened had one or both actually contracted the disease.

But it didn't do to speculate about the disaster which had only threatened. We'd have driven ourselves mad. In this age of easy communication when 'Let us know of your safe arrival' is a routine request for a telephone call, or a brief wire, I wonder what spirit of fortitude it was that let us wait days or possibly weeks to learn the fate of one who had ridden out of sight, to a destination where he was not expected, so that there would be no one to give the alarm for days at least, should misadventure occur.

The disaster we most feared was a horse's falling and disabling us. Possibly because this was our most common form of accident. Prairie-dog holes have been responsible for many a broken leg, both of horse and rider. Any rough country is always a menace. One man I knew rode fifteen miles with a broken leg, fifteen unbelievably rugged miles. Fortunately there had been help at hand to get him back on his horse.

But the most nightmarish vision of all was that of having a horse fall, flatten the stirrup, and find oneself caught by a foot when the horse got up again. For this we wore six-shooters long after any other reason for doing so existed. To shoot the horse was the only answer, in all probability. A six-shooter does give one a sense of security. We had a saying, 'A six-shooter makes all men equal.' I amended it to 'A six-shooter makes men and women equal.'

We thought little about typhoid or other gentler forms of kicking off. That I myself have survived to a ripe maturity is due to great self-control in not having committed premeditated murder and been hanged for it.

Not always, however, did our kill-or-cure methods succeed. One day a man looking tired and worn was dropped off at the ranch by a passing freighter. He explained that he had business farther on and asked the loan of a horse and saddle. So we gave this complete stranger a horse and saddle and believed him when he promised to return them in a few days.

The days passed and he did not come back. I remember how reluctant we were to believe that we had been deliberately victimized. Horse-thieves did not get their horses that way, and men 'on the dodge' who asked for a horse told you where they'd leave it for you to come and get it. But as time passed it began to seem that our confidence, for once, had been misplaced.

Still, we clung to hope, dreading, I think, to face loss of our confidence more than loss of the horse and saddle. Then one day John Cox from over in Nester Draw rode up, leading our horse.

'There's a man awful sick at our place,' he told us. 'He's got smallpox and he's out of his head, but he keeps ravin' about havin' to get this horse back to you folks. Yestidday the Magdalena Doc come by from Mangas where he'd gone to set a busted leg, and the Doc told us to give this sick man at our house lots of whiskey. The Doc wouldn't come inside the house; jest set in his buckboard and yelled over the fence. Didn't even want any of us to come near him. We've used up all the whiskey we had. My wife's plumb give out takin' care of him, so me and Gene have took turns nursin' him nights, but we got to get more whiskey for him.'

None of us doubted it. Hadn't a doctor shouted the prescription across the fence? The fact that the doctor had been afraid to enter the house, much less make any examination of the patient, did not militate against the confidence we placed in this long-range diagnosis. His prescription we felt must be filled at all cost.

In a three-man relay, we made a hundred-mile ride as fast as horseflesh could stand it. I did twenty of those miles largely in a gallop and turned the precious jug over to the last rider in perfect pony-express style.

I wish that I might report that the stranger got well, but he did not. Whether from smallpox or from whiskey, he died. Again neighbor Cox came to us, this time asking aid in burying the man. There was no undertaker to be called in, no coroner's inquest, no death certificate, no burial permit. There was in fact no cemetery, and of course no available coffin. There was, however, every necessity for prompt interment, it being midsummer, and hotter than usual.

Only two men were instantly available, a Mexican who worked for us and a chance visitor. Cox said: 'I'll git me back home, and help Gene make the coffin. He's rippin' the boards off the grain-room floor. If you all can, I wisht you'd have a grave ready so's we can git him buried and git home before dark. My wife wants him buried up at the old Flyin' V place, 'cause there's a baby buried there, and my wife wants this man buried beside this baby. She thinks neither of them'd be so lonesome. She's always fretted about that baby bein' there all by itself. She walked up there and put rocks on the grave and fixed it up not long ago. It's a little far away,' he went on, 'but if you all can have the grave dug, I reckon we kin meet you there 'fore sundown. My wife don't want to be at it after dark. She's had about all she kin stand. She ain't never had smallpox, neither.'

He turned and rode away, while the visitor, the Mexican, and I made ready to ride fourteen miles horseback, carrying digging tools, a long-handled shovel, a pick, and a crowbar.

The crowbar, being both awkward and heavy, was passed back and forth between us when it became too burdensome for one or the other to carry longer. When it came my turn, it was handed over to me without apology. The man from whom I received it surrendered it with relief and I carried it to the limit of my own endurance, with no added burden of having to listen or reply to polite murmurings of regret. We saved our breath for the business in hand.

Arrived at the spot where the baby was buried, we marked off a grave beside the little mound. We took our specifications from the 'Lament of the Dying Cowboy.' Graves, we knew, must be 'six by three.'

We began to dig.

It was a rocky ledge. The digging was painful. The rock strata grew harder the deeper we went. At the end of an hour we gave up. Only dynamite could have got down through that formation.

Even that tiny babe's grave must have been a heavy task for somebody.

With an hour's valuable time lost, it was feverish work digging a second grave at some distance away, where the ground was softer. My task, for the most part, was to stand on top and true up the corners with the crowbar.

As it turned out, 'six by three' was much too generous an estimate, for when the farm wagon arrived, just at sundown, we discovered that the coffin had been made strictly to measure and the deceased had been a small man. We wished that we had known it sooner.

But if we regretted useless labor, Mrs. Cox's regrets were more commendable. She had so wanted those graves side by side!

'It's allus so lonesome for that baby,' she breathed.

Yes, it was a lonely spot. A dilapidated windmill whose metal wheel had lost two of its blades creaked in shrill agony with every stirring of the wind.

One day, some time later, curiosity impelled me to dismount as I was passing by the one-room cabin near the baby's grave, and push open the door which swung lopsidedly on leather hinges. The unplaned floor was an inch thick with dust and the sign left by countless chipmunks. Sitting in front of the cold fireplace, as though waiting for its owner to return, was a little rawhide-bottomed chair. It was handmade, and unquestionably came with the first trek of pioneers into the Southwest.

Why had it been abandoned? Had the unknown mother of the dead baby felt that she could never again sit in it? At any rate, I could not bear to leave it to its pathetic vigil, and resolved to carry it home with me.

It was no simple matter to take the chair aboard a horse who harbored prejudices against serving as a moving van. Fortunately, from the corner of the house projected a wooden peg upon which it was possible to hang the chair by a rung. After numerous efforts

to get my disapproving horse close enough for me to reach the
chair, I finally succeeded in lifting it from the peg, a sort of merry-
go-round ride except that the prize was no brass ring.

I like to think that the chair is grateful for its refuge. I carried it
sixteen miles in front of me, and at the end of the trip my horse had
compromised but little with his prejudices.

We took it AND LIKED IT

Not many of our women neighbors got about as did my mother and her daughters. Not many had reason to, with their menfolks to carry the responsibility of looking after their cattle. It was this deadly staying at home month in and month out, keeping a place of refuge ready for their men when they returned from their farings-forth, that called for the greater courage, I think. Men walked in a sort of perpetual adventure, but women waited — until perhaps the lightning struck. One mother, carrying the body of her three-months-old baby, which had died suddenly of some infantile disorder, was being driven to town by a neighbor, her husband not being home at the time. Halfway across the plains, one of the team dropped dead from overdriving. All night the mother sat with the dead child in her arms while the man, riding the other horse bareback, went on into Magdalena to fetch back a fresh team. For him, that last ten miles was undoubtedly a longer stretch than a mere ten miles; for the woman, it must have seemed the long road to eternity. Again, coyotes played their part. We used to say they detected the presence of death with some macabre instinct. This night they sat close to the buckboard, with the dead horse lying in the harness and the dead child in the mother's lap, and howled the night through.

The terrible isolation and loneliness in which most ranch women lived called for the last reserve of moral stamina. The outstanding example in my experience of this sort of passive, unspectacular heroism was little Mrs. Eugene Manning, who lived in a box cañon at the base of the highest peak in the Datils. Months on end she and her small son stayed alone with only a very rare visitor, some cowboy perhaps who was riding the range and stopped long enough for a friendly greeting.

It fell to my lot to be present when her four-year-old for the first time saw another youngster. The visitor was also a four-year-old boy, himself not too accustomed to the presence of others of his kind. The two stood far apart, taking each other's measure. Between them, a thirty-five-foot lariat, the little Manning boy's principal plaything, lay stretched to its full length on the ground. The Manning child reached down and took hold of one end of the rope and instantly the visitor grasped the other end. Then, inch by inch, hand over hand, they approached one another, warily, cautiously. The rope taut between them, it was minutes before they arrived to within arm's length of one another. Not a word had been spoken, no sound had accompanied this steady coming together. Eyes had been steadily fixed upon eyes, but only the rope, familiar medium to both, formed a physical contact.

At last they stood face to face, a matter of inches of rope between them. They were oblivious to the adult audience, oblivious to everything but each other. Would they pull now, as a test of strength? We, the audience, waited.

Without warning and with apparently a single purpose, simultaneously they dropped the rope and flew at each other like a couple of cub wildcats.

'Don't interfere,' a man besought the two mothers. 'They're finding out something.'

It was a fierce little battle and soon over. A moment later they were playing happily together with the rope, two normal children.

'I guess he's got pretty bad manners,' both mothers apologized.

Ranch women took things in their stride. They had to, and it was always the unexpected that they strode along with.

One ranch mother I know was confronted with a situation that might well have daunted her, but which she took as just a pesky interruption in her routine duties. The ranch had one of the larger corrals of the neighborhood, and on this day it was serving to hold the 'drives,' small bunches of stuff which were successively driven in and penned. 'Stuff' indicates general range stock, cows with calves, bulls, steers, dry cows, yearlings, long and short, weaners, dogies — the whole ranch-stock gamut.

The corral gradually filled with new arrivals.

'You keep away from that there corral,' the woman of the ranch adjured her two-year-old embryonic cowpuncher, the sort of ritualistic admonition busy mothers fling out as they run.

Presently she missed the youngster and of course looked for him in the direction of the corral. He was not to be seen, but a dust cloud and a general uproar inside the corral was very much in evidence. She ran and peered through the bars.

In the center of the corral, in one end of a huge hollowed log which served as a salt trough and was now practically empty, sat her child squealing delightedly while about, back and forth over the trough, circling it, threatening to fall into it, fought two big bulls, bellowing, snorting, bent upon doing one another to death. Through the corral bars crawled the exasperated woman, dodged the head-to-head bellowing combatants, and snatching her infant, retreated back through the bars.

'Weren't you afraid of those bulls?' someone asked.

'I dunno,' was her reply. 'I didn't have time to think about *them!*'

Ranch women's life had its comedy side of course, as this story demonstrates. Most ranch owners frowned upon card-playing, and with good reason. Horses would stand all night with their *morrales* on, gates would be left open when they should have been shut, and even meals would be neglected if a good stiff poker game was in progress.

So the better-organized ranches forbade cards entirely and the smaller ones struggled with the problem. One of these latter was the INM, where the ranch women, Mrs. Starring and her daughter Lou, under extraordinary handicaps, were making a home for a bunch of winter hands. A card game got started with the usual demoralizing effects. The men simply would not attend to routine chores, which the women were forced to take over, nor would they come to meals when summoned. Exasperated over ruined food, and rebellious over having to do outdoor as well as indoor work, the two women finally reached the explosion point. They decided upon a hair-of-the-dog-that-bit-you cure.

They, too, set up a poker game, on the dining-room table. Stage property only. One of the women kept vigil through the window. The bunkhouse was situated directly in line. When a man emerged from the bunkhouse, the women hastily grabbed a handful of cards and began to manipulate poker chips.

'When we finish this game we'll begin to get supper,' the prospecting male would be informed. When he had retreated, the cards would be thrown down and more congenial pursuits resumed. Cold biscuit and a can of tomatoes purloined by one masculine scout served for the gamblers' first belated meal. The next day not even these slender rations were to be found. For two days the contest went on, until starvation forced complete surrender of the beleaguered bunkhouse forces.

'No use naggin' men,' Mrs. Starring said afterward. 'It never does any good.'

We never forbade card-playing on our place in the long winter evenings. We tried to make life as tolerable as possible. I remember how pleased I was to discover that ours was sometimes referred to as the 'ranch of the popping matches,' because we supplied the present type of tipped match instead of the blocks of sulphur-headed matches the fumes of which gave them their local name of 'hell-sticks' and 'choked a fellow to death before he could get his cigareet lighted.' Most ranches supplied 'hell-sticks.' But we didn't like gambling any more than Mrs. Starring had liked it. It was a nice problem, this fine line between entertainment and vice.

I thought to solve it the one winter I stayed home; I would play cards with the boys! We'd play in our dining-room and not in the bunkhouse, one sociable family! Meekly they came. I was bubbling with good will. We'd play poker for beans! The mere consciousness of having won, typified by the largest pile of beans, would be reward enough! Wouldn't it?

We played poker night after night. I bet recklessly. We had a winter's supply of beans on hand. My associates seemed to be exercising unnecessary caution in the manner of their betting. At times they seemed harried and confused — but we played on. One day I came unexpectedly upon two of them hunched over a slip of paper and overworking a stub of lead pencil. 'Damn it,' Bob Gard was muttering, 'I can't figger this out. Them beans of Miss

Agnes's just naturally ball it all up, but I'm doggone sure you owe me two-fifty.' I backed away before I was noticed. That night I told them I wanted to read. If they cared to play cards they could go to the bunkhouse. They accepted with alacrity.

With the cattle business the sole industry, and a working schedule of twenty-four hours a day necessary to conduct it, there was little consideration given to the comforts of daily life and practically none to the refinements. Women had to get along with what they had, which was precious little. Insistence would usually result in the men getting in a 'little jag of wood,' sometimes snaked in by a rope tied to the saddle-horn. Lucky indeed if insistence got it chopped.

I once overheard the Wheeler family working out the wood problem:

Mrs. Wheeler: 'Paw, chop me up a little jag of wood.'

Paw: 'Ed, chop yore maw up a jag of wood.'

Ed: 'Gus, Maw wants some wood.'

Gus: 'Joe, you chop Maw some wood.'

Joe: 'Virg, git a-holt of the axe and chop Maw some wood and git a move on you.'

Virg: 'Early, cain't yuh hear? Maw wants some wood.'

Early, moving toward the woodpile, mutters, 'Jest wait till I grow up and see if you lazy louses can make me chop wood 'cause I'm the littlest.'

Only when the welfare of the children was at stake did the ranch women become dictatorial. Like as not it was on the subject of milk. In a country where there was little else besides cows it might be supposed that milk would be plentiful. This is how we got it. One kept a lookout on the range for a likely-looking milch cow. Don't forget that the Texas longhorn and the range Hereford are not milk-producing breeds. When a cow was spotted that gave hope of supplying more milk than her calf could subsist on, she was brought in and her education as a domestic animal begun. We used the term 'breaking bronco cows' exactly as we spoke of breaking bronco horses, and sometimes the process was as exciting.

First you roped your cow, by the horns, and if she didn't put you over the corral fence before you could snub her to it, you tied her securely and the first step had been achieved. Then you took a shorter rope, one about four feet long with a non-slip noose on one end. Jockeying for a safe position and watching your chance, you flipped an end of this rope around the cow's hind legs above the knees, caught it and quickly pulled the smooth end of the rope through the noose, drew her legs tightly together, and tied the rope. Next you took your five-pound lard bucket, being an optimist, and standing well back attempted to squirt a stream of milk into the bucket. The calf on the opposite side of the cow was operating far more expertly in his own behalf and interfered seriously with your own efforts, but you tolerated his slobbery presence, for on these terms and these only would the cow stand as still as she did stand, which wasn't particularly still.

It is remarkable how a cow with both hind legs tied together can kick you winding, but I assure you she can. Assuming this has happened, you pick yourself up and try another squirt. Patience and an indomitable spirit will reward you, and you may ultimately hang your five-pound bucket on the gatepost with its precious quart or possibly three pints of milk, while you proceed to operate in reverse and untie the cow, after which you stand by while the calf does the 'stripping.' After this, you cut the calf off from the cow with the skill and technique of a bullfighter. In the end the cow goes out one gate and the calf another and milking time has ended.

Some cows never 'gentle,' while others will learn in a few weeks to stand reasonably quiet, although few of us in our early dairying experience ever risked milking without first hobbling the cow. The butterfat content wasn't high and butter-making was naturally left to the ranches, where there were women who had the makings of matadors and were willing to milk plenty of cows.

There came a time in the life of one such neighbor when she was compelled to relinquish the job to her husband. She had a baby and was totally unable to nurse it. Milk for the newborn was imperative. The husband rose to the emergency. Every two hours he went through the cow-milking ordeal and rushed to his wife's bedside before the 'animal heat' should be spent and fed the infant, first with a teaspoon and then with a nursing bottle improvised from a mustang liniment bottle with several thicknesses of porous cloth serving as a nipple. The baby came of hardy stock and was doing well, thank you, when I saw him ten years later.

Of course we were always casting about for some little epicurean luxury, so in early spring we often had lamb's-quarter greens and occasionally sheep-sorrel pie if a patch of sheep sorrel could be found. The acid-sweet of sheep sorrel makes delectable pie, but it takes so much of the short-stemmed clover-leaf-shaped plant that only when all hands gathered sheep sorrel could we hope for the luxury of a pie. Usually we had to be content with vinegar pie. The recipe for vinegar pie was as follows: Make a flour and vinegar base, seasoned with sugar, and cook until it thickens. It might be simpler to state the recipe, Make a good quality of paperhanger's paste and season to taste. But make no mistake, it's good! I once asked Mattie, a neighbor come to help us out, if she could make a vinegar pie.

'Oh, yes,' she said, 'and I can make a good imitation vinegar pie.' That left me guessing.

Our stock dessert was bread and 'lick.' Lick is syrup, molasses, or any viscous sweetening. There was a distinction between 'short lick,' sugar, and 'long lick.'

From present-day emphasis upon a balanced diet, it is interesting to look back upon our New Mexico ranch dietary of fifty years ago.

It consisted of meat, first, last, and always; potatoes in season, which means that we seemed quite unable to keep them from freezing in winter (building freeze-proof cellars called for just that much time away from hunting your wandering horses and cows); bread, a term which meant sour-dough biscuit almost exclusively; beans and sowbelly (salt pork to the fastidious); dried fruit; and, for a touch of luxury, 'canned goods.' Eggs? Not regularly. Too many predatory animals to make chicken-raising much more than a series of minor tragedies.

Any diet at all was the important thing. To become choosy about it was not good form. Of course, there were certain personal idiosyncrasies, such as pouring molasses over one's beefsteak, or, more generally, over one's bacon, although personally I never cared for either.

And while we are on the subject of ranch food, may I say a word for 'jerky'? Recipe for making jerky: When a beef has been butchered, and the neighbors have been presented with chunks (we didn't talk of 'cuts') thereof, and you know that even what is left will spoil before it can be eaten, take this surplus, cut in long thin strips, salt, and hang over the clothesline. Don't get excited about flies. It will dry so rapidly the flies will become discouraged. In a couple of days it will be as hard as a cedar chip. Put in an empty flour sack and hang out of reach of cats, dogs, mice, and chipmunks. To serve, eat as is, or throw on hot coals and roast, or, if time is no object, pound into a fibrous pulp, fry, and cover with milk gravy — and don't envy any city slicker at his banquet table. Of course, a healthy out-of-doors appetite is a great help.

Undoubtedly our diet was anything but scientific. 'You seem to have lived on meat and starches,' a careful eater once pointed out to me. 'And darned glad we were to get it,' is the only answer.

A cowboy's FORTUNE

Every ranch owner sent representatives to the roundups in the spring and fall — one or more men as his interests might require. In the early days in Texas, a 'work' might bring one hundred or more men together. Half that number was a full quota with us. Each man came with his bed on a pack-horse and his 'string' of eight to fourteen saddle-ponies. The chuck-wagon from that time on was his home. All of his personal belongings were wrapped in his bedroll. One piece of baggage and one only was his allotment.

A stranger on his way to the local roundup once stopped at our place for a meal. Something frightened his string. It may well have been one of our menagerie. Anyway, the horses stampeded, with them his pack-horse, carrying his all-inclusive bedroll. The man leaped from his chair, muttering, 'There goes the savings of a lifetime.'

It took Ray on one of our horses a considerable while to restore the man's lost fortune to him. It probably inventoried a seven-by-sixteen-foot tarpaulin cover, a pair or two of store blankets, although in my day homemade comforters were in general use, a few 'boughten soogins,' things that 'drove cowboys crazy' trying to decide which was length and which was breadth, as the saying went. I don't know how the word 'soogin' came to mean bedquilt, but I do know that the cheap ones were square and not quite adequate. The word 'soogin' reached us from Texas, as did many another phrase. It was a popular joke with us to tell some tenderfoot that we were very sorry, but we had to confess that all our beds had soogins in them, and then watch the look of apprehension settle in the visitor's eye.

One visitor put a certain cowboy properly in his place — an especially ignorant cowboy, I confess, but not too rare a specimen. The cowboy had laughed uproariously at the visitor's unconcealed distaste for sleeping in a bed infested with soogins.

'You should laugh,' retorted the visitor. 'I happen to know that you slumber in your bed.'

The cowboy turned purple. 'No man can say that about me and git off with it!' he roared.

Fortunately he had no gun. We rescued the visitor.

But returning to the inventory: Along with the soogins, the bedroll probably contained an extra pair of boots, socks, extra shirt, smoking tobacco, and any other oddments making up the quota of personal belongings. And the weight of that bedroll itself was something to ponder. Ah, no, it was not in the class with your modern sleeping-bag. But it was vastly more comfortable, defying wind and weather, snakes and beetles. It was his own retreat to which its owner could repair and feel that all was secure, unless it rained too hard, which sporadically it did. Then one was apt to sleep in wet blankets.

Much of the cowboy's equipment, and all that couldn't be bought in Magdalena, was ordered by mail. Our family did most of the mail-ordering for the community as a matter of fact: possibly because our roomful of books was impressive, or because our good nature was to be depended upon, we had become sort of public scribes. Legal documents to be interpreted or executed, important letters to be written, any one of a dozen services which our neighbors needed and which required 'book learning,' fell largely to our household to execute.

By some mysterious grapevine route it usually became known when we were getting off a mail order to Sears Roebuck, Montgomery Ward, or one of the firms which catered exclusively to the stockman's trade. Then requests came from the cowboys, who usually didn't possess a lead pencil, asking to have some of their small wants included in our order.

Patience went along with every order, for goods came to Magdalena by express or freight and lay there until we could go for them — an indefinite wait, often weeks. But when the package did arrive, it was an out-of-season Christmas. Bridle bits, gauntlet gloves, quirts, a set of hames, a kingpin for a wagon, a box of liver pills, a pair of shoes for some trusting soul who often had to fill them with wet corn and let it swell, thereby stretching the shoes to the requirements of comfort rather than style. Returning goods was such a heart-breaking process of long waiting that we avoided it if possible.

We always tried to notify the owner of the goods in time for him to be present at the unwrapping ceremony, but that wasn't always possible, of course, and we were frequently custodians of articles which belonged to someone who apparently had vanished from the face of the earth.

The rivalry between the partisans of Sears Roebuck and fans of Montgomery Ward, then as now affectionately known as 'Monkey Ward,' was almost as keen as the rivalry between followers of major-league ball teams. Should an article turn out to be unsatisfactory, the rival camp would exult, 'I told you you orter trade with ——' (the opposition). Neutrality was looked upon as a sign of weak character.

Flipping through the leaves of a mail-order catalogue, with a little cash on hand, was a favorite occupation. My most exciting adventure was assisting a prospective bride order a complete trousseau. She had all of twenty dollars to spend. It sufficed.

The cowboy of the era of which I write counted physical hardship as a normal part of life's routine.

'Why would he put up with it, for thirty dollars a month and his board?' — remember he supplied his own bed — the question is sometimes asked.

I doubt if he thought he was 'putting up' with anything. He wasn't given to philosophical analysis. He was merely about the business he understood, and enjoying it. I suspect that had it ever been successfully drummed into his head that a day would come when his profession would be exploited for its dramatic qualities, he would have been sadly perplexed and disbelieving. Had anyone told him that riding a bucking horse would become a histrionic profession, he would have smiled pityingly. To be sure, Buffalo Bill had started out with his road show, but never could we have been made to believe that it was a forerunner of a national industry.

Once I was besought by one of Buffalo Bill's talent scouts to join his show.

'*Me?* What on earth could I do?'

'I seen you ride that blue roan outlaw yestidday,' he replied, with more admiration than grammar.

'And you saw me keep him *from* bucking, didn't you?'

No, I've never yet let a horse buck with me if I could stop him. I can't see any sense in getting your head all but snapped from your shoulders, your spinal column whipped like a bullwhacker's blacksnake, your insides churned into jelly, even if you stay on, which I usually didn't — not if one could help it! As for making it a profession, that was to laugh!

Those who do it for high pay are 'putting up with' the greater hardship. At least some of us think so.

'High, WIDE, AND HANDSOME'

We usually had a dance whenever the roundup was in the neighborhood. Word went forth as widely as possible, often by the 'kid-on-a-horse' route, that there would be a dance at such and such a place. 'Come one, come all,' was the invitation, for we were the extreme example of a classless society.

I have known people to ride forty miles on horseback to attend a dance. I myself have gone as far as twenty-five, with my party dress in a flour sack tied to my saddle. Yes, of course it was wrinkled, but it was clean.

The dances started at sundown and continued until sunup. There were at least four or five 'gents' to every 'lady.' These latter ranged in age from Grandmother to little pigtailed Susie; anything feminine would do as a partner. No wallflowers in those days!

'Five, six, seven, and eight,' the master of ceremonies would bellow, 'get your partners and don't let good music go to waste.'

The music more often than not was Jack Howard, one of the great old-time fiddlers, who could 'sure make that fiddle talk.' When Jack Howard drew his bow across the strings, he wanted action. I can still see him, sitting on a stool on top of the table shoved in a corner, his eyes closed, a foot tapping out the rhythm of 'Sandy Land':

> 'We'll hoe potatoes in Sandy Land,
> Mighty fine taters in Sandy Land...'

Nothing, to my mind, approaches 'Sandy Land' as a dance tune — not even 'Turkey in the Straw.'

High-heeled boots pounded out the rhythms on rough floors; the lighter tap of feminine feet played treble accompaniment. Our square dances were a combination of dance and romping game made especially zestful from necessity of following the instructions of the caller.

> 'Balance all until y' git straight,
> Swing on them corners like swingin' on a gate,
> Bow to yore partners and pull yore freight.
> All drift south.
> First couple lead off to the couple on the right,
> Balance all.
> Ladies do-see-do,
> Gents you know,
> Four hands around and around and around,
> Birdie in the middle and around and around.
> Birdie hop out and the crow hop in,
> Three hands around and go it agin.
> All drift south.'

For hilarity I'll match limber Gus Wheeler obeying the call, 'Three hands around and gent cut a caper,' with any present-day dance routine. I remember, too, a time when Gus relieved the caller, whose voice was giving out, and that, too, was on the funny side:

> 'Here we go to Rackensack,
> Now turn around and go rackin' back,
> Everybody put on polite,'

howled Gus, and 'put on polite' we did, each according to his own idea of 'style,' which was the usual word in the call. Gus defended his substitution by guessing 'they meant the same thing.'

By midnight we womenfolks would begin to weaken. I remember Lora hiding under a table, concealed by the long cloth, and when this retreat was discovered, sneaking out to the barn and crawling into a manger, to sleep briefly before being mercilessly dragged back and made to dance. Often, however, she bought immunity by offering to play the harmonica and let the fiddler rest. And how she could make the harmonica sing!

Midnight supper consisted of coffee and cake. Every woman brought a cake, whether she came by wagon or horseback. Even when it is packed in a tin bucket it is no mean achievement to keep a layer cake intact for mile after mile on horseback. But one's social rating was judged by the cake one brought, and bring it one did, at whatever cost to strained muscles.

I don't know why we didn't bring pies. Probably because cakes were more easily served. And how we compared recipes, trying in particular to discover good ones which required fewer eggs! 'Half lard and half butter if you have it,' was the traditional recipe, 'and condensed milk is fine, but you have to have at least one egg.'

There may have been liquor at our dances, but it was not in evidence. Any man who showed symptoms of intoxication was promptly hustled out of sight, and kept there. 'Gents don't drink whiskey in front of ladies' was a social dictum. It was the era of the temperance crusade, the era when we sang (for the crusade had reached even into our backwoods society):

> 'We're coming, we're coming,
>   A brave little band;
>   On the safe side of temperance
>   We'll now take a stand.'

When our cowboys got drunk they did it without benefit of the society of 'nice' girls.

Moreover, pulp Wild West yarns and movies to the contrary, a cowboy did not wear his gun and spurs to a dance. High-heeled boots, yes; one couldn't dance barefoot, could one?

Toward morning the sufferings of my sex would become acute. Dazed with fatigue, I have dragged myself through the last hour of many a dance, praying for the sun to rise and put an end to my misery. A cowpuncher who would have gone to fantastic lengths to save a lady from discomfort in any other circumstances would be inhuman in his insistence upon 'just one dance more.'

Bill Hazelwood was perhaps the greatest offender in this. So we women once entered upon a conspiracy and promoted a leap-year dance for the sole purpose of retaliation. It was aimed at Bill Hazelwood as a public example. The other men were invited to be spectators to a sort of mental lynching bee.

If Bill Hazelwood had begun by feeling pleased at the evidence of his popularity, as time after time he was led out on the dance floor by some cryptically smiling lady with the glint of determination in her eye, his self-satisfaction was short-lived. Fortunately for our purpose, Bill's boots were new. After an hour of steady dancing, lines of suffering began to show in his face.

'Stay with it, cowboy!' his comrades encouraged from the sidelines. 'Keep a-steppin' wide, high, and handsome!' (Little did I think, when Noah McChristian yelled it at Bill Hazelwood almost fifty years ago, that that phrase would achieve immortality! It probably wasn't original with Noah, but we all thought it was at the time.)

Alas, Bill Hazelwood couldn't hide under a tablecloth. So the sadistic performance continued throughout the night, the victim too proud to cry for mercy, and his tormentors driven on by memory of his own previous ruthlessness.

Forty-five years later, I was sitting on the veranda of the rebuilt White House, reading over an old letter of mine to my mother, one which I had just unearthed from an old trunk. 'Dick Dean and Bill Hazelwood didn't act like gentlemen,' I had written in 1891, and was re-reading in 1935, when a large car stopped and a gray-haired gentleman, wearing glasses and looking every inch the substantial citizen, got out and came over to me.

'Pardon me, madam,' he said, 'but do you happen to know whether any of the Morleys are still in this vicinity? I have brought my family through Datil to show them where I once worked as a cowpuncher. My name is Hazelwood.'

Two minutes later we were re-living the dance and the other occasion when he and Dick Dean hadn't 'acted like gentlemen.'

'After that dance,' he confessed, 'I walked for a month like a horse with string-halt.'

'So I recall,' I rubbed it in; 'and what's more, I've never forgiven you and Dick Dean for not heading off those mules.'

He beckoned his family. 'I want you to meet this lady,' he said. 'Forty-five years ago I lost a bet on her. Another puncher and myself were riding up the cañon when we saw two mules running along a fence and a girl riding sidewise *bareback* on a horse and trying to head off the mules! Just beyond us the fence turned at right angles, and we knew the mules would follow the fence. "Bet she'll make the turn," said Dick Dean. "Bet she won't," I said. So to settle the matter we pulled off the trail and let the mules go by, with Miss Agnes, here, after them. She made the turn. Best bit of fancy riding I ever saw.'

'And the most ungentlemanly act I ever knew two cowpunchers to pull,' I reminded him. 'You know you should have headed off those mules instead of letting me risk a bad fall just to settle a bet.'

'Of course,' he countered, 'you *could* have stopped before you got to the corner.'

'With two men watching? Never!'

The proverb that pride goeth before a fall was proven to be fallible. Pride alone kept me balanced on that horse — impossibly, it seems to me now.

We thought IT FUNNY

Lᴀᴄᴋɪɴɢ the ordinary forms of entertainment, we invented our own. With the younger men, these were often little short of brutal. Possibly the most exquisite torture meted out in the spirit of fun was the operation known as 'goosing.' It consisted of pulling a few hairs at a time out of the temples and from above the ears. To make it more impressive to the sufferer, horseshoe pincers were sometimes employed, although a thumb and a knife blade are equally effective.

Then there was the process called 'jerkin' the chaps off of him,' a complete reversal of the fact, for it means putting the chaps on — with the victim stretched face down over a wagon tongue. A pair of leather chaps is a fairly cumbersome strap, but I've been assured that it is just as effective as a smaller one.

Once the majority of the outfit, which happened to be made up largely of youngsters in their teens and twenties, turned the tables on their two principal tormentors, big fellows who had been dishing it out from the security of their superior strength. Overpowering them by force of numbers, the insurgents bound them, stretched them out on the ground side by side, about a yard apart, and built a fire between them. Escape was possible only by rolling over and over with hands and feet securely tied. Thus frantically wiggling, they put on as ignominious an exhibition as ever two bullies gave a delighted audience.

I never knew a case of serious results from this sort of rough play, that is to say, serious to the point of injury; but I remember one sadistic performance which took place at the V + T headquarters with apparently no reason other than exuberance of spirits and no rational outlet for it.

Bob Gard was batching at the V + T. During his temporary absence, a gang of the younger element came in and found a big kettle of peeled boiled potatoes on the cold stove. When Bob and several companions returned, they were met with a potato barrage. No one seems to know on what basis sides were chosen, but it appears to have been a spontaneous lining-up of a minority of big fellows against a majority of smaller ones, presumably a fair division of brawn.

The formal battle began about sundown, and at sunup was in its last stages as a dozen men, utterly spent, battered, and bruised, still struggled feebly. Ray could not speak above a whisper for three days. The crew came to our place for breakfast, and before learning the reason for their ghastly appearance, I was all solicitude.

'We fit,' croaked a young sapling of a Texan with a half-closed eye.

'What did you fight about and who fought who? — yes, '*who*.'

'It wasn't about nothin'. We just fit.'

No further explanation.

Recently I asked one of the participants, now a man with grandchildren, if he could tell me why a dozen men had spent an entire night pommeling one another when there was no reason in the world for it. He rubbed his chin.

'Well,' he said, 'when my potato hit Bob Gard in the face, he grabbed me and that was the start. We just kept on.'

Of course, there were endless practical jokes. Stock among them was that of rattling a set of chain traces and yelling 'Whoa!' close to the head of a sleeping man, who very reasonably thinks the chuck-wagon team is stampeding and is about to run over him. His exit from his bedroll is explosive.

Seeing to it that the other fellow's horse pitches is routine on a frosty morning. Horses' humor is no better than that of their human brethren on cold mornings, and any unexpected happening will set them off. So yell and throw your hat under the feet of your neighbor's horse just as he mounts, and the chances are you'll have a nice little rodeo right then and there. It is not difficult to understand why we had so few gentle horses. We had so few gentle people!

Another favorite joke, when conditions were right, was to tie your saddle rope to a corner of a sleeping man's bed-tarp and pull bed and occupant into the pond. Naturally, this requires a pond, an accessory that wasn't always to be had, but if by chance camp was pitched by the side of a mudhole, the wary spread their beds as far as possible from its rim. It's very funny, of course, to see a wrathful man emerge in the middle of a pond.

Of course, these pranksters were the enforced early risers, the horse wranglers, or the men who had stood the last watch on night herd.

Work began long before daylight. To some wagon bosses, it was a matter of pride to have their outfit 'standing around waiting for light.' The horse wrangler would start to round up the remuda before he could distinguish a horse from a tree stump, and the rest of the outfit was presumed to have had breakfast and be ready for the day's drive when he returned with the horse herd.

It was then that we had our impromptu rodeos. It was not un-
common for half a dozen horses to go into action at one time. The
drive usually lasted until mid-afternoon, when, with the cattle
penned, if a corral was available, or 'thrown into the day herd,' if
one was not, the outfit sat down to its second and last meal of the
day. It was years before I became accustomed to three meals a
day. I still think it a senseless convention, wasteful of time and
effort. Many an old cowman who is in position to order the details
of his life comfortably or even opulently continues to adhere to the
two-meal régime.

Remembering the hardships which life at its best imposed upon
us, I often wonder at this deliberate intensifying of it in the name of
fun. The one thing, however, which was never done was to take a
man's horse and make him walk. That would have been a shooting
matter.

Then there was the practical joke that dragged itself out for
months on end and came to a head one day on Trinchera Flat. Although for a long time Lelia had lived on a ranch only forty or fifty
miles from us, we had never met. Cowboys going back and forth
between the two places began to carry tales to each about the other.
She was told how I had ridden such and such a bad horse; I was told
of her skill with a lariat, etc. Then came the story of the horseshoe-
ing. I forget which was supposed to have done it first. As a matter
of fact, neither of us had ever shod a horse until the tale came that
the other always shod her own, and the challenge thrown down was
instantly accepted. This rival, whom one had never seen, but who
was matching, feat for feat, one's own best performances, must of
course be outdone at whatever risk of limb.

Then, one day, we found ourselves together in camp. The men of
the two districts had set up temporary camp headquarters in order
to clear the rough country of wild cattle which had evaded the regular roundup drive. The outfit was short-handed and we two girls
were called in.

The first morning one of the men announced that he would rope Lelia's 'pet horse' for her from the remuda, and hung his string on a Roman-nosed, rolling-eyed beast which immediately went berserk. Lelia, a little green around the gills, looked at me, imploringly, I thought. Was I going to expect her to ride that insane bundle of horseflesh? Ray, meantime, had roped a fitting mate for him with the gleeful announcement, 'Agnes will take the monkey-shines out of this gentleman.'

However, as conspirators usually do, they had overreached themselves. Lelia and I compared notes. Thenceforth we began conspiring on our own account, resolved to make our tormentors pay for the sport they had been having at our expense.

But the funniest incident I ever saw on the ranch was not a practical joke. I had gone to call upon a newly-wedded pair, Henry and Ollie. Henry also enjoyed the monicker of 'Highpockets,' or, sometimes, 'Timberline.' He was mostly legs. They were the long, limber kind which buckled at the knees as he walked, suggesting that each step was in preparation for folding up like a jack-in-the-box. As I rode up, Henry was penning a bunch of range cattle in the corral a hundred yards or so from the cabin. In the doorway his bride stood watching.

Henry dismounted to lay up the corral bars. My arrival at that instant distracted his attention and he paused to greet me, thus giving his horse a moment in which to move out of easy reach.

Among the penned cattle was one big longhorn steer. We had only just begun to breed a pure Hereford strain, and Texas longhorns still often appeared in our herds. This particular longhorn had been 'showing fight' right along, and now, sensing himself trapped, he asserted the good old Texan spirit. He lowered his head and made for Henry, who had got but one corral bar in place.

Henry didn't climb the corral fence, or make for his horse: he started for the cabin with a head start of only the few seconds the steer had hung on the bar as he went over it. Those long legs of his folded and straightened, folded and straightened. Meanwhile, his bride stood in the doorway shrieking, 'Run, Henry, run! Run, Henry, run! RUN!' Back-seat driving in its purest form. Although the steer was raking at the seat of Henry's britches with one of its long pointed horns, and Henry manifestly needed all of his breath to finish the race, he nevertheless threw back his head and bellowed, 'What the hell you think I *am* doing?'

Tenderfeet

BUT it was tenderfeet who were the raw material for most of our jokes, practical or otherwise. Those who found themselves as far from home as a New Mexico cattle ranch in the eighties and nineties were alike in but one particular: they had been misfits where they came from. Sometimes their home climate hadn't suited them; sometimes their law-enforcement machinery hadn't suited them, or they it; sometimes — and I think this accounted for the greater number — the ways of civilization itself hadn't suited them. In any event, we always asked ourselves, 'What's *he* out here for?' One young tenderfoot who stayed a year with us, and who afterward became rich and powerful beyond most, came out to test the potency of New Mexico sunshine in making hair grow on a prematurely bald pate.

It was the health-seekers who gave us the most concern.

In those early days, before the caring for health-seekers became one of the Southwest's largest and best-organized industries, the 'lunger' was all too often advised to 'get out on a cattle ranch; it will make a new man of you.' It did, in countless cases, and many a New Mexico and Arizona leading citizen has come to eminence by that route. But it was hard on the ranchers. After the first few experiments had succeeded, more and more sufferers rushed to try it themselves, until they became no slight problem to the ranchers.

In my childhood the idea of tuberculosis being contagious was not widely credited. We received 'lungers' into our homes exactly as we'd have received a man with a broken leg. Possibly an atmosphere in which the sufferer did not feel himself a pariah accounted for the fixed conviction of many an old-timer that a greater percentage got well in those days than in these. But, of course, we old-timers can't be bothered with statistics.

If the stranger were actually ill, I like to think that we treated him considerately, that we made suitable allowances for his vagaries; but if we suspected malingering, we educated him.

The education of Ramsay is classic in the annals of our country. Young Ramsay told us he had come West because his nerves were bad. Now, 'nerves' was a disorder beyond the grasp of the cow-boy mind of that day. Young Ramsay from all outward appear-ances seemed to be in good health. So when he seemed to us to be pampering himself, it was decided that his cure could best be ac-complished by homeopathic treatment, along lines of the present-day theory of artificially inducing high fever to allay fever. We decided to give his nerves an artificial fever.

On this basis young Ramsay's cure was undertaken. With con-siderable pains. First Ray and Bowlegs sat up half the night gouging the lead bullets from a handful of forty-five-caliber car-tridges and substituting wads of cigarette papers. Blank cartridges were not a purchasable commodity. We made our own.

The next morning Ray and Bowlegs picked a quarrel, not with the nervous young Ramsay, but with each other. Ray had sud-denly decided, so it seemed, that Bowlegs's dog was no longer to be allowed in the house. This Bowlegs hotly resented. Where he went, there went his dog!

They kept it up all day, young Ramsay's nerves showing increasing strain as the enmity between the two heretofore good friends grew more and more violent. Finally, late in the afternoon, Ray lifted the surprised pup on the toe of his boot and tossed him out the open door. Bowlegs, with an oath, fired pointblank at Ray's stomach. Ray leaped behind Ramsay and from that vantage returned shot for shot. Nerves had apparently made young Ramsay more than ordinarily agile. But then, Ray was agile himself. He managed to keep the victim pretty much in the line of fire.

Ammunition gave out at the height of the treatment: it had been slow work digging bullets out of shells. With Bowlegs's last shot, Ray, groaning horridly, slumped face down to the floor, his fingers clutching a handful of blackened cigarette papers. The patient stood flattened against the side wall of the room, trying to back through it. Bowlegs turned to him: 'Of course I'll swear *you* done this,' he hissed.

Ramsay clutched at his throat. 'Er — er,' he gurgled, 'I'm going back home. My nerves just won't stand this sort of thing.'

'All right,' says Bowlegs, jamming his six-shooter into its scabbard. 'I'll give yuh time to git out of the country. It'll be a long while before Morley's missed. There's a horse in the corral. You can reach Magdalena before the morning train leaves.'

He did.

Mutual friends in the East reported: 'Young Ramsay's trip West did him a world of good. From a young egotist whose mind seemed wholly centered on his carcass, he came back a normal human being.'

'Them nerves of his'n sure got cured,' Bowlegs chuckled reminiscently.

But young Ramsay had his vicarious revenge. It seems a pity that he probably never knew it. A few days after the affair, I happened to be waiting at Baldwin's for the mail when Bob Lewis, then under-sheriff, came in with warrants for the arrest of two

Quemado Mexicans who had been involved in a gun fight that was no fake. Bob had heard echoes of the phony one and was all amused interest. At the finish of my report, and while Bob laughed uproariously, an idea seized me.

'Ray and Bowlegs,' I told the officer of the law, 'are camped only a little way off your route to Quemado. Why not go by and tell them you've come to arrest them instead of the Mexicans?'

Bob thought as highly of the idea as did I. No great hurry about apprehending the Mexicans. They didn't know he was coming and an hour or two more or less would make no difference. So Bob Lewis rode into the horse camp and confronted Ray and Bowlegs. He wore his badge on the outside of his coat, a false note that the guilty couple did not at once detect.

'Sorry I have to do this, boys' — Bob Lewis's manner was exactly correct — 'but you know I'm an officer of the law. I got two warrants here.' He produced them. The genuineness of the warrants was unmistakable, even though the distance was too great for the names inscribed on them to be read by the supposed owners of those names. The charges, however, fitted. Attempted murder.

Ray and Bowlegs were solemn-eyed and a little white around their mouths. That nervous tenderfoot! He *might* have done this!

Bob thrust the warrants back into his pocket.

'Got to look into a little trouble out at Quemado,' he told them, 'so I'll put you fellers on your honor to be right here when I come back. Can I trust you?'

'Yes, *sir*,' was the chorused reply.

Bob went off chuckling over that 'sir,' and Ray and Bowlegs sat down to take stock of their situation. 'Damn all tenderfeet, anyway,' was about as far as they got that night. They dared not leave camp and go about their necessary work lest Bob return and find them gone.

They were still pondering and fuming next day when Virg

Wheeler rode into camp and was soon relaying the current news. One item was to the effect that I had been seen talking to Bob Lewis.

'Ha!' It was then that Ray recalled the too obviously displayed badge and the fact that the warrants, while unquestionably the real thing, had never left the sheriff's hands. The charges had been read aloud in correct and impressive legal language, but the persons most interested had not been permitted to lay eyes upon the print. 'Ha!' said Ray again.

The final chapter unfolded the next day. Virg came dashing in to the ranch. 'Ray and Bowlegs been killed, resisting arrest!' he cried. 'Bob Lewis tried to handcuff 'em and they wouldn't stand for it.'

For one awful moment I believed him. I was to blame!

I looked at Virg again. His lips were twitching.

'Liar!' I said haughtily, and turned my back to conceal my vast relief.

We were never selfish with our practical jokes. The whole community was welcome to participate. Everybody, for instance, helped with the joke on Bob Matheson. He was a young Scot who as a tourist had drifted into our community during one of my absences at school, and, liking the place, had taken up residence at the home of a near neighbor — about twenty miles away.

His first effort at 'making a hand' was to help brand a three-year-old maverick bull. When the animal had been roped and thrown, Hi Adams, his host, whose horse was keeping the rope taut, yelled, 'Git down and hawg-tie him, Bob.' Justifiably, Bob, the inexperienced, demurred. 'Aw, hell,' cursed Hi. 'Wish Miss Agnes was here — she'd do it.'

A current ditty composed by Jack Howard, who fancied himself a poet as well as a fiddler, was responsible for Hi's statement. One verse ran:

> Miss Agnes rides the gray horse,
> Miss Lulu rides the brown;
> Young Milton ropes the mavericks,
> Miss Agnes ties 'em down.

At that instant young Matheson developed a distaste for the unknown Miss Agnes. Unluckily for him he did not conceal it. Promptly the other cowboys seized upon it as a weapon wherewith to make the young Scot's life miserable. He knew no American girls whatsoever, and by the time the romancing cowboys had made me out a female Paul Bunyan, always, of course, reflecting upon his own shortcomings in the cowpunching field, his dislike of me had become virulent.

When I arrived home for the vacation I was begged not to spoil the joke. Then followed a protracted hide-and-seek game. Young Matheson was determined not to encounter me. He would attend no gatherings of any sort lest I be present. He would not go to the post office on regular mail days for fear of a chance meeting. Of course each time I promptly heard about it. It became a community joke.

At last, one day Gus Wheeler came dashing up to our place on a sweating horse. 'Miss Agnes,' he panted, 'I jest seen Bob Matheson goin' to Baldwin's. You can git down there before he leaves if you ride like a drunk Injun.'

Bob was just coming out of the post office preparatory to

mounting his horse when I dismounted from mine at the same hitching-rack. He carried a white rawhide quirt ordered from some stockman's catalogue. It had just arrived in the mail. My eyes caressed it covetously, I confess, before they were raised to meet the cold eyes of the quirt's owner.

'What a beautiful quirt!' I murmured, turning on as much feminine allure as was possible on the part of a girl who shod her own horses. A feeble effort, but my best.

'May I present it to you?' he said, with what I recognized as a counter-effort to turn on hauteur.

With a courtly bow he handed it to me. 'Delighted,' I came back at him.

'Pray think nothing of it.' He was keeping his pose and would have probably come off victor had not Gus Wheeler at that moment let out a war-whoop.

'Haw, haw! Bob Matheson's done give Miss Agnes his new quirt. Haw, haw!'

Pose was manifestly impossible after that. Bob Matheson rode home with me.

Occasionally the tenderfoot turned the tables. Two young New Yorkers appeared in our midst one summer, chaps of such native common sense that 'loading' them lost all flavor. In fact, they soon put us on the defensive by 'loading' us about New York manners and morals.

One cowboy proved particularly gullible — until he happened to hear the young Easterners talking between themselves about a civic banquet they had attended in New York 'to the tune of five dollars a plate.' A sudden gleam lit up the cowboy's narrowed eyes. 'Ha!' he exploded. 'You've overplayed yore hand at last. They ain't no man livin' can eat five dollars' worth of chuck at one meal. You musta thought I was a easy mark to swallow a lie like that.'

That everybody in New York rushed into aisle seats in theaters and refused to let others, even ladies, pass until force was used, so that general free-for-all fights preceded every performance, was a yarn the cowpuncher had accepted without question. It merely corroborated his low opinion of New Yorkers. But five dollars' worth of ham and eggs and canned peaches!

Another New Yorker who did not run true to form — that is, to our idea of New York form — was Billy Mitchell. Billy Mitchell was big and husky and self-assured. He promised to be a fair target for our peculiar form of hazing. He submitted at first with disarming meekness, getting his bearings, we were later to discover. His chance came. He was put on a horse which had the habit of running away. 'Ha! ha! There goes one tenderfoot leavin' New Mexico headed for Arizona,' yelped the audience as horse and rider disappeared.

We waited for him to return, which he didn't do as promptly as was to be expected. Nor did he return in the succeeding daylight hours. This was getting beyond the joke stage. Everybody rode out to hunt him, shooting and yelling signals. Night came on and we built fires on hilltops. There was no sleep nor rest, but plenty of remorse. My mother paced the floor. The horse wasn't vicious, we knew, and after one uncontrollable burst of speed could be relied upon to quiet down. Billy Mitchell was a competent rider. Strange. And very, very harrowing.

It was noon the next day when Billy Mitchell came galloping into the ranch dooryard, horse and rider both looking in prime condition.

'Hurry up, you fellows!' he cried. 'A big grizzly got away with one of Nat Straw's traps and his dogs haven't come back. He's afoot and wants you to bring him a horse and come yourselves with your dogs and trail that grizzly.'

No time for further explanations. We knew that Nat Straw, famous bear-hunter, was camped at Blue Spring, and Billy's report bore all the earmarks of veracity. Horses were already saddled, of course, and all who were not still out searching leaped into their saddles and were off, leading Billy's mount for Nat Straw. When they were out of earshot Billy sat down and gleefully hugged his knees. Of course, there was no grizzly.

'Likely young chap, that there tenderfoot,' said Nat Straw to the crestfallen rescue party. 'I plumb enjoyed him. We sat around my fire and talked most all night.'

A summer visitor on one occasion offered to lead a pack-horse to Baldwin's store and bring back some needed provisions. The pack was tied on by somebody at the store and the tenderfoot started home leading the pack-horse. Somewhere along the line the led horse slipped its halter. A cowboy met the expedition some miles from the store. The tenderfoot, with a do-or-die expression, sat erect in his saddle, the lead rope grasped firmly in his hand, and the halter dragging on the ground. No pack-horse was in sight. The cowboy looked at the tenderfoot and rode on in silence.

'Reckoned he'd find it out in time,' he explained later, 'but he sure had a strangle hold on that rope.'

Less tragic, this, than the incident of another tenderfoot who left his saddle-horse tied to a tree while he climbed a promontory to admire the view, and could not go back to the spot where he had left his mount. It was years later when the horse's skeleton and rat-eaten saddle were found. The tenderfoot wandered for two days, at the end of which he was too hysterical to give any account of his journey.

Ray DISSOLVES

A PARTNERSHIP

At a very early age, Ray had begun to have dreams not only of getting the ranch back on its feet, but also of adding to the original property. Even while he was away at school, he had set out, with the aid and advice of certain of Father's old friends, to pull the ranch together. Because he was legally too young to transact business, he formed a partnership with an older local citizen, and thereby acquired his first lesson in the laws governing partnerships.

He was at school when some New Mexican friend wrote him that his partner had arranged to sell the cattle and to skip the country with the proceeds — all legally. I do not know what arrangements Ray made for quitting before the term expired, but I know that he arrived in Datil orey-eyed. By chance I arrived

home almost simultaneously from Ann Arbor, where I was study-
ing at the University of Michigan.

The second night after my homecoming, I was waked by a
gentle tap at my window and my name softly spoken.

'Get your clothes on,' Ray whispered. 'That damned skunk has
got our cattle rounded up and he's going to deliver them tomorrow.
I need help.'

Out the window I went. No one must know what was happening. The partner had the law on his side, and one hard day's ride
would take him over the border into Mexico. Of legal redress
there was no hope. But one half of those cattle belonged to us.

Ray had a saddled horse waiting for me, and a bunch of discarded gunny sacks. Swiftly we wrapped our horses' feet in the
sacks. In case you don't know, that's the way you avoid leaving
recognizable footprints. Then we rode silently away.

The cattle had been rounded up from the open range and put
into a small out-of-the-way pasture for the night. An abandoned
cabin stood in one corner of this pasture. But tonight it was not
deserted. To our dismay, light shone from the open doorway as
Ray and I came in sight. Cautiously we dismounted and with
utmost stealth made our way to a point where we could see what
was going on inside.

Sitting on bedrolls around the wreck of an old packing box were
four men, including the perfidious partner, playing cards. Not
only were they armed with the ever-present six-shooter, but a
rifle or two stood handy, and that was something else again.
The partner evidently knew something of Ray's temper and was
taking no chances.

'Got the nerve?' Ray wanted to know, as we made our way
back to the horses. 'They'll shoot.'

'I've as much nerve as *you* have, I'll thank you to know,' the
old rivalry flaring into life.

I am quite sure that if it hadn't been that neither of us was willing to be first to show the white feather this night, we would have abandoned the crazy enterprise then and there. If we had done so Ray, in all probability, would never have come to be one of the last of the great open-range stockmen of the Southwest. His college course was civil engineering, in a sort of tribute to the father he scarcely remembered, and he was, at the moment, balancing on the thin edge of indecision as to which field to choose for a life-work. To have lost all his cattle in this, his first business venture, would almost certainly have tipped the scales to engineering.

We began a silent roundup of that pasture. Twice, a man's figure was silhouetted in the bright rectangle of the doorway, as though he had come out to listen. A suspicious noise would have been our undoing. But luck was with us. The hooves of the cattle made no sound in the soft *vega* bottom, and we had not urged them along fast enough to start them bawling.

Even so, it remained always a mystery to the natives of the region how five hundred head of cattle could have been removed from a hundred-and-sixty-acre pasture right under the noses of four armed men set to prevent it. Providence sometimes takes care of idiots.

We got the cattle safely out through the lower gate, carefully replacing the bars, as an ironic gesture, and started the herd for the high country. After a half-hour we dared push them along faster, and presently we were yelling and slapping slickers at them, 'throwing them over the mountain' into the rough brakes of the Alamosa side.

We pulled up as the last yearling disappeared into the rocky depths of Red Cañon.

'Let him try to gather that bunch again inside of six weeks,' exulted Ray. 'Guess he won't collect any money on cattle he can't deliver.'

We arrived home just before daylight. The gunny sacks were

long since worn off our horses' feet. Possibly it wasn't actually necessary, but it did seem fitting for me to go in through the window.

Two hours later my mother came to my room. 'I hope you slept well, dear,' she said.

'M-m-mmm,' I replied, feigning sleepiness.

'You must enjoy the quiet nights out here after the noises of the city,' went on my mother.

'M-m-mmmm,' I said again.

Later I asked Ray what we should have done had we been discovered.

'Oh, you'd have gone in and played poker with them,' he replied brightly.

But he knew better. We should undoubtedly have been shot 'by mistake' — and with impunity to the killer, for we *were* trespassers — we *were* cattle rustlers!

Later Ray's partner himself decided to dissolve the partnership — the decision being made with Ray sitting on his chest. Chest-sitting was one of Ray's specialties. The man spluttered something about 'having the law on you,' but in the end thought better of it, since, from the only evidence at hand, those cattle, each and every one of them, had jumped a five-bar gate.

A night OF GOOD

CLEAN FUN

Not long after Ray and I prevented the legal stealing of our cattle, I forestalled the wholly illegal stealing of some of our horses. One night about dark, two young fellows arrived at our house and asked for lodging. As prospective guests, they were anything but reassuring: it happened that there was no man on the place that night, and it was quite evident that they were ill at ease. My mother, unlike her usual fearless self, was unaccountably frightened.

'I have a queer feeling about them,' she insisted. The white, strained look in her face was witness to the depth of this feeling. She had recently been seriously ill; and, overwrought by the brutal murder not long before of a hermit neighbor who was supposed to have had money hidden on his premises, she had convinced herself that these strangers were somehow involved,

and that they were abroad on another like enterprise. Tales of
our wealth had always been out of all proportion to the facts,
except that local standards of what constitutes wealth were very
low indeed. I was more concerned about her than about the visitors; and I felt that something must be done to ease her mind.

I had been conscious of open interest in me on the part of the
visitors, not surprising since they were so youthful — they were
possibly eighteen or nineteen — and for once I decided to make
capital of my sex.

'Would you folks like to play cards?' I said, after they had
eaten their supper in shifty-eyed silence. They exchanged glances.
Then one of them, rather self-consciously, said, 'Shore thing, miss.'

We set up the card game at one end of the dining-room and I
left open the door into the room where Mother lay in bed.

'Shall we make it poker?'

They grinned assent.

Now, poker has always seemed to me to be the only game of
cards worth wasting time over — if one is determined to waste
time. Poker is the ultimate of individualism. One goes it alone.

Our penny-ante began, and with it the usual banal wisecracks
and sad witticisms. We had hilarious fun, which became more un-
bridled as the hours wore on. We exchanged seats, walked around
our chairs, put coats on wrong side out, and did other puerile
things to change our luck. We groaned dismally, or exulted loudly,
over losses and gains; we called one another names and made
dire bodily threats upon one another. 'Gimme two, and watch me
cut Miss Agnes's throat and git back my pile she done stole from
me.' — 'Draw to yore hand, girl, draw to yore hand; think I'll
fall for that blazer?' — 'Now, Mr. Red' (the only name I knew
him by), 'here's where you land in your narrow grave, just six
by three, and the wild coyotes will howl with glee.'

Meanwhile, my mother was growing calmer. Better this uproar
than to lie and imagine stealthy footsteps in the dark. At midnight

we abandoned our card game long enough to make coffee, and I was thankful that I had experimented, highly successfully, that very day in the manufacture of doughnuts of sour dough.

After we had feasted and my guests had lavishly praised the doughnuts, we resumed play. Somebody was forty cents in the hole and must recoup.

'I ain't had so much fun since Moses was a nigger baby,' announced the man whose name wasn't Red. I have no idea what it was. 'Only, it shore grieves me to have to set in a game with two such loco-blossoms. I'll take four cards to keep my ace company. A royal flush, by golly!'

Toward daylight, when my staying qualities were weakening, came a gentle snore from the adjoining room.

At last I spread the deck face down on the table. 'High man rustles the pasture. Second man cooks breakfast. Low man lies down on the sofa and pounds his ear for a while.'

Argument as to whether the ear-pounding privilege should not go to high rather than low. Finally we draw. I must rustle the horses, he whose name was not Red cooks breakfast, and Red himself with exaggerated yawning throws himself on the sofa, and in a moment his less gentle snores play bass accompaniment to those issuing from my mother's bedroom.

When I step out into the clear chill dawn to rustle the horses, I know it is safe to leave my mother alone in the house with the men she has so dreaded. I know it, even when I discover footprints of their horses in places that proved that those strangers with whom I had spent the night in a poker game had reconnoitered before presenting themselves at the house, sure sign of unfriendly designs.

When I came back to the house, driving the horses before me, breakfast was ready. Every man in those days was a good cook. We decided to let Red sleep on, after I had with difficulty restrained his partner from pouring hot coffee into his open mouth.

We did rouse him, later, and make him wash dishes, over his
protests that it was a breach of contract.

They departed in mid-morning, promising to return some day
and prove masculine superiority at poker. I was twenty cents
ahead, and they professed shame at being 'cleaned out by a girl.'
I could see, however, that they were inordinately pleased by it.
This was my one exception in 'playing for money.' The circumstances I felt justified my making the game as entertaining as
possible.

Later there came to us confirmation of my mother's suspicions
that they were a brace of scalawags, horse-thieves, and cattle
rustlers, and that they had come with the undoubted purpose of
raiding our place. That they were the assassins was probably not
true. Remembering our night of 'good clean fun,' I refuse to
think so.

Our Neighbor

It would be entirely wrong, of course, to leave the impression that there was in New Mexico in the early days no law-enforcing machinery whatsoever. It was merely too far away to be useful in emergencies. Also, it did creak when in action. In our immediate section, at any rate.

The county seat, Reserve, is in the southwest corner of Catron County, with its back to the Arizona line. When comes high water, and with it hell, Reserve is cut off from the rest of the county until floods roaring down Box Cañon, through which the road winds, have abated. There is no telling what may happen when it rains in New Mexico in the late summer. The grass roots may be slightly moistened or half the landscape torn away by a cloudburst. In the latter case the sheriff might as well be on Mars for all the use he is to us.

To this day, there is only one line of telephone in Catron County, and that is usually down. It can be imagined on what slow pinions justice moved when there were also no automobiles and virtually no wagon roads. Any stranger whose presence was not instantly accounted for was reasonably presumed to be with us because it was less safe for him to be elsewhere.

Did we promptly convey these suspicions to the proper authorities and clear ourselves of any possible charge of having aided and abetted crime? We didn't. No matter how plausible our suspicions, we gave testimony only under compulsion. Ray once avoided giving testimony by leaving home on a dead run before he could get the bridle on his horse. I had the dickens of a time trailing him up later with the information that the deputies had gone and it was safe to come home.

We had to live with the outlaw in our dooryard, meaning our half of the county; the properly constituted authorities did not. If outlaws let us alone, which for the most part they scrupulously did, we reciprocated and let them alone. I am not defending, I am merely reporting. Remember that they had been guilty of no horror crimes. Kidnapping, except for the Charlie Ross case of the seventies, had scarcely been heard of. By far the greatest number of the misdeeds of our outlaws had been cattle-stealing, Texas cattle most likely, which to us New Mexicans seemed less than heinous.

Many of our New Mexico citizens had originally arrived at our border from Texas 'between two suns one jump ahead of the sheriff.' It was a commonplace pleasantry to brag how one had been 'officially escorted to the border' and how grieved had been the Texas authorities to see one cross it forever.

Even our most respected friends were sometimes in trouble with the law. There was the occasion when a guarded halloo called me from our ranch-house door to confront a very weary rider upon a very weary pony.

'They're after me, I got to get a fresh horse,' he told me. 'I'll see that he gets back to you.'

'What have you done?' I asked, as we hurried toward the corral.

Instantly I felt apologetic. What George may have done is his own business. But he forgave me as he saddled a fresh horse with a few sure motions.

'I didn't do nothin' to kick up a fuss about. Just shot a couple-three times as I was leavin' town. But it seems like Magdalena's gone plumb sissy. Old Foster had a posse on my heels before I hit the top of the divide.'

I, too, was indignant. George wouldn't shoot *at* anybody! For a posse to trail him fifty miles for so slight a matter as shooting a farewell salvo to a community which had shown him hospitality seemed base ingratitude.

So I told George I'd leave food the next day at the mouth of Kid Spring Cañon and he rode off. Meantime, I had gone into the house, so that when the posse arrived I could truthfully say I didn't know which way he went.

The posse was led by eagle-eyed Sheriff Foster, who later presented me with a photograph of himself in which the eyes had been pin-pricked lest his eagle-eyedness go unnoticed. A six-shooter was strapped low on his leg. I knew he felt he was a fine figure of a man. He strode toward the door.

'Yes, I've seen George. No, I don't know which way he went.'

'Wouldn't tell us if ya did, I reckon?'

'That depends. Won't you all get down and have some coffee?'

'And give George more time to git away?'

But the sheriff is being facetious. We all knew that George had already had all the time that was needed, and that hunting him in these, his own mountains, would make search for the needle in its haystack a simple matter by comparison. George is known to be quite as skillful in leaving no trail as he is in following one.

The sheriff's second cup of coffee, I remember, brought on a flush of moral fervor. Remembering the coffee of that day, I can understand why it would bring on something. The practice was not to empty out the grounds until the pot was too full for further brewing.

The effect it had upon the sheriff upon this occasion was to inspire him to lecture George vicariously through me. Didn't we young fellers know that when a country got civilized you couldn't go popping off your six-shooters around settlements? Et cetera. I took George's scolding with every show of meekness, but the sheriff's eagle eye pierced through the sham.

'Don't let me ever catch *you* shootin' up the town,' he warned 'Bein' a girl won't save you.'

I've never forgotten nor forgiven that dare, for I hadn't the nerve to take it.

Because the conventional system of administering justice was unpractical for us, we worked out a legalism of our own. Take for instance the trial of young Pedro Bustamente for shooting young Casimiro Gonzales's dog. The cur had snapped at the heels of Pedro's already fractious horse, which promptly 'turned his pack,' neat phrase for throwing its rider. Pedro picked himself up and shot the dog and Casimiro had the law on him. It was some time before any law was to be found, but finally Old Man Adams agreed to act. He summoned the litigants before him. Sitting impressively behind a table he had the parties to the action stand, their sombreros respectfully held against their chests. Their eyes were glued to the tome on the table before the judge. They looked upon it with awe, because they had never been permitted to look inside of it. It was a mail-order catalogue and contained pictures of ladies in their underwear. The youths' parents had never permitted so corrupting an influence in their homes. Just what might be in that forbidden volume besides indecent pictures of females in union suits the young men did not know. They did not question that it set forth the law covering their case.

Old Man Adams opened the book and ran his finger down a page of cuts of saddles and bridles.

'Ha, here it is,' he bumbled. 'It sez here, "If a dog runs out and bites at a horse, the rider of that thar horse has a vested right to shoot that thar dog."' He slapped the catalogue shut and pronounced judgment.

'You, Casimiro Gonzales, ain't got no redress. Case dismissed.'

The verdict was fully upheld by public sentiment. Dogs snapping at a horse's heels can be very trying.

I hunt GRIZZLIES

I N THE fall of 1895, it became clear to Ray and me that Mother could not be left alone to manage the ranch. One of us must stay home and help her. It was my contention that he should be the one to go to college; it was then or never with him, I reasoned correctly. The ranch had become increasingly his problem; and he was struggling with a decision which has baffled many a maturer mind than his: just how much immediate duty should be sacrificed in behalf of preparation for assuming the same duty later.

After long debate had failed to settle the issue of which of us should stay, we tossed a coin. The 'coin' was a chip from the woodpile on which we sat in conference.

'Dry side you go, wet side I go.' Ray spat on the chip and tossed it. I won, and he went to the University of Michigan.

So, merely because a chip fell wet side up, I did not go back to Ann Arbor. Thus it was that I happened to be in Datil in the early fall of 1895, ready to be overtaken by adventure. Now, the season before, General Nelson A. Miles had been Montague Stevens's guest on a bear-hunt which another guest, Frederic Remington the artist, later described and illustrated in *Harper's*. So exciting had been the sport that plans were worked out in detail for a repetition the following fall.

I was on my way from Magdalena in the spring wagon with a load of provisions, a routine freighting stint, when a little way out of town I met Montague Stevens. He had just received a telegram from General Miles regretting that since he had newly been promoted to Chief of Staff of the United States Army, he would be compelled to cancel the bear-hunt.

'And I was all set,' Montague Stevens told me, 'for a ten-day hunt. Dan Gatlin is at the ranch with the hounds. There is bear sign all through the Spur Range.'

Hope flared. 'Wouldn't I make an acceptable substitute for the general?' I said audaciously. 'I'll contribute the largest bear track anybody ever saw. Within a mile of our house, too.'

His eyes lighted at mention of the grizzly track, but the light quickly faded. 'Extremely sorry, Miss Morley' — we were very formal in those days — 'but hunting grizzlies isn't exactly a chivalrous pursuit. It *could* be extraordin'ly inconvenient to have a young lady along. As for the largest track anyone ever saw, I've been told of them before. Yours will have shrunk unaccountably, I suspect, by the time anyone else sees it.'

His ungraciousness was, of course, due to disappointment over the general's wire, and I tried to forgive it. I was unsuccessful, however: most of my life had been spent in non-chivalrous pursuits, and to have my veracity challenged about the size of a bear track was just too much.

I wrapped the reins around the brake handle and squared off.
'Now, see here ——'

Finally he capitulated. I had found the weak joint in his moral
armor. Although he didn't believe that my track was the biggest
in the world, he was a big-game hunter of long experience, young
man though he was, and my promise to lead him to it was more
than he could hold out against. I cannot forbear stating here and
now that I kept my promise. My grizzly turned out to be, if not
actually the biggest in the world, at least twin to the biggest specimen in the Smithsonian Institution for the same species. The
skull and hide measurements were sent there for comparison.

That ten-day bear-hunt, conducted from our home as the base
of operations, netted two grizzlies and one black bear, and four
others 'jumped' — seven bear in ten days! Male hunters will
probably scoff at the impressions which were uppermost in a girl's
mind and which have remained vivid throughout the years. As
concession to the male viewpoint, I'll say that there was a well-
trained pack of eight or ten bear hounds, and the guns were the
best of their kind. I carried no firearms, however. I was along as
supercargo, merely collecting in excitement my pay for contributing the first and biggest bear.

The bagging of it was so quick and so without adventure that
but for the grizzly's extraordinary size its slaughter would hardly
be worth the recounting. It had been curled up, asleep in the warm
winter sun, only a few hundred yards from where the hounds picked
up the track in the light snow. The bear made for a low range of
hills with dogs and riders in close pursuit. It rimmed around the
base of the first hill while we, the pursuers, kept just above it.
Dan Gatlin, riding at a run just below me on the steep hillside,
jerked his rifle from its scabbard, raised it, and fired. The bear
rolled over dead, the bullet centered in his heart. Just that easy.

You don't believe it, you old bear-hunters? Sorry, but that's
the way it was, nevertheless. It wouldn't happen that way twice

in a lifetime, but it happened that way once. It was too late in the day to skin the grizzly, and trusting to the freezing night ahead, we left it to be skinned the next morning.

On the morning following, we left home before sunrise to return to the carcass, but before we had gone a mile the hounds were off in full cry on another track. We couldn't have called them off had we wanted to, so great their excitement and so swift their flight.

This second bear had had a better start, and was in the rough country before the trail got hot. And what I mean, it was *rough* country.

It had been my amusement many times to point out our route to people and say, 'We came across there on a dead run after a grizzly,' and then to see polite incredulity settle in the listener's eye.

Years later, Montague Stevens and I together rode out on a vantage-point of a mountain range and settled the question. We located the exact shelf upon which we had found ourselves marooned and the gash in the mountain-side down which we subsequently slid. Neither of us would have come down it again for all the treasure in Kingdom Come — much less a grizzly bear. We looked at one another out of middle-aged eyes, and said, 'Were we ever such damn fools?'

We were, and that's why we found ourselves marooned on a narrow shelf which dropped off sheer for at least ten feet to the precipitous shale-covered mountain-side below. We had come down over a smaller shelf above, to find ourselves trapped on the second one. There wasn't footing for the horses to attempt to scramble back, and to go on down was quite impossible for them. Their bleaching bones would have been there yet had it not been that a pine sapling grew close to the edge of the rocky shelf. (They do grow in the most unbelievable places.) Without it, we should have been compelled to shoot those horses and make our own way home on foot, at least ten miles.

To avoid that, one desperate chance remained — and we took it.

Dan Gatlin tied his saddle-rope around the base of the sapling and slid down to the foot of the cliff; then Montague Stevens and I blindfolded the first victim chosen for the experiment, tied one end of a lariat around his neck, took a couple of wraps of the rope around the sapling, and backed the horse off the cliff. As he fell we sat back on the opposite end of the rope with all our strength, keeping it from paying out too fast from around the tree. It broke the force of the animal's fall. With Dan's assistance the horse was able to scramble to his feet, when he landed, shaking with terror, but uninjured.

The second horse also went down safely. But with the third came trouble. He had seen his two companions disappear over that cliff and he was strongly disinclined to follow them. He wouldn't let us blindfold him, and before we could subdue him and get our 'dallies' properly around the sapling, he reared and accidentally backed himself off, all but taking us with him. We did succeed in easing his fall a trifle, but he landed on his back wedged in the trough formed by a fallen tree and the steep upper mountain-side. Montague Stevens and I then slid down the rope.

The upturned roots of the fallen tree behind which the horse lay held one end of the trunk slightly elevated, affording a chance that it would be possible to ease the animal on down under it. The only tools with which to excavate were flat slabs of shale. In relays we dug, the horse meanwhile lying on his back, his four legs pointed to the heavens.

I don't know how long it took us, but it seemed endless before we had sufficiently dug out beneath him to allow him to slide on down and be helped to his feet. He showed injury, but how bad we were not certain.

Leading the three horses, we slipped and slid the rest of the way down the shaly mountain-side, the animals threatening to slide on top of us at every step. To get the full picture of my part in the adventure, please remember that I was wearing a riding skirt as well as several other ordinary skirts beneath it as protection against cold, since the thermometer often falls to below zero in those high altitudes and this was a cold spell. For years thereafter bits of my clothing were found hanging to twigs of trees along the course of that day's run. Cowpunchers collected them as souvenirs.

We reached the base of the mountain finally, and stopped to consider our next move. The decision was made for us. The far-off baying of hounds came to us faintly. The timbre of it told us the bear was fighting the dogs. But Montague Stevens's horse was standing on three legs! He had hurt himself seriously enough to be out of the running.

'Get to the dogs as fast as you can,' Montague Stevens said to Dan Gatlin. 'I'll see that Miss Morley is cared for.'

It was my moment of sweet revenge. 'Did I hear something about bear-hunting not being a chivalrous pursuit? I expect you to live up to the terms of the covenant.' I had the saddle off my horse. 'I'll ride your horse home if he recovers; if not, I can walk ten miles.'

'Unthinkable!' protested Montague Stevens. 'I can't' — don't forget the broad *a* — 'I can't think of it. It's utterly preposterous, I can't allow it ——'

Chivalrously protesting, he was, nevertheless, transferring his saddle to my sound horse, and a moment later I was alone, afoot, in a desolate mountain fastness, with a sub-zero night coming on. As a matter of fact, not one of those considerations assumed the least importance in my mind. I had matches and a knife, and had but to reach out my hand to get all the fuel I needed for a fire. I knew where I was, and I knew that all the wild animals had been scared away from that immediate neighborhood by the dogs, had there been danger from them in any event, which there wasn't.

The possibility of spending the night where I was held no terror

Nor did a ten-mile walk home, if that should be the final decision, one which would depend upon the horse's recovery. I felt that he was suffering more from shock than injury and that an hour's rest would restore him to a state where he could be led slowly, even if not ridden.

I found a comfortable spot where the slanting rays of the late afternoon sun had taken the chill from the ground, and lay down and dozed for an hour, the horse standing almost over me, as if in grateful companionship. When the sun went down, and a sharp chill had taken the place of its pleasant warmth, I put the saddle on the horse and led him for a few test steps. He took them without limping too seriously and, still leading him, I started homeward. It was one o'clock in the morning when I arrived, benumbed with cold, my clothing in tatters, and quite ready to testify that bear-hunting really wasn't a chivalrous pursuit.

Dan Gatlin was already there. He had attempted a short-cut to head off the bear in country with which he was not sufficiently familiar, got himself trapped behind miles of rimrock, over which he didn't know the trails, and, finally, completely baffled, had given up trying to find either bear, dogs, or companions and had headed for home. He had reported to my mother, 'The last I seen of Stevens he was a-tellin' of Mis' Agnes "I cawn't leave you here alone" and a-saddlin' up as fast as he could, still yellin' back after he took off at a high lope, "I cawn't leave you here alone, it's beastly unchivalrous, don't-cha-know."'

Dan Gatlin's mimicry of his employer's English accent was always funny, but on this occasion my mother didn't laugh. She was waiting for my return.

Toward daylight, Montague Stevens came in. If he was weary, his elation quite overshadowed the fact. He had overtaken and shot the bear. It took a full hour for him to tell us the details. Every lunge of every member of the hound pack at the fighting bear was pictured for us. I wanted to feel sorry for the bear, until

I remembered what the carcass of one of our milk-pen calves had looked like when we found it one morning, too far from home, with bear tracks all around it. Cattle losses from bear had been heavy that season.

Now we had two dead bear, at least twenty miles apart, on our hands.

After a few hours' sleep we decided to return to the one Montague Stevens had just killed, because one of the hounds had not yet come in, and we hoped to find him. We did, keeping vigil over that dead bear.

It was again late afternoon before we got the carcass skinned and quartered. The green hide was thrown across my sidesaddle, over the horse's indignant protests, and to my own subsequent acute discomfort. The men each swung two quarters of bear meat across their saddle-horns. The country was densely timbered, and when dusk came we missed the trail and the three of us found ourselves also trapped on top of a long reach of rimrock that, for all we knew, stretched for miles in both directions. The wretched thing about rimrock is that unless you know the trails you may be going in exactly the wrong direction while trying to find a way off. We did just that, and by the time darkness had settled we were completely lost.

The men threw the bear meat away to lighten the load for their horses, but the head and hide were too valuable for that, so to me fell the extremely difficult and disagreeable task of keeping that slippery, sliding green hide under me. Because I was so much the lightest in weight, it had to be my horse who transported it.

We came perilously close to quarreling before that ride was finished. What about? About everything, anything, nothing. Overstrained nerves. We weren't on speaking terms when we finally arrived home after midnight. I recall sliding down off that sidesaddle, the bear hide coming along with me, and announcing as I staggered out of its greasy folds, 'Take your old bear hide:

I never want to see the confounded thing again.' Under my breath: 'Nor either of you.'

But a night's (what remained of it) rest brought us all back to normal, and we were friends again when we set out next morning to bring in the hide of the big bear we had killed the first day. By now it had lain three days where it fell. Winter days are sometimes warm, no matter how cold the nights. They had been too warm for a bear three days dead to be a pleasant object to handle. We hauled the hide home in a wagon. I shudder to think what would have been the demand upon me had it been impossible to reach the spot with a team.

Score to date, three days hunting, two grizzlies.

Montague Stevens consulted his list of reported bear tracks. Half of the local gentry had sent messages to him to 'Come git Big Susie,' or 'Clubfoot,' or various other grizzlies popularly referred to by name, for the ranchmen of that day found tracks, whether of man or beast, as individual and as easily recognized, even after long intervals, as faces. Often as I had seen it practiced, and try as I would, I could never acquire the art, almost mystic, of reading the story of the past and the future in a half-obliterated impression of a passing foot. But ability to do it by those gifted in the art not only supplied us with a great deal of our local news but guided our behavior in no small degree.

Montague Stevens decided to investigate Billy Swingle's report of a recent bear track in his cañon. Billy Swingle was locally known as 'the cliff-dweller,' because he looked as though he might have belonged to some extinct race. He seemed desiccated like a mummy come to life, and he had a habit of appearing and disappearing as though materialized and dematerialized on the spot. I cannot explain these uncanny vanishings of his any more than I can explain the same phenomenon on the part of a Navajo Indian. All that can be said is: Now you see them, now you don't.

'Seen anything of Billy Swingle lately?' was part of every exchange of news. We all carried him more or less on our conscience, especially as he grew older and more feeble.

'Still gittin' his "tricks 'n' traps" together so as to leave the country,' was the usual reply, in Billy's own favorite phrase. When, in the end, he did get his 'tricks and traps' together, or rather had it done for him by a distant relative who also carried him on his conscience, he survived it only a few months. One of his last plaints to me was:

'This here high cost of livin',' he grumbled, 'is gittin' too much for folks to stand. Know what it cost me to live last year?'

I couldn't hazard a guess.

'Fifty dollars,' he said, and waited for my horror to show itself.

Yes, it could be done, and I do not doubt Billy's word, and I know it killed him when he had to stop living at that level. To be sure, he 'rode chuck line,' and became a sort of community charge, but at no time was he a pauper. He was merely disinclined to sell any of his horses, and he had some good ones. He broke them by tieing them with a rope to the chain I had first seen over on the Alamosa, 'where the Injuns kilt the Mexicans.' It was a good scheme: a bronc could run to the end of the rope without breaking his neck, because the chain, though it weighed some three hundred pounds, would give a little since it was unattached to anything solid; and yet it was so heavy that it could not be dragged far. It always pleased me to see the chain which I associated with that ancient tragedy put to so humanitarian a rôle in social progress.

The argument still goes on as to whether Billy Swingle was eighty or ninety or a hundred when he died. In my childhood I thought he was then a hundred. The last time I saw him we were having our pictures snapped, standing side by side. He was saying to me, 'Well, when me and you packed the dirt to make this here country, you was just a little trick. I remember you had trouble with them big boulders up Thompson Cañon' — and cackling delightedly at his joke. Maybe, standing alongside of him, I looked as old to the urchins who gaped at us as he had looked to me forty-five years earlier.

Billy started on the hunt with us in the early bitingly cold morning, assuring us that he would lead us straight to a fresh grizzly track. We were riding single file in the tortuous roughs at the head of Swingle Cañon when somebody noticed that Billy was missing. No one of us had seen him go.

'He'll turn up again in a month or six weeks,' said Dan Gatlin, untroubled. 'Or somebody will find a mummy in a cave and identify it as Billy,' added Montague Stevens, equally unperturbed.

With Billy gone before he had located a track for us, we changed our course, and almost immediately the dogs set off in full cry. They had picked up the trail of a mother bear and two cubs, not in Billy's report. Of the subsequent chase, only a word can be said: If one respected life or limb, one did not try to keep up with Montague Stevens as Montague Stevens rode in those days of bear-hunting.

We had raced a mile or two following the cry of the dogs, and trying to make short-cuts where possible in order to overtake them. Of the three of us, I knew this particular section best, and was leading out around the skirts of Crosby Mountain, when the one ridiculous incident of the day happened. Dan Gatlin told it later in a saloon in Magdalena something in this wise:

'We was a-ridin' along single file, Miss Agnes in the lead, when we heard a snort up on the mountain above us. We'd woke a grizzly as big as a Missouri mule out of a nice nap, and he was comin' down that mountain with blood in his eye a-hittin' the ground only once't in a while. Miss Agnes she looked up and seen that b'ar and [with infinite scorn in his voice] she run! Then Stevens he looked up and he seen that b'ar and *he* run [more scorn]. Then *I* looked up and seen that b'ar and [here Dan's voice broke into a high falsetto] *I* run.'

My own memory is of a huge dark shape hurtling down the

mountain-side directly at us. When finally I succeeded in bringing my horse out of his stampede at least a half-mile away, I seemed to be the only living thing in a vast solitude of mountain range filled with primordial quiet.

There was no bear, no sound of dogs, no Montague Stevens, no Dan Gatlin. Nothing but a quivering horse under me, and a pounding heart in my chest. Which, it seems, was exactly the case in which my two companions found themselves, as we all reported when, after much hallooing back and forth, we got together and compared notes.

From all indications, the bear had been as surprised and as determined to get away as ourselves. Had he singled any of us out for attack, he could have overtaken his victim with ease, for on level ground or in a downhill race, a grizzly can overtake a horse. He lumbers more clumsily uphill but 'turns all holts loose' when he starts down. So, a tip to any of you who may go chasing grizzlies: Keep on the uphill side of him.

Feeling decidedly sheepish — for our rout had been completely ignominious, without the slightest claim to presence of mind or bravery on the part of any one of us — we decided to go on in the general direction we supposed the dogs to have taken on the trail of the first bear, the one with the cubs.

Omitting account of one or two tense moments after we finally caught the faint sound of distant baying, I'll bring the picture to the moment when Dan Gatlin and I found ourselves on the edge of a patch of slide rock several acres in extent which lay close under the top of a precipitous peak. It seemed in defiance of the law of gravity that this loose shale remained in place at all. For the first time thus far on the venture, I was downright scared. It just didn't seem possible that a horse could hold his footing at that angle on such an unstable foundation. To have slipped would have meant a plunge downward of five hundred feet.

Dan Gatlin started his horse across it without looking back at me. But somehow I knew that he was aware of my terror, and wanted to reassure me without the injury to my self-respect which mentioning the matter would have involved. He reached into a trouser-pocket, drew out a large claspknife, and began to operate on a fingernail.

'When I git a hangnail,' he observed, with what seemed the utmost nonchalance, 'I got to cut it off right now.'

I still maintain that cowboy chivalry is the truest in the world. Dan Gatlin was to show his again that day. We climbed out over the top of the peak and looked about for Montague Stevens, who had somehow got separated from us. We were now on the north face and snow lay at least a foot deep, and so solidly crusted it could bear up the weight of our horses. The icy surface made horseback travel impossible, however.

While debating what to do next (I didn't like the idea at all of going back over that slide rock nor yet of taking another step on that ice slide at which we had halted), we suddenly heard the dogs so close that it was startling. The wind until now evidently had been in the opposite direction, carrying the sound away from us. We not only heard but saw them almost simultaneously.

Far down the mountain-side the whole pack was bunched together, yapping on that shrill excited note which proclaims that the quarry is at bay. They were lunging in and out at the base of a great overhanging boulder.

'She's denned up,' Dan Gatlin said, his own voice carrying the same note of excitement. Then he broke into a short laugh.

'I ain't lost no grizzly bear. If that fool Englishman wants to go on foot a-shootin' of a mad she-bear outen her den, it's all right with me, but far as I'm concerned, I just ain't out no bear.'

He was right about it having to be done on foot, if at all. Even that would be perilous over that ice-encrusted snow.

Montague Stevens finally joined us and after a brief survey of the situation decided that he would go down and reconnoiter

He slid from tree to tree, in a series of short toboggan-like dashes

Arrived at the theater of action, he signaled us to follow. We fastened our horses' bridle reins to the branches of near-by trees and started down. Dan Gatlin carried his rifle. He also had his six-shooter in his belt. Montague Stevens was similarly armed. As I have said, I had no weapon.

Looking back on the idiotic performance, I wonder how three presumably sane people could have engaged in it. Just above the boulder which formed the roof of the bear's den, and a little to one side of it, a Douglas fir sapling stood slim and erect. I was told to climb as high as its branches would sustain my weight.

'Grizzlies don't climb trees,' Montague Stevens assured me. 'You'll have a ringside seat. I'm going to fire into the mouth of that cave and bring her out. When she comes, you, Dan, be sure you get her before she gets me.'

As if this were not madness enough, Dan Gatlin must add to it. Another attack of chivalry had seized him.

'I'll tell you what, Miss Agnes,' he said, the light of inspiration in his eye, 'you shoot the bear when she comes out. 'Tain't every girl can say she's killed a grizzly.'

He passed his rifle up to me.

If Montague Stevens was dubious about this arrangement, he likewise was too chivalrous to make objection. 'I'll shoot into the den, then I'll drop back out of range of your fire,' he coached me. 'When you see her head over the top of the boulder, shoot. You can't miss,' he added confidently, whether to reassure himself or me I don't know.

Dan Gatlin stationed himself at the base of another sapling, 'just in case.' Retelling it later he said, 'I clumb and I clumb and I clumb, and when the excitement was all over, by golly, I was three feet off'n the ground.'

Montague Stevens shot into the mouth of the cave and leaped back as planned. I had drawn a bead on the spot where the bear's head must appear. But no head appeared. And thereby all our well-timed calculations went by the board.

'By Jove, I must have killed her,' said Montague Stevens, and took a step forward to peer into the den.

At that instant, the earth shook. Something like a subterranean roar filled the air, and a great dark hulk came out of the den with the momentum of a cannon ball. I was already sighting along the rifle barrel, finger on trigger. Just as I pressed it, it seemed to me that it was Montague Stevens's head and not the bear's which showed in the notched sight of the barrel. Then certainty of it swept over me and turned the world black, for at that same instant Montague Stevens fell and lay absolutely quiet. He had toppled backward over a fallen log and his legs lay across the trunk seemingly lifeless.

Only one who believes he has killed a human being can know the spasm of agony which fairly stopped my heart's beating. Then, somewhere, out of a void of frozen fear, I heard Dan Gatlin's command: 'Shoot her agin, Miss Agnes, shoot her agin!'

Mechanically I tried to obey. Ignominious the confession — I snapped the trigger without having thrown a fresh cartridge into the chamber! Then I was aware of Dan Gatlin at the foot of my tree yelling at me. I dropped the rifle into his hands and threw my arms around the slender top of the sapling's upper trunk to keep myself from toppling to the ground after it.

But Montague Stevens had not been shot. He had accidentally tripped as he sprang backward and was momentarily stunned by the fall. Luckily for him, the full dog pack had pounced upon the bear and she had turned to fight them.

I recall seeing the two half-grown cubs standing over Montague Stevens and then I heard the crack of his six-shooter and knew that he was not dead. Relief was almost as great a shock, and I clutched my sapling trunk more frantically than ever.

The mother bear, shaking off the dogs, started around the mountain in one direction, the two cubs in the other. Apparently every-body was at too close range or too excited to have made a direct hit, and in a moment bear and dogs were gone and my two companions were scrambling up the mountain-side to where their horses were tied. I was too dazed to move. I felt unable to unwind my arms from around that sapling's trunk. Rigor mortis itself seemed to have taken possession of me.

I suppose I didn't stay there for as many hours as it seemed. It may have been only minutes; but when I came somewhat to my senses, there was no evidence of life around me, animal or human, and the tree shadows were elongated on the white snow.

Then I recalled the tradition that a mother bear will deliberately, as a protective ruse, run in an opposite direction from her cubs, only to return when she thinks the danger past to the spot where she left them. I didn't want that bear to come back and find me up as in-adequate a tree as that sapling. I slid to the ground and began to climb the icy slope to my horse. At every step I felt the bear's hot breath upon me. Imagination had broken through all barriers of reason; I was just a badly scared girl in an awesome setting. The north side of Crosby Mountain at twilight, with the suggestion of grizzlies at every turn, may, I think, without exaggeration be termed awesome.

Gasping with exhaustion, my lungs on fire from the effort of trying to run up an icy mountain-side at an altitude of ten thousand feet, I finally reached the place where I had tied my horse.

He was not there. A broken branch was evidence of his having jerked loose, presumably when the other horses left with the two men on them. Two courses lay before me, to collapse in sheer panic and freeze to death, or to gather myself together. I made an effort in the latter direction. I'd asked for this, hadn't I? I'd been warned that bear-hunting wasn't a chivalrous pursuit. Was I to whimper now that the warning had become reality?

I'd never been eaten by a bear yet, I assured myself, and the chances were I wouldn't be! I set out on my horse's well-defined trail. The fragment of limb which dragged from the bridle rein had left a clear scratch in the snow that could be followed rapidly, so long as daylight lasted. I overtook him just before the shadows deepened into utter blackness.

The nearest ranch was the JL and I headed for it. The horse had found an easier descent from the peak than the way we climbed up, and by the time I caught him we were well down on the relatively gentler slopes. An hour's ride brought me to the JL Ranch and a surprised welcome.

Montague Stevens came in later with the dogs and no bear. He had seen neither mother nor cubs again. It was after daylight when Dan Gatlin arrived, reporting still another bear jumped and killed by another of those miraculous shots of his.

Remember, Montague Stevens had but one arm. But he has probably more bear to his credit than any man living, unless it be professional hunters. It was the next season that he killed the bear who was, so I insist, the famous Big Susie.

'The healer' COMES TO DATIL

How tragic my mother found her life has been indicated, I am sure, by much of the foregoing recital. Certainly it was a succession of disappointments and failures, for whose explanation she sought answers in many directions. I remember Lora once greeting her upon her return from an absence: 'What's the name of your new religion this time, Mother?'

That she was Grandmother McPherson's daughter was not without its influence, although Grandmother McPherson's simple formula for salvation — 'Republican-Methodist-Teetotaler' — had never seemed to her divinely authorized. But that a right formula did somewhere exist, Mother unquestionably believed, and with a fervor equal to Grandmother McPherson's own she sought it. The day came when at last she believed she had found it.

In the summer of 1895, a golden-bearded, blue-eyed, six-foot-tall Alsatian cobbler named Francis Schlatter appeared in Albuquerque. He had just walked from California across the Mojave Desert, living on little but bread made from unleavened flour which he baked himself, and almost no water. This walk is considered impossible, yet the fact that he made it is amply authenticated.

Arrived in Albuquerque, he announced that as a final act of spiritual preparation for his life mission, 'the Father' had bade him fast for forty days. This fast took place in the home of people we knew, and, according to them and scores of others, including newspaper reporters, was genuine. At its finish, one who was present recorded that he ate a substantial meal of 'fried chicken, beefsteak, and fried eggs.' No ill effects followed.

His fame became of headline importance, but it was not until he appeared in Denver later in the same summer that Mother saw him. She was one of thousands who stood in line to receive his blessing, one that was reputed to carry healing.

Lest the conclusion be jumped at that it was only the weak-minded who stood for hours waiting to touch the hand of this peasant cobbler with his little-understood powers, let me say that on the special trains that were run into Denver to accommodate the throngs who believed in him were many intelligent and well-to-do people. A person who was at the end of the line which formed daily and stretched out for many city blocks at 6 A.M. counted himself lucky to stand in Schlatter's presence by noon. As many as five thousand in a day passed before him. In good journalistic style the newspapers gave accounts of healings claimed and miracles performed. In the line three stations ahead of my mother, a crippled negro woman inched painfully forward, hour after hour. Arrived at last where Schlatter stood in the gateway of the yard to a modest home, where he was being harbored, the negro woman stretched forth her hands to grasp those of the man before her. An instant later she threw her arms in the air and shouted, 'Praise Gawd, he done healed me, and he done give me back my dollar!'

Yes, he gave back all money proffered. That was never disputed. He took no pay.

Day after day he received the lame, the halt, and the blind, the rich and the poor, the educated and the ignorant. I refer you to the Denver daily press of the period, to the press of the whole United States, for details, and for claims of cures.

It was a reporter's paradise.

Then Schlatter disappeared, leaving behind him thousands of disappointed people. It was a disappearance that seemed miraculous, for he vanished on a big white horse. For weeks the boys of the press vied with one another in efforts to find him — solely for his news value. He was reported seen here, there, everywhere, only to have every clue fail. From the newsgatherers' standpoint it was exasperating and the determination to find him grew apace. The hunt assumed incredible proportions. Every white horse within a radius of several hundred miles was held suspect, but none of them was Schlatter's horse, Butte.

Then one winter night, seven weeks after he had seemingly vanished from the earth, a man who was doing some temporary work for Mother in Datil came to where she sat before an open fire reading, with the startling report: 'There's a man lying beside the barn and he had the gall to put his horse in the haystack corral. It's a great big white horse that'll sure make a hole in that stack by morning. I told the man to come over to the house or he'd freeze to death and he answered that he must be invited. He's *poco loco*, I guess, but he'll sure freeze if he stays where he is.'

A few moments later, Mother met the stranger with the cry, 'Francis Schlatter!' He nodded gravely. 'The Father has directed me to a safe retreat. I must restore my spiritual powers in seclusion and prayer.'

He had ridden the seven hundred miles between Denver and Datil in midwinter, much of the way in desolate rugged country, the last stretch across forbidding Putney Mesa, where snow lay over a foot deep. Yet Butte had arrived in exceedingly good condition.

For almost three months, Schlatter remained in an upstairs room, venturing out only when the coast was unmistakably clear. Two occupations engrossed him during this time: he dictated to my mother a manuscript of considerable length, which she later published under the title he gave to it, *The Life of the Harp in the Hand of the Harper*. The rest of the time he spent in swinging a bronze club very like a forty-pound baseball bat, as a drum major might swing a baton. It was a feat requiring prodigious strength, but he did it tirelessly. He said that it was a practice imposed upon him by 'the Father' and he must obey or lose his power.

Mother read him the newspaper accounts of the search still being made for him, to all of which he replied, 'When the time has come for me to reveal myself, the Father will tell me.'

Finally, one day a Mexican woman who came to do the washing noticed an extraordinarily large flat-heeled footprint in the yard, not at all the sort of imprint made by a spike-heeled cowboy boot. She suspected rightly whose it was — not surprising, with the big white horse still in the barnyard.

Immediately Mexicans from Quemado, from Mangas, from outlying ranches, began coming on flimsy pretexts, camping in the dooryard, and Mother was hard put to it not to lie outright. At last, Schlatter said to her, 'I must go.'

He saddled Butte, tied the brass rod to his saddle, and mounted. Then turning to Mother he said: 'Walk with me. I have things to tell you.'

She walked by his side for three miles, and by herself in a sort of rapt ecstasy the three miles' return trip. She believed! He said:

'You will have what will seem to be certain evidence of my death brought to you. The world will laugh at you for rejecting — but reject it! I shall not be dead. I will return to Datil. The Father has told me that Datil is the place He has selected for New Jerusalem. Wait for me.' Then he bade her go home.

Again he vanished, and for a decade impostors in unbroken succession appeared throughout the country claiming to be the original Schlatter, but all differing from him in the detail of returning any money proffered. A Los Angeles court sent one false Schlatter to jail, and all others were discredited. Meanwhile Mother waited with unfaltering faith. Nothing mattered any more. Schlatter would return and the world would be freed from its shackles.

My own part in the story was slight, but, slight as it was, baffling. As I have said, I did not go back to college that fall because I felt that one of us should remain with Mother. Her search for the Formula was engrossing her more and more. She spent longer hours in letter-writing and shorter ones on material concerns.

But since little ranch work goes on in midwinter I had decided in January that I could go to Stanford. I left her to her letters — letters to most of the leaders of thought of that era in this country, and not a few in foreign lands — and entered upon another bout of my battle to get an education. I had been gone only a day or two when Schlatter appeared at our house.

As usual, I returned to Datil for the summer vacation. As I approached the house riding with Mother in the buggy in which she had come to Magdalena to meet me, I gasped in surprise: 'WHAT is that?'

A design stood out boldly on the front of the west wing of the house, a design that I can best describe as a bent cross, the upright curving counter clockwise so the crossbar curved slightly upward. It was about ten feet high and it appeared to have been painted on the logs with whitewash.

'I thought I would let you see it first,' Mother said, uneasily, I felt. 'Perhaps it may help you to form a right judgment.'

'But what is it? Who put it there?'

'Nobody knows how it got there,' Mother told me. 'It appeared when Schlatter left.'

I hesitate to repeat the surmises that we all indulged in but stick strictly to facts. No tracks showed where someone had brought a ladder; there was no ladder on our place, nor whitewash. Our dog had not barked in the night.

'What do you think it means?' I asked, and it was my turn to feel uneasy, dreading what her explanation might suggest.

'Well' — Mother seemed to be choosing her words carefully — 'the upper part is a sort of map of the pilgrimages which the Healer' — she spoke the title reverently — 'has already taken: north and south from Cheyenne to El Paso, east and west from Topeka to San Francisco, and back to Denver, then to Datil; I interpret it as meaning that he will finish the cross by going deep into Old Mexico. I interpret it as meaning that until the cross is completed by his journeyings I must wait for him.'

I looked at her with troubled eyes.

It was in Old Mexico that, ten years later, the newspapers thought they had discovered him. A clipping was handed to my mother which told that under a tree in Chihuahua had been found a man's skeleton, a peculiar metal rod, a weather-faded Bible with the name Francis Schlatter on the fly-leaf.

'He told me to expect this,' Mother said quietly. 'He is not dead. He will return.'

Thereafter we walked in the presence of one who was with us but not of us. The home life went on around her but she was no longer interested in it. She was now sure that a short-cut into the Eternal City was to be opened through the tortuous mountains of human struggle.

A call ON THE BRIDE

In THAT summer of 1896 there occurred the most momentous social event within the experience of that country — before or since. There came to dwell among us an English lady of quality, newly become Mrs. Montague Stevens. She had defied all parental opposition to come and marry her childhood sweetheart.

News of her arrival reached us by word of mouth when someone came out from Magdalena with the description of her gorgeous attire and her quantities of impedimenta. 'Gorgeous' was the news-bearer's word for it. Mrs. Stevens insists that it was a conventional traveling costume, although she confesses that her hat did have a long ostrich plume.

I had promised the young bridegroom that I would as promptly as possible call upon the new bride. Montague Stevens's ranges adjoined ours. It was a mere matter of seventy miles between our respective dwellings.

First of all, I drove into Magdalena to pick up my friend Lelia, who also wished to extend the hand of hospitality to the newcomer. When we got back, there came a blow almost fatal. Ray needed the team. Hot was the argument as to which were the more urgent, his affairs or mine. With masculine ill-logic and general bone-headedness, he clung to his position that, his being business whereas mine were merely social, his were the more important. As if that had anything to do with it!

Anyway, he took the team to haul the chuck-wagon. Lelia and I could wait a few days until they found the runaway mules, the regular chuck-wagon team. We refused to submit to such cavalier treatment.

'If there were two horses left on this ranch who had ever looked through a collar in their lives, we'd drive them,' I fulminated.

'We might *make* a couple of them do it,' suggested Lelia, inspired.

That was a thought! And what sweet revenge lay within our grasp! Revenge not merely for this episode, but for the long practical joke they had played upon the two of us. For Dudley and Paint, the pet horses respectively of Ray and Bowlegs, were still on the ranch.

To understand the extent of this revenge, one must know that the attitude of the cowpuncher toward his private mount, his show-off horse, is comparable to a jewel-collector's attitude toward his noblest gem. Lest Lelia and I even ride them, Dudley and Paint had had their shoes pulled off and they had been turned out barefooted into the largest horse-pasture. The possibility that they should ever be subjected to the ignominy of wearing harness had been too far-fetched for consideration.

The more we thought about it, the more it seemed to us that not only our convenience but the cause of woman's emancipation from male dominance demanded that we make our trip as planned, and that we emphasize our defiance by making Dudley and Paint haul us.

They were gentle enough ponies, as ponies of that day went, and we decided that we could shoe them ourselves. So, putting on leather chaps, we valiantly went to work. It was a backbreaking job. Dudley in particular had the habit of taking as much weight as possible off his remaining three legs and transferring it to your two as you held up the one of his you were operating on. We were the better part of the day getting those eight shoes on, but in the end we surveyed our handiwork with justifiable satisfaction.

The next question was whether or not to set aside another day to break the horses to drive. In the end we decided against this as a waste of time. They might as well learn by going in the direction we wanted them to, as to learn meandering all over the landscape.

So the next morning we set out in the buckboard, with Dudley and Paint looking back over their shoulders at us, in understandable bewilderment. They had been required to do many peculiar things in their lives, but never this. They were not vicious, but they were confused and finally exasperated. We had finally got them down to pulling side by side rather than each trying to go in a different direction, when we came to where the road led across a wide arroyo. We plunged into it. But at that instant a cow's head appeared over the rim of the opposite bank.

Now, a cow was the one thing that might have been supposed to be reassuring to those two ponies, but evidently not. With the first evidence of singlemindedness they had yet shown, they turned and tore up that arroyo bottom, the buckboard wheels throwing clouds of sand in our faces, as Lelia and I together tugged at the reins.

The arroyo narrowed, as they all do at their source, and as we swished around a bend the horses suddenly found themselves wedged between two sheer banks, unable to go a single foot farther. I crawled out on the buckboard tongue between them and held their heads until Lelia got the traces unhooked and the buckboard towed back far enough to permit me to worry those ponies about face. No hope of making them back. They had contributed their all when they went forward.

Ultimately we got out of the arroyo on the right side and resumed the trip. We made it to the Z-P that night. Half a dozen men but no women were there. We were treated with deferential cordiality. There had been a gun fight on the ranch a few days previously, to which a newly made grave almost in the dooryard bore grim testimony. Two of the men present had been involved and the details of the affray were rehearsed for us.

No official investigation of the affair had yet been made. It was presumed that the sheriff would come out from town when he got around to it. Just now he was too busy dealing with a case where there was less certainty that the victim needed killing.

A night's rest, and time to give the subject serious consideration, left Dudley and Paint with the conviction that this practical joke on them had gone far enough. It took all the men on the place to get those rebellious ponies back into harness, and there was much ominous headshaking among our hosts about what would happen when the ponies' masters discovered the sacrilege. Lelia and I were leaving that bridge to be crossed when we came to it.

The first few miles after leaving the ranch were covered in record time, Lelia and I clinging to the buckboard desperately as it careened behind the merry ponies. The country was fairly flat and the horses kept reasonably well to the wagon tracks, which, by a slight stretch of imagination, might be called a road.

Only one mishap delayed us. In topping a sparsely wooded ridge, Dudley decided to go on one side of a sapling and Paint on the other. The pole struck the sapling dead center and snapped. It was a sort of fracture rather than a clean break, and with baling wire, without which no one traveled, we were able to bind on a splice. Miraculously, it held.

It was just sundown when we drove through the NH pasture gate and up to the steps of the Stevens residence. It was a big well-built log house standing against a backdrop of pine-forested mountains and facing down a wide-open draw. Mrs. Stevens was washing clothes in a tin washtub set on a packing case in the side yard. She wore an apple green taffeta petticoat, a rose boudoir jacket, and a large flower-trimmed leghorn hat. She took her hands from the suds, wiped her very lovely white arms, and came forward to greet us. That she was glad to see us was revealed in the soft depths of the most beautiful brown eyes I had ever looked into.

Her husband and the other men of the ranch, she explained, had gone to the roundup. She was alone at the moment, save for old Dad, a white-whiskered patriarch whom we had all known since ever time was. The ranchwoman whom her husband had engaged as maid-of-all-work had departed the day after the arrival of the new mistress.

'It was really most surprising,' Mrs. Stevens said. 'I said to my housekeeper, "We'll not dine until your master" (broad *a*) "arrives," and she whirled on me and said, "I'll have you know I ain't got no master" and off she went. Evidently in America one does not speak of oneself as master to the servants.'

'One does not,' I assured her. 'Not in Socorro County, at any rate.'

To record this call in its mere outward aspects would be something like describing Stonehenge as large rocks lying in a circle and saying nothing of their significance in the imagination of a race. More boxes from England had yielded their contents in the form of hangings, tapestries, silver plate that had belonged to more than one earl; but an Arbuckle's Coffee packing case served as woodbox beside the fireplace. Equally violent contrasts were in evidence on all sides. To do us honor, our hostess dressed for dinner as she might have done had she been entertaining us at her country place in England. Her black lace gown was by Worth. An engraved ruby ring, reputedly a stolen idol's eye, was but one of her jewels of historic lineage. This was not ostentation. It was a simple act of courtesy such as she had grown up to consider fitting.

At dinner there was imported curry from India, and rare vintages of wine; and Dad served the tomatoes in the can he had just opened by cutting two gashes in its top with an axe. Throughout, our hostess made smiling quips that invited us to enjoy it all with her. After we had retired to the 'drawing-room' — but not before Dad had begun to clear away the dishes — she played the piano and sang for us, in a voice whose natural beauty the London Conservatory of Music had skillfully enhanced. The log ranch house, one hundred miles from Magdalena, nearest point of civilization, rang with melody fit for the angels to hear.

The spell was broken by the entrance of Dad. 'Time to feed the dogs,' he announced, stroking his long beard with the air of a man sidestepping responsibility. Mrs. Stevens thanked him and asked us if we'd like to see her feed the dogs.

Now, feeding the dogs was no matter of throwing a bone to Fido. There were forty Fidos whose cash value was probably twenty thousand dollars. There was a pair of Russian wolfhounds from the Czar's kennels; there were blue-ribbon winners from New York dog shows; the breeds were varied, as Montague Stevens had the idea of developing a strain that would be the ideal hunting dog for the peculiar conditions of the country.

The food consisted of cornmeal boiled with chunks of meat in a huge cauldron. There was always enough ready-to-die-anyhow range stuff to supply the meat. Into a forty-foot trough Dad ladled out the portions. Mrs. Stevens stood by with a blacksnake to preserve order. Suddenly from nowhere appeared a stray burro. In an instant the pack of forty were in full cry after it. Across the flat went the burro, nose in the air, tail high, hee-hawing its terror. At its heels the pack yelped in every key. A distressing tragedy was in the making.

Gathering up her black lace skirts and brandishing the black-snake, Mrs. Stevens took out after the dogs. 'Come back here, you Czar; come back here, you Czarina,' she commanded. Her voice, trained by the London Conservatory to carry above the orchestra, carried distinctly above the braying burro and the yelping dogs. The dogs knew its note of command. One by one they slunk back. Mrs. Stevens shook down the lace folds of her skirts, handed the blacksnake to Dad, and led the way back to the house.

'Montague attends to this when he is at home,' she apologized.

The duties which she was later to assume, with a similar lack of hesitation, have insured her a place in the hearts and memories of our entire community. She rode countless miles to minister to the afflicted. Possessed of a natural flair for relieving lesser ailments, she gave to many a distracted ranch mother the sympathetic interest and simple home remedy which was all that was needed. To-day, she might be thought to have practiced medicine without a license, but when I recall some of those early-day examples of medical practice on the part of the few doctors who came into our midst with licenses, I think I should have felt quite as safe under the ministrations of Mrs. Stevens.

But it was not only to the physical needs of her neighbors that she gave her bounty. She catered, at least on one occasion, to that universal longing of her sisters for personal adornment. A rancher's wife so unsuccessfully concealed her covetousness of one of Mrs. Stevens's gayer gowns that its owner presented it to the lady. Some days later four other ranchers' wives arrived in a buckboard and announced, 'We've come t' look over them dresses yore sellin'.' It developed that the first rancher's wife had bragged of the 'stiff price' she had paid for her gown, a pathetic little falsehood to bolster up self-respect.

Today if asked 'Would you knowingly do it over again?' she smiles faintly and looks at her husband. 'If Monte were there, I'd think it would be worth it.'

Because of knowing Mrs. Montague Stevens, I think I understand the English. The world will do well not to make premature prophecy of their decadence. Only once do I remember having seen Mrs. Stevens flinch. She had just received a letter from her aged mother in England. It said: 'I sincerely hope, my dear child, that you have a trustworthy coachman. I would feel easier in my mind if I were assured of it.'

If Montague Stevens ever had a trustworthy horse, none of us knew it. As for a trustworthy coachman ... well ...

But of course all this was of the future into which the young bride, mercifully, could not peer when she so graciously entertained Lelia and me on this our first formal call.

Our return trip was comparatively free from untoward incident and we arrived home with everything reasonably under control, save, possibly, our own emotions. The day of reckoning was at hand. Both Dudley and Paint had slight galls where the unaccustomed horse collars had rubbed. Should the hairs come in white, as usually happens, they would go to their graves bearing this badge of dishonor.

Ray and Bowlegs had not yet come back, and Lelia and I nursed those galls as tenderly as a mother nurses a chafed baby. We debated whether to pull the shoes off the horses and pretend we hadn't seen them since they had been turned out, or to face Ray and Bowlegs with a 'cat-eaten-the-canary' expression. Finally we decided to give no ground. Hadn't we been fighting for a principle?

With this somewhat feeble defense, we awaited the deluge.

It came!

Many years later the four of us found ourselves together and bystanders were all but forced to interfere. The only thing which saved Lelia and me from physical violence at the time was, I verily believe, the fact that the galls vanished and no white patches appeared.

I drove Lelia back to Magdalena and reckoned the total time and mileage consumed in this social call:

2 trips to town and back...	4 days, 200 miles
NH and back.............	4 days, 150 miles
Total..............	8 days, 350 miles

Which is far and away the greatest effort I have ever put forth to fulfill a strictly social obligation. Even counting it in, my average is considerably below a civilized normal.

The hotel service

WAS HOMELIKE

THE informality of Magdalena's hotel service was calculated to put guests at their ease — always provided, of course, that the guest's idea of ease coincided with that of the management. The homelike touches were many; for instance, keys to doors were often missing. When the town was crowded in the cattle-shipping season it was accepted as a matter of course that male guests would share their quarters with subsequent arrivals, friend or stranger, even to three in a bed if the emergency became sufficiently acute.

Among those who occasionally transacted business in Magdalena was an abnormally shy chap. His self-consciousness in the presence of unaccustomed women verged on the pathological. He never looked toward a family wash on the clothesline, and turned scarlet to the roots of his hair at the hint of a feminine overture. We females scarcely dared say 'Good afternoon,' so keen was his distress sure to be. It naturally became a sort of community game to attempt to trap him, a game in which he invariably was winner.

One night he rode into town late and near the point of exhaustion from sixteen hours in the saddle. He inquired about a room at the hotel. A young squirt, with a sense of humor all his own, was acting as night clerk.

'We got just one bed left,' he told the weary traveler. 'When you get yore horse put up at the livery stable it'll be ready. It's a double room and Dwight Craig's in the other bed, but you can go in quiet and not wake him up.'

Gratefully the tired youth agreed to the arrangement and was soon back from caring for his horse.

The night clerk had been busy meanwhile. When the new guest returned the clerk picked up the lamp from the desk and lighted the way down the dark hall. Arrived at a door, he spoke in a whisper.

'You won't need a light, I reckon. Dwight was plumb give out hisself, and I reckon you won't want to disturb him. He's in the bed by the south wall. You can fall into the other one quiet like.'

Considerately, Dwight's uninvited room-mate tiptoed into the darkened room and crawled into the bed on the north wall as noiselessly as possible. The night clerk retreated, grinning. To the late loiterers in the barroom he explained the reason for his mirth. Their appreciation made the pool tables tremble. The joke spread to the rest of the town's night owls. When morning came there was a waiting audience in the hotel lobby. But time passed and nothing happened. When waiting finally became irksome it was decided to force matters. Opening the door of the bedroom without knocking, the delegation had its reward.

From under the covers of the bed by the north wall appeared a wild-eyed stricken face and a hand. For an instant only. A flick of thumb in the direction of the other bed and the face and hand disappeared once more beneath the bedclothes. What the spectators saw across the room was a very still form in the bed and, draped across chair and dresser, articles of apparel that had never belonged to Dwight Craig but did belong to the waitress.

The clerk approached the occupant of the other bed and spoke casually: 'Ain't yu' goin' t' git up a-tall today?'

Deeply muffled was the reply: 'Fer God's sake git her out-a here. Why didn't the damn fool lock her door?'

The clerk's voice didn't crack. 'All right, you lay quiet and we'll get her out.'

A moment of mild commotion was followed by a shrill feminine shriek. The figure in the north wall bed was seen to cower lower under its coverings. The clerk approached it and spoke again. 'All clear. She's done grabbed her clos' and drug it.'

How long it was before the victim of the raw hoax discovered that only a dummy had shared his room and that the waitress had been enriched by the equivalent of a week's tips for the loan of her apparel and her shriek, no one was ever to know. The bashful youth mounted his horse and left town, his business, whatever it may have been, unattended to. How long he had lain slowly suffocating under the quilts or how long he would have continued to do so was any man's guess. His only reference to the incident, so far as we know, was a question he was heard to propound some time later. He wanted to know what the chances were for successfully suing a hotel for criminal negligence.

I could readily sympathize with his point of view, due to an experience of my own in the same caravansary. I had had an ulcerated tooth. I went in town to consult a traveling dentist whose credentials consisted of his own advertisement and whose tools were an assortment of probes and forceps in a small black case. Like all his other victims, I was placed in a kitchen chair and held down by two strong men. One of these, in my case, was the faithful Corky Wallace, a sort of family factotum whose services had run the gamut from cook to bronco-buster.

'Now I'll give her an anesthetic to quiet her nerves,' the dentist announced. Weakly I tried to suggest that it was too late for the anesthetic, but he had put a pellet in my mouth, and I had obediently swallowed.

I recall Annie the chambermaid helping me into bed and saying as she withdrew: 'I'll leave the light burning and your door unlocked and will look in on you later. Now go to sleep.'

My next conscious thought was, 'Here's Annie,' and I was trying to formulate a cheerful 'Hello' when I had the illusion of its being Corky Wallace who stood at my bedside instead of the chambermaid. Funny. That I had been given some sort of dope was my first mental reaction, and I didn't like the feeling. To dissipate it I said firmly, 'Hello, Annie.'

'Hello,' said Corky, a bit thickly. I sat bolt upright. Was this Corky or was this Annie? My head was whirling and I seemed unable to assemble my wits.

'Besht friend ever had,' said Corky — or Annie.

'Sure,' I said a little wildly and fell back on my pillow, while the universe spun and I gradually lapsed into peaceful oblivion, a voice carrying ever and ever more faintly to my dulling senses, 'Won — three hundred dollars — all yors — besht friend — ever — had ——'

The late morning sun full in my face waked me. That was a queer dream I had last night, I told myself. I put a hand out from under the cover and for the second time sat bolt upright, my fingers laced around a packet of paper bills, fives, tens, twenties! The packet had been lying on my chest.

I shook my head violently to make sure that I was not still dreaming and then counted the money. Three hundred dollars! There was just time to slip it under my pillow when Annie bustled in.

'Have a good night?' She was all motherly concern. 'I looked in once and you were sound asleep, so I didn't come back.'

'Did you leave my door unlocked?' I wanted to know.

'Oh, sure. Couldn't lock you in, could I? Besides, nobody was goin' t' bother you, was there?' I realized that these were purely rhetorical questions. Annie was going on chattily: 'Big poker game last night, I hear. They say Corky Wallace cleaned 'em all out and broke up the game about three o'clock this mornin'. Then he got drunk and passed out cold. Seems like somebody rolled him and got all the money, something like three hundred dollars. He's sobered up some, this mornin', and says he can't remember what happened. Corky's one what oughtn't ever to drink,' Annie went on piously, 'he's such a plumb gentleman when he's sober.'

'Has he no idea what he did with the money?' I probed.

Annie shook her head. 'He claims he don't. Claims somebody stole it off'n him. Says he'll make whoever done it hard t' ketch if he ever does find out.'

I wrestled with the problem for a couple of days — until I felt reasonably fit physically. Then I caught Corky alone. 'Here,' I told him, 'is the three hundred dollars you asked me to take care of for you.'

His look of blank amazement did not appear to be feigned.

'I never asked you to keep ary money for me,' he insisted, refusing to touch the packet.

'Of course you did.' I pressed the packet into his hand. He stared at it as though he had never seen it before.

'Who yu' tryin' t' pertect?' he said at last.

'You,' I told him, and while he was trying to figure that one out, I shot home the moral: 'You and I both better keep our wits about us, no?'

Civilization CATCHES UP

WITH US

Even after horseflesh began to give way to the internal-combustion engine in our part of the world, we rather clung to our point of view.

'Bad Man' Pete was a perfect exponent of it.

He was called 'Bad Man' because his looks were awe-inspiring, whether artificially or by nature, I was never sure. Certainly Nature furnished him the raw material, for he was a huge man, bull-voiced, with shaggy eyebrows and hairy forearms, but Pete took full advantage of all this. He let his walrus mustache grow to unbelievable proportions, didn't cut his hair, and wore two six-shooters long after most of the men of the country had ceased to wear one. But in spite of it all he gave one the feeling that an overgrown baby was throwing out dark hints about a murderous past.

At the time in question Bad Man Pete was engaged in the very prosaic pursuit of regularly hauling freight with a mule team across the San Augustine plains.

One night, long after schedule, Pete came in and explained his delay.

'What do you think happened to me?' he rumbled. It sounded like some old bull defying a younger rival of whom he's just a little afraid. 'Well, I met up with one o' them blank-blank horseless kerriges out in the middle o' the big sand. The blank-blank driver wouldn't turn out of the road quick enough and his old tin can skeert my mules. They r'ared around till they busted the wagon tongue. So I jumped down off'n my wagon and drawed down on the loco blossom with both my guns.'

My sympathies went out to innocent motorists who couldn't possibly have turned out of the road except to get badly stuck in the sand.

Pete went rumbling on.

'"Ya don't get away from here till you pay fer the damage," I yelled at him. The feller was sort o' shakin' and he sez, "How much is the damage, mister?" You bet he called me mister.' Pete's tone suggested that this was a high but unaccustomed honor. ' "Well," I sez, "considerin' as how ya should 'a' turned out of the road when yo' fust seen me, I think ya orter be made to pay and pay good, and what's more yore goin' to."'

I was still suffering vicariously with the motorist.

'That feller's voice sort o' squeaked' — Pete was deferring the climax as long as possible. '"How much is it, mister?" he says again.'

' "It's a *dollar*," sez I, "and don't think yore goin' to git off with one dime less."'

Triumph rang in Pete's bass notes.

'Did he pay?' I asked, trying hard to keep my voice steady.

'Yo' bet he paid' — Bad Man Pete brought out the silver dollar. 'This here's *it*. He never made no fuss about doin' it, neither. Seemed like he couldn't git that dollar to me quick enough. I tell you the's times a feller has to git tough in this world to keep from bein' pushed around. No tellin' what these fellers with their little play wagons will come to.'

I could see that Pete was expecting praise for his display of moral courage.

'I'm sure you did right,' I told him. 'How long did it take you to splice your wagon tongue?'

'Only a couple of hours. That was workin' for mighty good wages, I'll tell the world.'

My own great concession to a new age was to abandon the sidesaddle. Why, for ten years, I continued to ride sidesaddle is a mystery to me now. I recall the steps that led to emancipation.

First, I discarded, or rather refused to adopt, the sunbonnet, conventional headgear of my female neighbors. When I went unashamedly about under a five-gallon (not ten-gallon) Stetson, many an eyebrow was raised; then followed a double-breasted blue flannel shirt, with white pearl buttons, frankly unfeminine. In time came blue denim knickers worn *under* a short blue denim skirt. Slow evolution (or was it decadence?) toward a costume suited for immediate needs. Decadence having set in, the descent from the existing standards of female modesty to purely human comfort and convenience was swift. A man's saddle and a divided skirt (awful monstrosity that was) were inevitable. This was in the middle nineties.

'I won't ride in the same cañon with you,' protested Ray, when I first appeared thus clad.

'Put that promise in writing — you might forget it,' I snapped.

And forget it he did. Vehemently he denied only a few months later ever having said it, wherein he was not unlike many another penitent who has rushed into delivering a premature ultimatum.

Our Jekyll–Hyde Lives

OUR Jekyll-Hyde lives were never so hard to reconcile as they were during these years of the middle nineties. Ray, for instance, suddenly found himself one of the nation's early football stars. While he was at the University of Michigan he was still quite small; he was known there as 'Little Morley,' no more than a promising quarterback. The following year, he went to Columbia.

Decidedly, he didn't like his first taste of New York City. He was far less a personage there than he had been in New Mexico. A letter addressed 'Towhead, New York City' would probably not have reached him! In fact, he insisted that in his first week in the nation's metropolis not a soul spoke to him voluntarily. That was something new in his scheme of things.

Then one day a young man who had known him in Michigan called and found him throwing his belongings into a suitcase. He was leaving on the night train and New York be damned! He'd go back where people were humans. But there were the hours before the train left and the friend persuaded him to go with him to watch football practice. The friend managed to get the ear of Coach Sanford. Looking him over with expert eye, Coach Sanford decided that Ray, who had suddenly put on stature and was no longer 'Little Morley,' had the general build of a football player and suggested that he put on a suit and get out on the field. Flat refusal was Ray's first reaction to the invitation; then an inspired idea came to him. For every slight he had received he'd leave imprinted in some New Yorker's mind the memory that he had passed through town.

The trail of bruised and battered and toppled-over football players he left behind him in the next half-hour was, so he thought, bidding good-bye to New York forever. Incidentally it was a show to delight the soul of a football coach. When he returned to the dressing-rooms he couldn't have left town had he wanted to, not if it had taken the police force aided by the fire department to stop him! Columbia needed football players like him, for Columbia had never yet beaten Yale. Ray helped do that, hence his trunkful of clippings.

It was always amusing when our two lives confronted each other. On a train coming home from New York Ray once fell in with a young West Point graduate enroute to his first army assignment. The young West Pointer obviously had 'background,' but even so he seemed flattered to have made the acquaintance of a ranking football hero.

Arrived at El Paso, the two registered at the same hotel and dined together. In the evening the West Pointer announced that he would like to do a bit of slumming through the tough joints which then flourished in that city.

'Better leave all your valuables in the safe,' the hotel clerk advised. Sound advice, which was heeded.

As Ray, followed closely by the wide-eyed West Pointer, pushed open the swinging doors of the most notorious of the gambling-dens, a man leaped from the dealer's chair at one of the faro tables and fell upon Ray.

'If it ain't old Towhead!' he squawked. 'Boys, let me give you a knockdown to my old pal, Towhead Morley. Him and me done stole many a longear together.'

Doctor Jekyll fell away. Mr. Hyde emerged. 'Jack Creighton, you old spavined maverick!' Ray cried, pumping his friend's arm. 'What you doin' in store clothes?'

Followed many questions back and forth, Ray bringing himself up to date on local gossip. He learned that Three-Fingered Mike was 'on the dodge,' and that Shorty was 'doin' a stretch in the Santa Fe pen for gettin' caught at stealin' a beef.'

Ray insists he honestly forgot the presence of his West Point companion until a chilly 'I think I'll be returning to the hotel' reminded him. Ray couldn't think of the right things to say on the strained trip back to the hotel, so utterly hopeless seemed any attempt to explain our peculiar society to one so newly arrived. In silence, the two entered the hotel lobby.

The clerk greeted him. 'Mr. Morley, Mr. A. A. Robinson, president of the Santa Fé Railroad, discovered your name on the register and wants you to communicate with him immediately.' The West Pointer listened with growing puzzlement as the clerk rambled on: 'Mr. Robinson says he was associated with your father in the early days of the Santa Fé, and he asked me to tell you how anxious he is for you to get in touch with him.'

The West Pointer gulped. 'Well, Morley, you seem to have intimates at both ends of the social scale,' he murmured. 'I had just about decided that you were an impostor and not *the* "Bill" Morley at all, but a come-on man for a gambling-house.'

One of my guests at the ranch was a sorority sister. In time she confessed that before she left for Datil 'the sisters in the bonds' had taken her aside and said to her: 'Grace, we want you to take careful note while you are visiting Agnes. You know, Agnes worries us. She seems to be a truthful enough person generally, but we just can't believe all the things she tells us about that New Mexico cattle ranch. Just keep your eyes open and report.'

Three weeks on the ranch — and Grace wrote the sisterhood, 'I want to report that Agnes' stories indicate admirable self-restraint on her part.'

That was after she had attended one of our dances and had overheard a discussion between two of our gayest young blades. They were undoubtedly inspired by Grace's college-bred presence.

Said one, 'No, sir, "Pass them molasses" ain't right.'

'Why ain't it right?' demanded the other.

'Because it orter be "Pass *those* molasses."'

In spite of the fact that Ray was at Columbia, where he coached football for a season after he graduated, and I was finishing a somewhat disrupted college course at Stanford, we managed by a sort of remote control to hold the ranch together even though loose-endedly. Competition in the cattle business was not especially keen then, and the land simply lay there supporting a few hundred head of stock who in turn partially supported us. Ray, of course, bore the real brunt of the responsibility. It was a period during which he wavered between civil engineering and ranching as a life work: but because he was at heart Mr. Hyde, ranchman, the civil engineer faded and disappeared.

The schism between my own opposed lives was made permanent when in 1899 I married Newton Cleaveland, whom I met on the Stanford Campus, and became a visiting Californian — for New Mexico always remained 'home' to me. I am still married to him after more than forty years, during which time we have on occasion put to an inconclusive test the question of what happens when an irresistible force meets an immovable body. For a short period, soon after our marriage, Newton tried living in Datil. He now stoutly maintains that he liked it, but I know full well that when he had planned to use a team on the following day he expected the team to be available, which was more than the rest of us did. After he had wasted just so much time and energy looking for straying horses he decided that his time and energy could be better spent looking for gold mines: they have at least the virtue of not moving about after you start to look for them. We returned to California, and from then on the ranch became Ray's in a strictly legal sense, but Mother still lived there and that gave me a valid reason, until her death in 1917, for 'going home' at frequent intervals. 'Going home' was a phrase which Newton accepted with becoming tolerance. Even after her death I could always find a plausible excuse if not a valid reason for continuing to 'go home.'

Ray, too, for all the singleness of his purpose to be a ranchman, married on the right side of the line. After a very brief and ill-fated marriage to Bessie Cresson while he was still in Columbia, he married Nancy Brown, a New York girl, who had been one of his fans when he was a football hero. Nan made valiant efforts to adjust herself to a standard as far removed from the ones 'to which she had been accustomed' as East is from West. Spasmodically she succeeded. In retrospect, from what she insists upon calling her 'declining years,' she swears she loved it all. I believe her.

Lora, by all means the most respectable one of us, went Jekyll in her first marriage and Hyde in her second. Her first husband was Perry Warren, recently of Yale University, where his too studious temperament had caused a breakdown, and to recuperate from which he had been sent West.

I first met Perry at a neighboring ranch where he was trying, with but little success, to adjust himself to the conditions which seemed essential to his recovery. It was not the physical privations that were bothering him but the utter intellectual barrenness. He welcomed my fairly grammatical use of the King's English as a drowning man might welcome a floating spar. I invited him to come and stay with us and he accepted the invitation with alacrity. He transferred his boxful of uniformly bound volumes of the classics, his silver-mounted military brushes, his meerschaum pipe, to the small cabin which served as the guest house on our place. He stayed more than a year. He never became a cow-puncher himself but cowpunchers liked him, even though 'he couldn't ride a mountain-side without holding to a tree.'

Perry and I got on famously but entirely unsentimentally. That flame was left for Lora to blow into life, she with her gentle lady-like manner which nonetheless did not militate against an excep-tional gift for the practical. Perry announced the engagement to his family in New York and the storm broke. A scion of the house of Warren, one related to General Joseph of Revolutionary War fame, to marry a Western nobody!

Then indeed did the practical side of Lora come to the fore. To this day I probably should not have known any of the twigs or branches or possibly even main stems of our family tree on either side had Lora not unearthed them to flaunt in the faces of the family-tree-worshiping Warrens. She dug out the fact that Morleys all but matched Warrens twig for twig.

It was other considerations than 'difference of station' that made the marriage impermanent. She married again, and any-body who has the hardihood to say that this time it was she who married beneath her station will have the whole Morley tribe unto the second generation to fight. Tom Reynolds never attended any institution of higher learning, but for what it takes to make a man I'll enter him in any list of salt-of-the-earthers. They still live in Datil.

Ray Morley THE LEGEND

Of course Ray was to me always the kid brother who needed taking down a peg, but I could see that he was becoming a tradition before my eyes. He was one of the people whose presence seems to cause the very air to vibrate. 'Ray Morley's in town' was a phrase that acted like an electric current through a quiet community. Spirits rose and loud laughter echoed wherever he appeared.

Mother's early but shattered dream of becoming a cattle tycoon became reality in Ray's case. If ever anyone looked the part of cattle king it was Ray. Just under six feet tall, broad of shoulder, narrow of hip, bewhiskered and wind-tanned, he belonged in the loud clothes of the typical ranchman. Possessed of the strength of half a dozen average men, he was an endless source of tales of daring and of muscle. One incident to which I was witness will indicate the character of his physical strength.

One of the ranch cabins had sprung a leak in the roof and I had climbed up to locate the thin spot in the dirt covering. Ascent had been by way of cleats nailed to a perpendicular post set flush against the wall. From the top of the house I saw Ray. He was riding a young bronc and experiencing the usual difficulties with an unbroken horse. Sidling up toward the cabin, he called up to me asking what I was doing. Before I could explain he had dismounted and was climbing up the makeshift ladder. In one hand he held the end of the long lariat the other end of which was tied around the horse's neck.

'That horse will jerk away from you sure as shootin',' I told him.

'I can hold him,' Ray told me. He was now standing erect on the edge of the flat roof. The bronc, believing himself free, ran to the end of the rope. I held my breath. Of course Ray must let go or be jerked off the roof. He didn't let go and he wasn't jerked off. He braced himself, and the bronc came to the end of the slack with a sudden halt. Ray tottered but held.

'Maybe I better get down,' he said with elaborate casualness, and proceeded to climb down. Although the horse continued to lunge on the rope he did not succeed in breaking loose. Ray remounted and waved to me airily. He did everything airily.

Surprisingly enough, though, he did not drink. Only one tale ever reached me of his having drunk too much. On this occasion he had come into Magdalena on a bitterly cold night, half frozen and slightly ill. The hotel-keeper, kindly Mrs. Chisholm, insisted upon prescribing a remedy. She handed him a glass half filled with hot water, and a bottle of Jamaica Ginger, a patent medicine much in vogue. Ray filled the glass to the brim, almost emptying the bottle, and gulped it down. His subsequent efforts to remain poised and dignified were thought to be exceedingly funny, the more so because of the novelty of the exhibition.

'I thought it *was* ginger,' he said afterward.

Under his management the Morley ranges had become enor-

mous, even in comparison with neighboring ranges. His ranch comprised about two hundred 640-acre sections to which he held title
by patent or by perpetual lease, and possibly treble that number
which he controlled by virtue of the location of the watering places
or by National Forest permits. Computed in acres it would have
crowded a half-million, but nobody so computed it. It was forty
miles in this direction, twenty in that, ten at the lower end, always
miles and more miles.

That Ray was arrogant as well as human and friendly there is
no doubt, but the arrogance was toward life in general and not
toward people in particular. That he sometimes bowled people
over as he went his single-purpose way is also beyond doubt, and
that he made enemies in the process naturally follows. But his
enemies respected him. It is notable that the one man who carried
his grievances into print waited until after Ray's death to do so.
Ray always had the better of it when it was a man-to-man proposition.

No situation seemed to daunt him. When the arroyo was at
flood and he wanted to cross, he plunged in. When the torrent
carried him fifty yards downstream and flung him out on the same
side from which he had entered, he plunged in again, all but drowning himself and his horse. His reason for taking the risk was
merely that he wanted to cross the arroyo.

My own principal grievance against him was his apparent obliviousness to time. 'Time goes right along and I go right along with
it,' he would say when brought to book for being late to an appointment. On this theory he was apt as not to arise with the rest of us
when somebody said 'Bedtime,' but instead of going to bed he
would announce, 'Well, I guess I'll go up to Santa Fé' or wherever
he might have business. Then we would hear his horse's feet or
his car's wheels as we dropped off into comfortable sleep. He slept
less than anybody I have ever known, ate abstemiously and was
apparently indifferent to what he ate, a personal idiosyncrasy

that he imposed upon the other fellow. His cow outfits always 'lived hard,' not from any intention upon his part to exploit but because he entertained the notion that what satisfied him would probably satisfy anybody else. In this he was, of course, mistaken.

Lou Gatlin once expressed the opposite point of view. Ray had fashioned a robust Lazy Susan table from a Model T wheel and hub, for the ranch headquarters. 'I done played that 'ar wheel for three years now,' Lou grumbled, 'and nothin' ever come up but sowbelly and beans' — a picturesque exaggeration possibly, but containing an element of truth.

Dane Coolidge, on one of his literary 'prowls' in search of authentic local color, came upon Ray's kindergarten outfit at a critical moment. They were almost out of provisions and sick unto death of the monotony of what they had been eating. Dane, with a well-stocked chuckbox, including canned fruit, descended upon them like a heavenly visitant. He reported the boys' plight to Ray.

'Make men of them,' said Ray, but sent immediate replenishments — of the same old monotonous salt pork and beans, potatoes and flour. Along with it, however, went something of his own buoyancy of spirit and his cheery good will. The boys laughed even while they cussed. Most people did in dealing with him, from the congressional committee before whom he testified half insolently in behalf of the cattle industry, to the quaking sheepherders whom he caught poaching upon his range. He made his points with a good-natured directness that swept complacency or hypocrisy aside and more often than not left his opponent laughing at himself.

He could with fair reason be called anti-social. He did not think in terms of massed men but of challenging situations. He appeared to believe that everybody else was as ready as he to bring tireless effort and self-denial to a tough job. He worked prodigiously hard and felt superior to nobody and, by the same token, inferior to nobody. He stood on his rights and expected his opponents to do likewise — and let the best man win. When there was no issue of opposed rights he was boon companion to high and low — if they afforded amusement, which practically everybody in that era did. As a matter of fact we were all uncompromisingly self-contained If that be anti-social, make what you will of it!

Ray LIED ENTRANCINGLY

For a person who caused so many other folks to break into loud guffaws, Ray was curiously quiet in his enjoyment of the ridiculous. A low chuckle, accompaniment to a twinkle in his eyes, was his only outward sign of amusement. I've noted this quietness in many an old stockman.

One writer of Western tales who averred that 'young Ray Morley laughed aloud' did not know him. But the people whom he made to laugh aloud and who are still laughing aloud in retrospect are countless.

Once he had the whole county, if not the state, laughing; or more properly those who weren't hopping mad and rushing into print about it. A school teacher at Reserve had wandered into the near-by mountains and got herself lost. She probably hadn't mastered the elementary rule of our section: If lost, keep going downhill. When search parties did not find her, the sheriff dashed to Datil in his new Franklin sedan, the first sedan, I think, to have come snootily into our Model T touring-car lives. He came for Rock, our veteran hound, cleverest trailer of the pack.

Now, Rock had never ridden in anything. His own stout legs had served him well enough, and he assumed the attitude that it was too late at his time of life to indulge in the nonsense of the younger generation. It took all hands to load him into the sheriff's shiny new closed car and an extra man to keep him from jumping through the window, once aboard. Put on the teacher's trail, he almost immediately met the lady on the outskirts of the town, which she had finally happened upon without benefit of outside help.

Rock was promptly returned with thanks, heartfelt thanks, for he had been an unqualified nuisance and the lady's rescue was no addition to his long list of achievements. But here was material to Ray's hand. He presented a formal bill to the State Board of Education for three hundred and fifty dollars for the lease of one hound dog and the complete ruination of said dog. He represented that whereas said dog had heretofore been content to walk, he now insisted upon riding in limousines, and whereas he had heretofore been invaluable in tracking down grizzly bear, mountain lions, wildcats, and such predatory animals, he now refused to pick up the trail of anything less than schoolteachers.

The State Board of Education, Ray was sure, would acknowledge the justice of his demand for damages, but he did not wish to be unduly insistent in pressing his rightful claims. He would make the State Board of Education an alternative offer. He would sell the dog outright to them for three hundred and fifty dollars. It was an opportunity he was sure the Board of Education would jump at, in view of their known difficulty in securing teachers for Catron County. Rock would find them a schoolteacher on command at any time.

At least one member of the State Board of Education thought the letter was funny and turned it over to a newspaper editor, who thought so too and printed it. Did everybody laugh? No, not everybody. The paper received a barrage of letters from indignant taxpayers warning the School Board against squandering public funds on a 'holdup' and berating Ray for his lack of public spirit, his eagerness to profit by human distress, and particularly for his gross overevaluation of any hound dog that ever bayed of a moonlight night.

But the most laughed-at of Ray's victims was — myself. Reverberations of that laughter are still heard in the Datils. It probably won't die out so long as a man is alive who remembers anything about it. Ray met me at the train in Magdalena upon one of my homecomings. His face was bruised and an egg-sized knot protruded back of his left ear.

'Tell you about it later,' he promised; 'too long a story right now.'

'Later' was after lunch, in the lobby of the Aragon Hotel. The lobby was filled with acquaintances, by design, as I was to discover. When I could restrain my sympathetic curiosity no longer, I asked, '*What* happened?'

'Well,' said Ray, 'you won't believe me if I tell you. But the fact is, a wild man hit me with a club.'

I met this with the equivalent of 'Oh, yeah' — whatever it was we used before that labor-saving phrase was invented to relieve thinking.

'I knew you wouldn't believe me' — Ray sounded injured. 'No use trying to tell you.' His manner dismissed the subject.

'Well, something hit you, that's evident,' I conceded. 'Let's have it.'

'I tell you, a wild man hit me, and John Fullerton and Bert Beagle and Milt Craig and all these fellows here saw the wild man after I captured him. Didn't you?'

They all assured me they had. They described him minutely. Ray had brought him in and had lodged him overnight in the jail. The whole town had seen him. There had, in fact, been an article in the papers about him. Hadn't I seen it?

No, I hadn't seen it. I searched the faces about me for signs of duplicity and found only frank open countenances. I had no recourse but to believe the tale thus far.

Where was the wild man now? I was not to be trapped if I could help it.

He was being held, it appeared, in the Las Vegas insane asylum pending arrival of a scientific commission from the Smithsonian to study his case, because this wild man was so very wild it was a question whether he might not even be subhuman, or possibly a survivor of the cliff-dwellers.

While I was pondering this, Ray went on rapidly: 'I was riding along under the north rim of the Datils — you know, north of Stiver Spring, not far from Skeleton Spring' — he paused for me to nod remembrance of the locality — 'and I heard my horse suddenly snort. Then I saw something in a juniper tree, and took down my rope and started toward the tree when the thing came at me with a club. It moved so fast that before I could get my wits together, it hit me alongside the head.'

Ray gingerly rubbed the black-and-blue knob behind his ear.

'I was knocked out for a minute and when I came to, I saw four of these things, the male that had struck me, and a female, and two young. I don't know whether to call them cubs, or children, or what.'

This was the time to have remembered Annie Shoemaker's admonition about not letting my imagination get away with me, but like most admonitions, it failed in the crisis. I had often amused myself by building mental tales of a survivor of the ancients, some lone member of a lost race who still lived in one of the many caves in the north face of the Datils. Now here was Ray with a roomful of corroborating witnesses making those fantastic yarns real. Nobody could tell a story as Ray could: I hung on his words.

'Well, I took in after the creatures and roped the male. He put up a battle, I'll tell the world. Almost scratched my eyes out before I got him subdued.'

Ray's face looked it.

'But finally I got him tied and then I took in after the rest of them — the wife and children or whatever they were. But they'd got too good a start and disappeared around the base of a cliff where I couldn't follow. So I gave up and came back.'

I was there on the scene myself. I saw everything with perfect clarity.

'Ray Morley!' I cried passionately. 'You should be ashamed of yourself.'

'Why?' he wanted to know.

'*Why?*' Emotion fairly choked me. 'Why, for not turning that father loose and letting him go back to his family.'

'And deprive science of a tremendous opportunity to ——'

I wasn't to be mollified.

'Science doesn't count in a case like that,' I stormed. 'You were downright inhuman!'

A look of utter penitence spread over Ray's face. 'I guess you are right,' he confessed abjectly. 'But the best of us will err at times.'

It was that last sentence that did it. I snapped out of my trance amid the thunderous laughter of half the town.

I had swallowed one of Ray's tall tales — even I!

'You are a bunch of liars,' I informed those present with what dignity I could command. But they still swore that they hadn't lied, not in one word they had told me.

In the end the facts came out.

Ray was chasing wild cattle in the place he had so vividly just described and his horse had carried him into a protruding spike that was a short dead limb of a tree. It had caught him behind the ear and then before he had recovered another branch had raked him across the face.

On his return to the ranch he was confronted with a harassed neighbor who had in his car a creature that seemed scarcely human. Naked, with hair hanging below his shoulders, his speech unintelligible guttural gasping noises, the creature truly seemed less than human. The neighbor explained:

'Found him wandering on my range. He run when he first seen me, but in the end he let me get up to him. I know what he is. He's a deef-and-dumb Injun who's been run off by his tribe for bringin' 'em bad luck. I don't think he's loco. I think he's just deef and dumb. He'll eat, sort o' like a dog, but he'll eat. I didn't know what to do with him, so I brung him over to you.'

'Thanks,' said Ray.

So those men in Magdalena had not lied after all. It had been a beautiful coincidence that Ray had been hit alongside the head by a tree limb the very day he had been made custodian of a starving, scarcely human fellow-being otherwise doomed to die. He was in the state institution the last I knew, waiting, I presume, for that scientific commission from the Smithsonian.

Corky IS TRIED FOR MURDER

BEFORE New Mexico achieved statehood — and what a hulla-baloo there was over that, the 'whites' fearing domination by the 'Mexicans' — our judges were all appointed from Washington. Many a newly arrived judge had his legal education considerably added to by his experience with New Mexico courts of law. Whether the trial of 'Corky' for murder was more or less fantastic than the average, I hazard no opinion, but I know it had its astounding features, and that I had an unwilling part in them.

Although our establishment was his headquarters, Corky had taken up a homestead some miles distant and, by the exercise of unusual thrift and self-denial, had accumulated 'a nice little bunch of cows,' a hundred head or so. Both ranch and cattle he finally contracted to sell to a new arrival in the community, a man with a wife, baby, and sister-in-law, who made up the family group. The purchaser moved on to Corky's place but neglected the detail of paying for it.

For months the meek-spirited Corky made mild representation that he would like a little on account. After having dispatched this message on one occasion, the reply came back by the messenger, 'Better stay on your own side of the mountain. Climate's better over there.'

Whether this observation about the weather constituted a threat or not was later to be argued at length in both Spanish and English. At the time Corky called it a 'threat,' and promptly rode over to the other side of the mountain. It was late afternoon of the same day that I saw him sitting on his horse, several hundred yards from our house, motioning to me.

'I had to kill McCullough,' he said, breathing with almost as much difficulty as my run was causing me to breathe.

'He shot first. I'm takin' out. Got no witness on my side.'

Believing his story, I begged him to go immediately into town and give himself up.

'And rot in that Socorro jail until my case comes up? Not me. I'll give up when they're ready to bring me to trial.'

The sheriff's posse roamed the hills day and night, our place being kept under the closest possible surveillance. If Corky obtained food from our storehouse, I can honestly swear that I never knew it, nor, under the circumstances, would I have countenanced it. I believed that he would be exonerated, so I should have continued to urge him to give himself up.

Other friends who believed in his innocence (although it is not at all certain that they made that a condition) gave him sanctuary until court should convene, when it was understood he would surrender for immediate trial. In all probability, he would have succeeded in forcing the law to accept these conditions, but for one of those trifles that have been the undoing of many a carefully laid plan.

Corky owned but one pair of boots, an especially fine pair, with his initials handsomely stitched on their tops, and he customarily wore them in the style still in vogue in smart cowboy circles, which is to say, with one pant-leg hooked over the notch in the top of one boot.

When there was well-founded suspicion that these particular friends were keeping Corky hid, Under-Sheriff Bob Lewis, who knew his cowboy lore, sent a man unknown to Corky or his host to the host's house to see whether any stranger was about. There was, the spy said, a man with EW (Corky's other name was Ervin) stitched in the leg of a boot! — once again proving that slavish devotion to style carries its penalties. Very stupid of Corky? The undoing trifle is always very stupid.

Some of us who were Corky's friends went immediately to the McCullough house to see if we could find proof of his innocence. Three bullet holes were distributed as follows: one in the jamb of the outer door, one in the headboard of the walnut bedstead which occupied one corner of the room, and one in the wall directly opposite the foot of the bed.

Those three bullet holes told the story exactly as Corky told it. He had stepped from the brilliant outdoor sunlight into the open door of a darkened room. Before his eyes had adjusted themselves to the dim light so that he could see who might be in the room, a bullet pinged into the doorjamb behind him. He then saw McCullough standing beside the bed. Sidling along the inner wall and drawing his own gun, Corky returned fire. His bullet hit the headboard, just as his enemy's second shot from the foot of the bed crashed into the wall behind him. Both shots missed by inches.

The men grappled at this point and Corky succeeded in knocking the six-shooter from his opponent's hand. Struggling, the two fell through the open doorway, just as Mrs. McCullough rushed from the second of the two rooms and attacked Corky, frantically trying to get possession of his weapon.

'Hold him while I get my gun!' yelled her husband as he turned back toward the door. He never reached it.

Both Mrs. McCullough and the sister-in-law, who had been witness to part of the scene, testified to the substantial correctness of this account, the main discrepancy being about the first shot.

'He came in a-shootin',' both women testified on the witness stand. Obviously improbable, when he could have had no idea as to the position of anybody in the room. Furthermore, the bullet fired at the man standing beside the bed did not range from the door but from the wall ten feet to the right of it. The bullet hole in the doorjamb, on the other hand, did range from the side of the bed.

I helped make careful measurements of the room and remove the doorjamb to be used in evidence.

Tom Tucker subpoenaed me as a material witness and I went into Socorro to see Corky. Bob Lewis ushered me into his cell just a moment before the appearance of Elfego Baca, Corky's defense attorney. This gentleman was a Mexican who spoke halting English.

'I was the first man in thees jail,' he announced, with every evidence of pride. 'They had me in here before the roof was on.'

'You're wrong,' contradicted Bob Lewis. '*I* was the first man in this jail. They had me in here when the walls were just high enough to keep me from climbing over 'em.'

Lest the argument grow heated, I hastened to inject, 'Well, this is the first time *I*'ve ever been in it.' To Corky I said, believing my words, 'You won't be here long.'

His attorney led me outside. 'I'll tell you what to say on the weetness stand,' he told me. 'You learn it good and come to my office and I cross-examine you like the deestrict attorney do, so they can't treep you up.'

'They can't trip me up,' I said. 'I'll just tell what I know.'

'Tell what you *know!*' he repeated the words, as if he had not heard them aright. 'Tell what you *know* — in a *murder* trial?'

'Why, yes,' I persisted in my innocence.

He laughed shortly. 'Nobody tell what he know in a *murder* trial,' he explained patiently. '*They* lie, *we* lie, *everybody* lie.' He waved his hands expansively.

'Corky isn't lying,' I insisted. 'His story holds up from start to finish. He'd better not lie.'

'We lie for him,' said his attorney. 'Nobody tells the truth in a *murder* trial.'

He was a good prophet, insofar as this particular murder trial was concerned. The jury was composed of nine Mexicans and three — well, just what am I to call them now that the useful word 'whites' is taboo lest it offend sensibilities? New Mexico Mexicans are Americans of four or five generations' standing, even when unmixed with Indian blood, so the word 'American' cannot be used to distinguish between Mexicans and non-Mexicans. There is an effort today to avoid the difficulty by substituting the word 'Spanish-Americans,' and calling the others 'Anglos,' but this has the fault of glaring inaccuracy in many cases and also of perpetuating the objectionable hyphen idea among us. Anyway, three of the jury were not Mexicans — or must I say, not Spanish-Americans?

The other nine understood no English. The judge on the bench understood no Spanish. Most of those in attendance, spectators and court attachés alike, understood more or less of both languages. The entire proceedings were conducted through an interpreter. There were some marvelously proficient interpreters amongst us in those days, individuals who regarded both languages as their native tongue. The professional interpreter reached his apotheosis in the state legislature, where even to this day his services are required.

I have engaged in many a conversation when Spanish and English were used with as little discrimination between an English and a Spanish word as though words had been cards dealt from a deck, differing only in the color of their backs.

'Oye, amigo, how far down este camino before I hit the trail that goes otro lado Arroyo Seco?' The answer might be: 'Tres millas and you better quidado because there's been mucha agua coming down Arroyo Seco. Better wait till mañana.' I doubt if we said 'tomorrow' once in a hundred times. 'Mañana' is such a satisfying word.

In Corky's trial the interpreter took his stand just below the judge's bench and spoke rapidly in an emotionless monotone. The district attorney was also a Mex — Spanish-American — who spoke English with even less accuracy than opposing counsel. The widow in deepest mourning appeared in court, carrying her baby, about whose arm was tied a black ribbon.

The taking of testimony began. As it proceeded I squirmed more and more restlessly in my seat. 'I'll nail *that* one,' I said to myself time after time. 'Wait till I get on the stand.'

'Thees was premeditated murder of the foulest kind!' roared the district attorney, and the interpreter monotonously picked up the words as they fell from his lips. 'Do I need to tell thees jury that when a cowboy goes to a ranch and ties hees horse to a fence post he does so because he knows sometheeng ees going to scare that horse and he is not taking chances on eet's running away? Every señor on thees jury knows that no cowboy ever ties hees horse.'

It was with the utmost difficulty that I, at this point, restrained myself from waving my hand and saying, 'Teacher, please, may I speak?' I doubt if the judge would have been unduly surprised had I done it, so many innovations had confronted him in this, his first court session in New Mexico.

The horse that Corky had ridden that day was one of the rare exceptions which could never be taught to stand by dropping the bridle reins. He was never taken to roundups for that reason. To catch him after unthinkingly dropping the bridle reins I had walked to the point of exasperation more than once — until I finally gave up and accepted the fact that no amount of stepping on those dragging reins and yanking the bit until his mouth bled was an effective object lesson. So we always tied Ginger.

When I saw how damaging to Corky this testimony that his horse had been tied to a fence post could be, I could hardly wait to refute it. But wait I had to as day after day the case dragged on.

Then suddenly, to my consternation, the defense announced, 'We rest, Your Honor.'

I had not been called to the stand; the diagram of the room in which the shooting had occurred had not been introduced in evidence, although there can be little doubt that it would have determined without question who shot first; above all, Corky's innocence had not been established.

Each attorney made his charge to the jury. The district attorney accused one of the defense witnesses of being a 'double-header.' I thought the judge looked a little nonplussed until it dawned upon him that 'two-faced' was probably the word. Corky's attorney, wiping his eyes with a bandanna, quavered, 'Gentlemen of the jury, you can tell by looking at thees defendant that he has a heart as soft as pudding; do you want to see the daisies growing over hees grave?' I glanced at the prisoner in the dock and thought I detected a faintly amused glint in his eye.

It was one cock-eyed murder trial from beginning to end. The defense attorney hadn't really defended and the prosecution hadn't made a case. The judge thought so too, from the tenor of his instructions to the jury. In a voice in which irritation was ill-concealed, he virtually ordered acquittal.

The jury filed out. The judge with an air of resignation sat back and relaxed. The spectators did not move. We were waiting for the jury to file back.

The bailiff came in and spoke to the judge. 'All right,' snapped His Honor. 'Take them to supper. The court will reconvene at eight o'clock.'

But it was four days later before that jury filed back into the courtroom, four days of uproar that had made sleep impossible for anyone within a block of the courthouse. Howls, curses, and sounds of splintering furniture had come from the open window of the jury room. Underneath the window a man with a shotgun across his knees had guarded against jury-tampering.

On the last day I met Elfego Baca. 'I can't stand this strain much longer,' I told him.

'Don't you be scaired,' he reassured me jovially. 'I got three men' — he held up three fingers — '*three* who won't give in — not eef the roof fall on them.'

'But nine men can't possibly think Corky's guilty,' I argued.

'Oh,' he said, 'nine men are probably saying he ees innocent.' And he winked at me.

His wink told me that he had put three men on that jury with instructions to prevent *any* verdict!

When the courthouse bell finally announced that the jury was ready to report, the town turned out. Twelve bleary-eyed, battered men stumbled into the jury box. The foreman addressed the court in Spanish and the interpreter informed His Honor that the jury could not agree. The prisoner was remanded back to the custody of the sheriff. And thus ended Chapter One.

Popular indignation immediately ran high. A committee of prominent citizens waited upon the judge and proposed to raise a twenty-five-thousand-dollar bond for Corky's release on bail. The offer was accepted and Corky returned to the ranch. Thus ended Chapter Two. Allowing bail to a man charged with first-degree murder was accepted as a matter of course. We now began to make plans for a second trial to establish his innocence.

Chapter Three opened with the county elections and the selection of Elfego Baca to succeed his former opponent as district attorney. Several months later, in this capacity, he dismissed the case.

'Why,' I asked Corky, 'didn't he clear you at the first trial?' Corky's reply was, 'He only got my ranch that time; it took another bite to get my cattle.' Corky's manner was that of a fatalist.

Although, to outward appearances, he was his old mild-mannered self, thereafter, we who knew him realized that a dead man walked among us. And one morning just at daybreak the guests in the Allen House in Magdalena were awakened by a wild shriek. Missouri Pete rushed into the lobby in his underwear, just as he had leaped from bed.

'I-I-I t-t-told h-him to r-ro-ro-roll ovver and g-g-g-git on h-h-his own s-s-s-side of the b-b-b-b-bed,' he stuttered, 'and when he w-w-w-w-wouldn't do it I g-g-g-g-give him a p-p-poke and, Mother of Heaven, he was s-s-s-stiff! I done sl-slept all n-n-night with a d-d-d-dead m-m-man!'

So passed Corky.

The Literati. ARRIVE

As TRANSPORTATION became less precarious, the steady influx of visitors to the ranch became a matter of some moment. The invited, the uninvited, and the self-invited came in unbroken procession. I think every rancher of that era will bear me out when I say that the food bills averaged twice the normal amount required by the household, and many a little ranchman has given his guests credit for his bankruptcy.

From the 'chuckline rider,' the stray cowboy who wintered by moving from ranch to ranch until his welcome was worn too thin for even traditional Western hospitality to sustain the fiction, to the guests who lingered with us for a year or more, as some of ours did, we entertained all sorts and conditions of people. One summer, representatives of twelve different colleges were our guests at one time or another during the vacation period.

The most memorable, perhaps, of our numerous visitors were the literary folk who in later years came seeking 'material.' Some, like the Dane Coolidges, were genuine friends whose advent was always hailed with delight and whose stay was always too short. Others sometimes gave us quite a lot to think about.

One of our ranch hands came in one night with the mail. He handed over his burden, with the exception of a bulky package which he held as he might have held a bomb.

'This here,' he explained, 'is for me, and it sure puts me in one jackpot.'

Sympathetic interest brought out the cause.

'It's like this,' he went on. 'I got a letter from my sister. She ain't like me, she's educat-id. She went to a business college back in Missouri and learned to write on a typewriter. Well, my sister is a secretary or somethin' for a woman what writes books. My sister told this writer woman that she had a brother who was a cowboy, and the woman says: "That's fine. Now I can write cowboy stories. Cowboy stories is going to be popular," so she done wrote a cowboy story and my sister done sent it to me to crittersize, as she calls it.' He looked ruefully at the unopened packet in his hand.

'I'm supposed to read this here and crittersize it.' His tone was despairing, 'Me, I never read a-tall, 'cept when I don't want to think, which ain't often.'

I knew what was coming, but waited.

'Mebbe,' he said, and there was pleading in his voice, 'you'd read it and crittersize it. I'll shoe a horse for you, if you will. I'll shoe two horses for you' — most potent of all bribes.

So I read the manuscript, with decidedly mixed feelings. It was good reading; but the author knew nothing of the cow country Each cowboy in this tale had his own tin washbasin and individual towel and cake of soap. I thought of the community towel to which we were accustomed; and the story of the man from New Mexico, the man from Texas and the man from Arkansas. It runs like this: The man from New Mexico washes his face and throws out his wash water. The man from Texas comes along, washes his face, and leaves the water in the basin. The man from Arkansas comes along and washes his face in the water the man from Texas has left in the basin.

Of course, the order varies according to the state in which the story is told, but there is no disagreement about there being but one basin to a ranch and one towel to a basin. So when I came upon a row of shining tin washbasins and a strictly sanitary face towel hanging above each basin, I was, or thought I was, prepared for anything. But I wasn't.

In this tale the heroine, a tender-hearted creature, had raised a 'pet two-year dogie,' named Peter. (Of course two-year-old Peter was not at all a dogie but a robust young bull.) The tenderness of his mistress's heart had succeeded in saving Peter from the cruelty of branding-iron or marking-knife.

Hero quarrels with heroine and rides off by himself. His horse falls and breaks its own neck and hero's leg. Hero lies three days with broken leg, ranch people apparently being incapable of following his tracks and finding him. Anyway, they don't. On the third day, Peter wanders into the foreground and gives hero an inspiration. With his suspenders (dead giveaway that he's no cowboy) he hogties Peter. A little vague here about getting Peter on his side with all four feet bunched together, but broken-legged hero does it. Boy, what suspenders!

Hero removes one of his spurs, beats it between two stones into a branding iron, builds fire (suspenders still holding), heats branding-iron, and brands the letters H E L P from stem to stern on Peter's port side (suspenders still holding). Then hero, with one good leg, flops Peter over and brands a large mule shoe $\cap$ on Peter's starboard ribs. He then unties Peter, who instead of charging hero trots home to bellow his wrongs to heroine. He presents himself broadside and she reads H E L P. He reverses the billboard and she sees the mule shoe. (Reader suspense here: *What* does the mystic mule shoe mean?)

But our heroine is not mystified; she knows it means Mule Shoe Spring. She surmises that hero needs help. But why such a superman should seems strange. Here occurs one of the emotional crises with which the tale abounds. Heroine's indignation over the desecration of Peter the Pet is pitted against love for broken-legged Hero, the Heroic. She doesn't know whether to organize a rescue party or let him come hopping home on his good leg. Of course her tender-heartedness prevails and hero is rescued, little the worse for wear.

I'm sorry I do not know the name of the makers of those suspenders.

'And why the hell did he go to the trouble of beatin' a spur out straight, even if he could of?' one cowboy to whom I read the tale snorted. 'A spur held between two crossed sticks makes a purty good branding-iron as it is.' The tale continued: Villain is being pursued by posse hastily recruited from local experienced cowhands led by sheriff. They pursue to roundup where seventeen other equally experienced cowhands sit about campfire.

'Seen anything of villain?' sheriff demands. Well, a stranger had been there a short time before, asking for food, seemed hungry and looked like a villain, shifty-eyed, nervous. All had noticed it. Ha! and what kind of a horse was he riding? Sherlock Holmes sheriff wants to know. Might be helpful in spotting villain. Seventeen experienced cowhands look sheepish. 'We didn't notice,' in mass confession.

For the exigencies of the plot this was a necessary development. As a picture of a bunch of early-day cowboys it ranks with the criminally insane in literature. I should have been forewarned and handed the manuscript back to its rightful crittersizer, but I didn't want to shoe those two horses myself, so in fulfillment of my side of the bargain I sent it back to its author, with exhaustive footnotes and reams of criticisms as tactful as I could find words for. With vast relief my cowboy collaborator shod the horses (they were the rebellious ones) and we thought the incident closed. We were very much mistaken.

On return from his next trip to Baldwin's for the mail my literary colleague burst into my presence waving a telegram. 'I done rode home on a high lope,' he explained breathlessly.

Telegrams were rare. They came from Magdalena by mail, possibly a week after their sender had trustfully committed them to the telegraph company. This one, however, had lain only four days in the post-office. A stout-hearted cowpony had covered the last few miles of its journey with record-breaking speed.

I tore open the envelope, while the messenger watched my face anxiously.

'Is it bad news?' he asked with manifest sympathy. I nodded. Then I read the telegram aloud:

THANKS FOR THE FINE CRITICISM STOP   FEEL IT NECESSARY TO CONFER FURTHER WITH YOU STOP   PLEASE ENGAGE ROOM AND BOARD FOR SELF AND SECRETARY SOME PLACE YOUR IMMEDIATE VICINITY STOP   LEAVING FOR DATIL THURSDAY NEXT STOP   PUBLISHER DEMANDING BOOK IMMEDIATELY HENCE HASTE.

It was signed by a woman I knew only as the employer of the sister of our cowboy employee! It developed that the public knew her name better than I did.

But to our domestic crisis. 'Engage room and board for self and secretary some place your immediate vicinity.'

'Engage big corral for herd of steers your immediate vicinity' would have been a comparably reasonable reverse telegram.

The secretary's brother had been making mental calculations

'They're in Magdalena right now,' he concluded, 'and seein' as how it's my own sister, I reckon I got to go meet them. Can I borry the team and buckboard?'

Thus it was that we became 'source material' and for the first time realized that there was supposed to be 'dramatic value' in the life we lived. The secretary carried a notebook with her constantly, and at a raised eyebrow from her employer would whip it out and fill a page or two with those curlicues which were our first vision of shorthand.

'Would you mind saying that again' — and we'd say it again, feeling very self-conscious and very foolish.

Finally Ray, the ever-resourceful, took matters in hand.

'If it's local color she wants, I say we should see that she gets it,' he confided; 'all hands be ready for a buffalo hunt.'

Gravely we informed our guest that a few buffalo still roamed about and we felt sure she would find local color in participating in a buffalo hunt. Of course buffalo never came onto the mountains, but the lady novelist didn't think of that. She swallowed the buffalo hunt, hair, hide, and hump.

We rode forth, a half-dozen of us, armed to the teeth. The lady came along on our most trustworthy nag. The bewildered 'buffalo' was waiting, long-suffering old Tude, reliable packhorse of the remuda, accustomed to having almost anything lashed to his back. But he didn't like a grizzly bear hide. His whole demeanor advertised outrage. Bowlegs had released him and vanished only a moment before. He was still standing uncertain about what was expected of him when a bunch of yelling, shooting horsemen broke through the timber.

The lady author was far, far in the rear, clinging for dear life to the 'knob' on her saddle. Tude decided to go home, and started. He finally got there after a several-mile enforced detour and after all our ammunition had been fired into the air.

At that the lady author, seeking her local color, saw some extra-

fine horsemanship, but, alas, she was not grateful for this contribution to the source material in her stenographer's notebook.

'A very silly performance,' she pronounced coldly, as she slid
heavily from her saddle.

Nevertheless she continued to sell 'Wild West stuff' and retired
in the fullness of time to a pontifical position in a literary colony.

Gene Rhodes

Reasoning that if 'Peter the Bull' could find his way into print, I should be able to write a story myself, I did, and it was published. I bought a buggy with the forty-dollar proceeds. Riding in the buggy to the post-office one day, I took from the hand of the post-master a thick square undersized envelope, addressed in fine but not too legible handwriting. The letter began 'Dear Madam' and was signed 'Eugene Manlove Rhodes.'

Eugene Manlove Rhodes! The name was faintly disturbing. I'd heard much of a 'locoed cowpuncher down 'round Engle' named Gene Rhodes, who enjoyed a reputation for 'ridin' anything that wears hair and goes on four legs,' but who was a bit cracked; for didn't he carry around in his bedroll an enormous scrapbook (it had

once served to hold samples of men's tailoring goods), and didn't he
put poems clipped from magazines and newspapers in this scrapbook, and didn't he sit by the campfire of nights and read these
poems over and over? This and many other like evidences of de-
rangement were all that I knew of an individual named Rhodes —
one who couldn't conceivably carry the middle 'name of Manlove.

With considerable difficulty I read the letter. Gene's correspondents will sympathize. The writer, it seems, had read my published story, and by one of those occasional freaks, found it practically identical in plot with an unpublished story of his own. How
had it come about, he wanted to know, that I could take an incident
so typical of our country that we had both seized upon it for a plot,
and turn it into cash? He was minded to do the same if I could suggest any sure-fire formula. With many apologies for the unwar-
ranted intrusion upon my valuable time, and scarcely able to hope I
would deign to answer, he subscribed himself my humble serv-
ant.

Suddenly I remembered. There had been a story in Charles F.
Lummis's little magazine, *Land of Sunshine*, published in Los
Angeles, signed by one Eugene Manlove Rhodes, but of course at
the time I had not associated it in my mind with bronco-busting
Gene Rhodes of local renown for his daredevil horsemanship.
That *Land of Sunshine* story was literature as well as life; the life I
knew, the life its author knew, but my Gene Rhodes its author?
Scarcely.

But I answered Gene's letter at considerable length. I had had
my second story accepted by now and felt qualified to pass out advice about 'the writing game.' Anyway, the advice I gave Gene
was sound. I told him to get in touch with Bob Davis, then editor
of the Munsey Publications. Mr. Davis in his dealings with me had
been kind. In the same mail with my letter to Gene went one to
Editor Davis, in which, referring to something encouraging he had

said in his latest letter to me, I wrote, 'I prophesy that this Eugene Manlove Rhodes will make Agnes Morley Cleaveland look like thirty cents.' And was I a true prophet!

Kind Mr. Davis replied promptly: 'Tell the young man to send something along and don't be too discouraged. You may find that all Rhodes do not lead to ruin.' The last tale I had sent to Davis was based upon an idea Bowlegs had furnished me — that of kidnaping the stenographer of our late literary visitor and forcing her to write something worth a cent a word, which was what our guest had told us was her recompense. Of course, we regarded this with exactly the same skepticism that Gus Wheeler had entertained about the five-dollar-per-plate banquet. Bowlegs seemed to hold the notion that it was the typing that gave such incredible value to words. My fantastic story had been about a man who knew where Adams Diggings were and hoped to finance his proof by the proceeds from a 'cent a word' forced out of a Smith-Premier.

Bob Davis promptly wrote to Gene and invited him to submit a story. Although Davis rejected the story, this was the turning-point in Gene's career. However, with that overgenerosity in giving credit so characteristic of him, he always insisted that his letter to me was the turning-point, that it was a toss of a coin: if I deigned to answer, he would turn from cowpunching to literature; if from my barren heights of the 'arrived' I did not answer, he would take it as a sign that he must stick to what he could do — ride a horse — and leave letters to others who seemed to him better qualified.

That Davis accepted my stories and not Gene's was proof of his discernment, for Munsey was using mere yarns, and Gene was writing literature. 'Too much the essayist,' was the Davis verdict.

I subsequently read Gene's stories in the more literary type of magazine and gave up writing, in discouragement. I could never hope to compete. My action disturbed Gene no end. He labored with me as long as he lived, and after his death a mutual friend reported to me that in his last interview with Gene the latter had said, 'You tell Agnes Morley Cleaveland I'm goin' to haunt her from the other world till she goes back to writing.'

One of his own futile efforts to encourage me had been what he and I called the 'Cleaveland-Rhodes Cattle Company.' It proved on the contrary to be the capstone of my resolution to quit that 'writing game' about which I had so smugly advised Gene some years earlier.

A ridiculous incident had occurred in Datil. Corky, whose eyesight wasn't good, had 'stolen' a longear presumably belonging to the V + T Cattle Company. The presumption was based upon mathematical probabilities. It developed, however, that the longear had been following one of Corky's own cows. He had, in short, 'stolen' a calf from himself. Gene enjoyed the tale hugely when I told it to him. He saw a story in it and insisted that I write it. I insisted that *he* write it. Indignantly, he declared that he did not appropriate other people's 'material.' This seemed to me straining at gnats, for it was he and not I who saw the fiction value in the episode. I made up an elaborate Christmas card and presented Corky Wallace's calf to him for a Christmas present. He promptly informed me that he had stolen too many cattle to be 'hornswoggled' into stealing Corky's calf by any such raw subterfuge. It has become a matter of literary controversy whether on occasion Gene did or did not steal beef. (Practically all of us claimed to have done so on occasion.) But he wasn't going to steal this particular calf. I tried to reason with him that his logic would leave only Corky the moral right to turn the calf into literature. We both were forced to admit that was out.

Meantime, as Gene reminded me in another letter, the calf was growing up. We had a maverick on our hands. Something had to be done. 'We'll both write the story,' was the compromise, and the 'Cleaveland-Rhodes Cattle Company' came into being. Gene gave it the title 'The Prodigal Calf.' In the face of this stroke of genius, I went completely dead and useless. I could draw no inspiration from that calf. Finally I told Gene I was sick of the critter and proposed that we barbecue it and set up a hamburger sandwich stand instead of trying to run a cattle company, after the cattle business had fallen upon such evil days anyhow.

Gene replied that we should finish what we had started, and commanded me to 'climb upon that typewriter and stay there until the prodigal calf has yielded us some profits.'

But it was no use. The calf proved as stubborn on paper as had Aunt Laura's in the flesh. It died on Charles K. Fields's desk when 'Cheerio' was editor of *Sunset*. Charlie objected to my name as collaborator with the far better-known name of Eugene Manlove Rhodes. I told Gene to take my name off, and he became a good exhibit of a man with apoplexy.

In that years-long correspondence of ours, Gene revealed a passion for the underdog that, in a less balanced temperament, would have carried over into sentimentality; but Gene knew too well the value of personal effort to have made the mistake of wanting to withhold its discipline from anybody. He had the same problem of dual lives with which I had always been confronted. In no small degree our friendship arose from the fact that when we were together we could usually make the transitions from one life to the other without explanation or apology. Only once did the transition become difficult. One summer he spent some time with his mother on the outskirts of Pasadena and I happened to be spending some time in Los Angeles. I had an automobile but Gene hadn't, so I would call for him and deliver him back home after our expedition, whatever it might be, was over. He had been long enough in a conventional setting to feel that he should express regret at this reversal of rôles, until I reminded him that our cattle-country code held it to be the highest form of compliment to allow every fellow to do what the situation demanded of him and to assume that he wanted to do it. Gene gave in, until the night we went to a Hollywood Bowl pageant. It was after one o'clock when we drew up to his

door. He started to protest at allowing me to make the long drive
home at that hour of the morning.

'Don't weaken, pardner,' I admonished. He watched me drive
away, and I knew that my insistence on going alone was giving him
a bout with his double code.

Then coincidence played neatly into his hands. The morning
papers carried the story of a holdup perpetrated during the night
by a 'short-haired female bandit.' By special delivery I received a
marked copy of the paper with an appended note: 'I now understand, but you might have trusted me. — E. M. R.'

Some of our happiest jaunts were visits to the studios of Ed
Borein and Maynard Dixon. On these occasions we were all experts together, not in the field of art — far from it in Gene's and
my cases — but in the field of life as it was jauntily lived in 'the
wide-open spaces where men are mean,' as Gene parodied the old
saw.

Then there was the evening spent in Will Rogers' home, when
Gene egged me on to 'tell one,' after he and our host had each had
his turn. It was fun not having to make a frame for our stories —
just to be able to tell them as they happened, sure of being understood. I recall that Will Rogers said: 'I don't like villains in my
pictures. I never had a villain chasin' me round, ever, in my life,
and I don't like 'em doin' it on the screen. But I got to take it, I
s'pose, in the interests of art.' This led to a discussion not of what
constitutes art, but of what constitutes a villain, and a mutual
agreement that none of us quite knew.

On the occasion of my first visit with Gene to Maynard Dixon's
studio — this was later and in San Francisco — I had the fun of
relating to them both the story of how I was able to accede to a
request Gene had made of me very early in our acquaintance. This
was the story: Maynard Dixon had lost all of his personal posses-
sions, including his studio properties, in the San Francisco fire of
1906 and had gone to New York City and there reopened his

studio. Since he was illustrating some Western stories, he needed cowboy accoutrement — boots, chaps, hats, etc., used ones — for his models. Not having too much money, and the market for these things being far more restricted than it is today, he was faced with a problem. He put it before his good friend Gene Rhodes: how was he to get his 'props' at the least possible cost?

Gene happened not to be in New Mexico when he received the letter, and forwarded the Dixon request to me, expressing the hope that I could help his friend 'out of a jackpot.' The obligation to help a friend of a friend out of a jackpot was not to be lightly thrust aside. I held Maynard Dixon's letter in my hand as I stepped from the post-office to the sidewalk in Silver City, where I happened to be at the time, but I hadn't any clear notion of what I could do about the request, especially with that 'cheaply as possible' clause in it. How did I know what Maynard Dixon in New York considered cheap? Certainly cowboy paraphernalia was never inexpensive as we figured expense.

I lifted my eyes from the sheet in my hand and looked into a pair of eyes I had never seen before, but they were friendly understanding eyes and they belonged to a young cowpuncher whose way into the post-office I was blocking.

'You are just what I'm looking for,' I blurted. 'I'm in a jackpot.'

Sympathy shone from those friendly eyes at once. 'It's shore too bad for a lady to be in a jackpot,' he answered me earnestly. 'Kin I help?'

We stepped aside and I read him Maynard's letter and Gene's note passing the buck to me. Then I looked at him appealingly, passing the buck along.

'Leave it to me,' he said gallantly. 'I'll rustle around and see what I can scrape together. Meet you at Kelley's saddle shop when I come in from the ranch next Wednesday.'

He didn't ask my name nor I his, nor was there any mention of money.

The following Wednesday, I shipped to Maynard Dixon these goods:

1   stock saddle and saddle blanket in better than fair condition
1   still sightly Stetson hat
1   run-over-at-the-heels-but-wearable pair of cowboy boots
1   pair concho-mounted leather chaps
1   one-eared bridle
1   pair of drooped-rowel spurs
1   rawhide quirt
1   metal-studded pair of leather cuffs

My rescuer scratched his head when I asked him the amount of the bill I should enclose to Maynard Dixon. 'Wa-a-al,' he drawled, 'that's a little hard to say. I won't charge you for the things I stole, but I had to promise one or two of the boys I'd pay 'em. I reckon if I don't show up at the ranch with about sixty dollars they'll take it out of my hide.'

I saved his hide for him and Maynard promptly reimbursed me, many times over, for in addition to his letter of thanks and his money order, came a painting of a girl and a man riding together across a twilight-lit desert toward a hazy purple mesa. The picture was inscribed to me.

When our house burned in the memorable Berkeley fire of 1923, and with it everything except what I could carry out in my hands, Maynard Dixon's picture was one of the two or three objects I had the presence of mind to rescue. It had always stood in my thoughts as a living link between those two lives of mine. Its loss would have been unbearable.

Years later, Maynard Dixon stood before it and speculated whether or not he had improved any since painting it in 1908. He hasn't, no matter what more enlightened critics than I might say. Into that picture went everything that a man can say with a paintbrush. Gene agreed with me.

In that years-long correspondence of ours, we found ourselves in pretty general agreement on most subjects. And it is for that reason that I am presumptuous enough to believe that I know what he would be saying were he alive today and confronted with the world as it is. I cannot hear him saying much about 'keeping out of war,' but I can hear him shouting defiance to the world in behalf of keeping out of slavery, personal or national. He was never known to shun a fight. How far he went out of his way to encounter one is another of those unsolved literary problems. I know that he carried numerous scars about which he talked little, and that he enjoyed the reputation of being 'a bad man to fool with.' Those who talked least usually were.

One of his visible scars was a slightly drawn little finger. A youngster I knew who had heard something of Gene's past brushes with fighting men asked him about it.

'Oh, a fellow cut me with a knife,' Gene told the wide-eyed boy.

'Did he do it on purpose?' the questioner asked hopefully.

'Oh, no. Accident.'

Gene waited for the disappointment to register, and then added, 'The guy was aimin' at my heart.'

That more than one guy had aimed at his heart is unquestionable.

From his mother, who visited many times in our California home, I heard many tales of his childhood — stories of unselfishness that made his a truly noble character. One story she told me concerned his mature years. Gene had a slight and not unattractive impediment in speech — difficulty with the letter *r*, hence difficulty in pronouncing his own name. It is impossible to reproduce in type his exact enunciation, but strangers often mistook his 'Rhodes' for 'Thodes.' One day, so his mother related, three strangers rode into his horse camp and asked for Mr. Rhodes. 'I'm Thodes,' Gene politely informed them. 'But it is *Rhodes* we want to see,' the visitors insisted. Gene regarded them for an instant in silence and then turned and bellowed to a comrade some distance away, 'Hey,

Pete, come over here, and tell these sons-of-guns what my name is and find out what they want.'

It developed that they wanted to buy horses. Gene had horses he wanted to sell, desperately. The trade was made, the horses were rounded up and put in a corral. The money Gene greatly needed was about to be handed over when he casually asked what they wanted the horses for. The would-be purchasers told him they were buying for one of two belligerent nations which were at war on the opposite side of the globe.

Gene walked to the corral, laid down the bars, and drove the horses out. 'I'm on the other side of that war,' he said nonchalantly. Quixotic? But Gene!

Later, in Hollywood, he was to throw away a glittering cash offer because the Script Department insisted upon a band of cowboys raiding an immigrant train and stealing the immigrant girls.

I was stepping into my car to drive to Pacific Beach to visit him and 'Mary and Martha,' his inspired name for his wife, when the telegram announcing his death was handed to me.

At that instant a door closed and a key was turned in the lock, for nobody else will again paint the life we lived as did Gene Rhodes. To no one else has it been given to live it and to immortalize it in words of sheer genius. That he called me friend goes far toward balancing life's ledger with its violently fluctuating record of triumphs and disappointments.

We were NOT FARMERS

ALL the pamphlets issued by all the chambers of commerce, with their pictures of hayfields, bean patches, and dairy herds to the contrary notwithstanding, New Mexico, as a whole, cannot be rated as an agricultural state. But we're coming along, brother, we're coming along.

That small segment of New Mexico at the time about which I write was strictly a cattle-raising community. Had there been no cattle, however, there could have been a natural hay crop far oftener than there was; for the native grama grass grew in such abundance that it could frequently have been harvested in the cañon bottoms and on the wide stretches of plain. Occasionally when the season was exceptional, say once in seven years, the grama outstripped the cattle and we had a hay crop nevertheless. Then other work stopped and all hands turned out to put up hay.

First, there was a rush to put long-disused machinery in order, and more particularly to find teams which would not go into hyster-

ics at the unfamiliar sight and sound of mowing-machine and hay-
rake.

I recall a ride of my own, perched on the high iron seat of a rattle-
trap mowing-machine, behind a supposedly gentle team of mules.
But when the sickle-blade began to clatter behind them, these
mules took the bits in their teeth and did a splendid job of running
away. I couldn't throw that sawtooth blade out of gear, and my
dreams were haunted for a long time by the memory of it as the
mower bumped and slithered over the rutted landscape.

Only a skill in maintaining balance, and possibly composure,
acquired by years on top of a horse, enabled me to ride that bucking
mower without being thrown in the path of the sickle-blade. However, mules and I returned to the hayfield uninjured, to be greeted
with, 'Well, ya sure pulled leather *that* time! Why didn't you spur
the thing in the shoulder?'

No heroics; albeit I rather fancied myself a hero — until quitting
time, when I was assisting in unharnessing this same team of
mules. They had been transferred to the hayrack and had plodded
along serenely all day, apparently having completely forgotten
their earlier brainstorm.

I was on one side of the team, Jesse Simpson, the foreman, on
the other, unhooking and unsnapping, in synchronized teamwork
— or should have been. But I didn't unhook my second trace in
time, and by some perverse instinct that mule team sensed that it
was attached to the hayrack by a single strap of leather, a good
stout trace, to be sure, but only one of four. Away it went. Away
went the hayrack with it, at first sidewise, then end over end.
Jesse on horseback brought the mules back eventually. We never
troubled to pick up the splinters that had been the hayrack. As
Jesse laid up the corral bars behind the mules, he observed casually,
'Book-learnin' sure is a great thing.'

We knocked together another hayrack and moved camp up to
Chavez Cañon, whose whole floor was a mauve-and-purple carpet,

with nap a yard deep. The feathered-top grama in full bloom gives the illusion of deep-piled plush. The first swath made by the mowing-machine seemed desecration, little less than cutting into a holy carpet.

The hay crew was what might have been expected — every able-bodied adult who could be drafted, regardless of age or sex. There were three girls, a local ranch girl, a visitor from Los Angeles, and myself. There was 'Old Man' Campbell, a dour recluse Scotchman who stubbornly held to the theory that there was gold in these here hills and spent his life digging tunnel after tunnel — in vain. There was young Bob Matheson, also Scotch, who kept his fellow countryman on his conscience and did not let the old man go too hungry or too cold and, greatest service of all, let him dig without interference or ridicule. There was a 'lunger' who insisted he was equal to any man in the crew and *almost* proved it. There was Jesse and a few others.

We worked like beavers every moment of daylight. The rake followed directly behind the mowing-machine — no need to allow time for curing. Hay cured in process of handling in this high dry climate. The new hayrack came along as soon as the winnows were raked together and carted them off to the stacks — slightly lopsided stacks, possibly, for we were not farmers, and it had been at least seven years since anyone had had opportunity to exercise whatever small hay-stacking talent he possessed. But the haystacks grew. It was all idyllic — except for one circumstance. Two of the men had been 'jarring at each other' from the beginning — some old feud fanned to flame by the exasperations of life in camp.

Then one day I came unexpectedly around the corner of a haystack just as one of the feudists slid off of it, pitchfork in hand. His adversary, similarly armed, stood waiting. Jousting with pitchforks has unpleasant suggestions, and I interposed my unexpected self between the two squared-off knights with an air of what

I hope was nonchalance and announced that dinner was ready. I'd seen the waved towel signal.

We walked to camp together, I chatting brightly between the two of them. But there was no deceiving myself. The bad blood had begun to boil. I saw both of them unobtrusively take six-shooters from their bedrolls and strap them around their middles — no hollow gesture in that era.

Julia, the Los Angeles guest, saw it too and whispered a question to me.

'Got to break it up, somehow, or there'll be trouble,' I whispered back. 'Something must stop it.'

What more potent than a premature explosion! I cast about for some, any, plausible pretext. There it was! The coffee-pot was boiling over.

With a yip of simulated rage, I leaped forward and kicked the coffee-pot ten yards out of camp. 'What loco blossom filled that pot too full?' I demanded, 'and who put too much pork in the beans?' The bean pot followed the coffee-pot. 'No use to have bread without coffee or beans,' and the dutch oven upset into the fire.

Then I sat down on a bedroll and burst into tears. 'I can't stand it, I can't stand it!' I blubbered. 'It's too much!'

'Can't stand *what?* What's too much?' Solicitous questions came from all sides after a moment's shocked silence.

'Everything,' I brokenly assured the would-be comforters. 'Everything's too much. Life is too m-u-c-h!'

The dazed audience exchanged apprehensive glances.

'Pretty hot sun out there,' someone diagnosed.

'It isn't the sun,' I protested fiercely. 'It's life. I can't stand *life* — ow-o-oo!'

Julia, the only one who was prepared for the act, played her part. She put a comforting arm around my shoulder and murmured vapid nothings.

Whether the two for whose benefit the phony brainstorm was staged realized what was happening or not, I was never sure. But the ruse worked. Solemnly they retrieved the coffee-pot and the bean pot. One began to mix a fresh batch of biscuit dough. The other 'built' a new brew of coffee, being careful not to fill the pot too full.

Before the second meal had been prepared and eaten the atmosphere was once more tranquil. The two belligerents apparently decided they could stand life, even if I couldn't, but it was some time before I dared explain my sudden aberration to all of its witnesses. Meantime, I went about with the stigma upon me of an heretofore unsuspected tendency to throw fits.

Haying continued with all speed — until the **next** interruption. 'Old Man' Campbell had arrogated to himself the task of building the fires — all of them. He was as set in his conviction that he alone was competent to build a campfire as he was that there was gold in Kid Spring Cañon, and we were disposed to humor him on both counts.

But one day, the old man was not about when I thought a fire should be built, and built one. He came upon the scene when the bootleg fire was blazing triumphantly. I apologized and attempted to explain. It was no use. The old man was deeply affronted. He sat himself down on his bedroll, his rifle between his knees, the picture of despair.

'I'm really *very* sorry,' I repeated weakly. 'I didn't stop to think ——'

Apparently he hadn't heard me.

'I'm no good any more,' he muttered, as if to himself. 'I can't even be trusted to build a fire. No place left in this life for me. I'm through. I guess I better kill myself.'

I was genuinely distressed at the seriousness with which he had taken my breach of our established camp routine, but words did no good so I turned to other tasks, and when I looked again the old man was not there. No one had seen him go.

'He'll be back,' we all reassured one another. 'Nothing to worry about.'

But he didn't come back; not that night, nor the next day, nor the next. Haying stopped, of course, and we scoured the countryside. Young Matheson's distress was great. A common highland ancestry was evidently a tight bond.

For my part, I knew I should feel like a murderer if we found his body, with his gun still in his hand, under some piñon tree. When I hear radio calls for missing persons, I sometimes think of this puny search of ours, a dozen tiny ants scurrying about looking for a lost comrade in endless uninhabited miles. On the fourth day, word came that the old man was in Magdalena. We never discovered how he got there.

The rain, against whose threatened coming we had been feverishly competing, overtook us before we got back from our search and our harvesting was at an end for the season — which is to say, for the next five to seven years.

Today we old-timers argue the question of whether rabbit brush is 'taking the country.' Those who rise to its defense say that it affords shelter for the cattle against the strong spring winds and tends to deter soil erosion. Moreover, the miles upon miles of woody-stalked, gray-green-leaved bushes that often grow shoulder-high blossom out in the fall into a mass of bloom that even to prejudiced eyes is a glorious riot of yellow and gold.

But against these advantages, there is the fact that the rabbit brush is marching up and down our flatlands wiping out the grama grass as it marches. And that's bad, very bad; for we cattlemen lived and moved and had our being because of grama grass.

Our most important contribution to the horticulture of the West, however, is the piñon tree. A species of pine, it is too scrubby to be used as lumber, but it does furnish fuel of a quality unsurpassed and unsurpassable. I stand on that statement, defying all challengers. The piñon is as resinous as pitch pine, but is a denser wood and

burns longer. A rich piñon knot, too heavy to lift, can be set afire
with a single match (if you're skillful about it). When it gets to
burning, stand back or scorch.

Aside from having warmed the Southwest for a countless number
of generations, the piñon tree bears a crop that has furnished food
for the same generations, and is today one of considerable commercial value. The piñon nut is known to the trade as the pine
nut, possibly because there is no letter ñ in the English alphabet
and the pronunciation of 'pinyon,' were it so spelled, would be
pinion instead of pin-*yown'* as it should be. I feel personally
affronted when I am offered at a candy store a small cellophane
bag of 'pine nuts,' price ten cents, and am told they came from the
'pinion' tree.

I'm accustomed to piñons in carload lots or even warehouse lots!
I believe it was fifty carloads that went out of Magdalena in our
best piñon year. The wholesale house who shipped them told me
they'd drawn a single check for thirty-five thousand dollars and
Magdalena is only one of a dozen shipping points in New Mexico
alone. There is also Arizona, Colorado and Utah. Eastern candy-
makers and more particularly New York's pushcart trade furnish
the market, and there has been a steadily increasing foreign demand. The nut's oil content is as rich as its food value is high.

But, alas, the piñon is a rugged individualist and bears its crop
not with any regularity, but when it gets ready. Whatever the
natural conditions which determine when it bears and when it
doesn't, they have not yet been established. Possibly they will be.
Meantime, it pleases me to think that the piñon tree is doing as it
pleases when it pleases.

Certainly good piñon years are unpredictable until it is too late
for adequate planning. This may explain why no attempt has been
made to cultivate piñons. It is only in recent years that owners of
land with heavy stands of piñon have made any effort to prevent
all and sundry from coming on to their property to harvest the
crop.

When the season is good and the market reasonable, pickers will receive up to ten cents per pound. A good wood rat's nest will yield as high as fifty pounds for about three minutes' work in destroying the nest and shoveling out the nuts. But wood rats' nests are the nuggets in the run-of-the-mill mining for piñons. The far greater yield is from the fallen nuts under the trees, after the first hard frost has burst open the cones and sent the nuts showering down.

The technic of picking piñons is to sit oneself under a tree and begin to pick. It's tedious but strains no muscles other than those used in shifting position, a hardship which can be mitigated by the use of a Chinese fanlike split-bamboo rake, a labor-saving device which I claim credit for introducing.

When the field surrounding the particular tree under which you are sitting and laboring has been fairly well cleaned up, you spread a wagon sheet under the tree and shake down more nuts and half-opened cones and twigs and débris generally, which may or may not be worth while. It's always a question, for there are so many more trees at hand where the reaping may be better without this hullabaloo.

There are those, especially the very young, who gather piñons flat on their stomachs, inching their way along like ponderous lizards in a sandy wash.

An entire family gathering piñon nuts at ten cents a pound can have done very well at the end of a season! The piñon crop has tided many a homesteader over a hard winter.

If one makes a serious business of it, of course one goes into camp and stays. In piñon years, the night campfires of piñon-pickers glow on the landscape near and far.

Indians flock from the reservations and the unemployed, white, black, and brown, from the towns. In every sort of vehicle, so long as its wheels will turn, they overflow into the piñon country, on a sort of combination picnic and working for a living hegira. There

are no rent, light, telephone, water, or heat bills to torment, and
the piñons can be eaten, if worst comes, so it is little wonder the
piñon pickers become something of a problem to the permanent
residents of the community. In fact, many owners of patented
land have been forced to forbid entry to this increasing horde, who
scare away the cattle even if they don't butcher them (which they
sometimes do), and who clean out the fuel which the rightful owner
had reserved for his own use. In countless other ways they consti-
tute themselves a nuisance if not a menace.

A large sheep-owner recently posted his range against piñon
pickers, on the ground that he wanted to fatten his sheep on the
nuts. Sheep, hogs, and turkey will on a good piñon diet put on fat
at a miraculous rate. Every Southwest housewife and schoolteacher has occasion to dread a good piñon year. Piñons are little
globules of fat encased in brittle brown shells, and when stepped
on leave a grease spot that has been well ground into the rug.
This is the housewife's plaint. The schoolteachers object to the
sharp crack, crack all over the schoolroom as the nut shells split
in two between skillful young teeth. There is an especial skill in
eating piñons which makes detection difficult, or would, but for the
crack. The experienced piñon-eater slips a nut into his mouth,
works it into position with lips and tongue, and bites down on its
one angular edge. The shell falls away in two halves, which may be
adroitly spat out without the fingers having gone near the mouth
after the nut has once been delivered.

The invention of a piñon silencer would be a boon to the school-
children of the southwest. Teacher could never catch them at it.
There are countless inventions for shelling them. Rolling between
two boards isn't bad.

One young man teacher of adequate height, whose rural log
schoolhouse stood in a piñon grove, was driven to the use of drastic
measures. When school reconvened after each recess he lined up
the student body. Each boy he grasped by the ankles and held

aloft and shook vigorously until all the piñons secreted in pockets rattled down. The girls he put on their honor. Moreover, they had fewer pockets. He reported that the method was only partially successful. The youngsters enjoyed the game. It delayed the pursuit of knowledge.

On the long winter evenings when we first came to the Datils our favorite recreation was to play mumble peg in a shallow box of packed dirt and eat piñons, spitting the shells half across the room into the open fireplace.

And a long solitary ride can be made far more tolerable by a pint or so of piñon nuts in the chaps pocket. Passing the jar of piñons is a gesture of hospitality for the ranch hostess, but the uninitiated may suffer as much embarrassment on first being offered a piñon as do those who have an artichoke set before them for the first time. If I were trying to unmask a pretender, one claiming to be a Westerner, I'd hand him a piñon nut. He might successfully imitate our dress, our speech, and our manners, but unless he'd had long practice eating piñons he'd give himself plumb away.

Indians PLAYED

THEIR PART

Sʜᴏʀᴛʟʏ before her marriage to Tom Reynolds, Lora had taken up a homestead of one hundred and sixty acres just outside the Eastern Forest boundary and adjoining part of Ray's property. Ray had discovered this vacant quarter-section after the general belief prevailed that no such 'close-in' land remained, and had assisted Lora in getting herself appointed postmaster to one of the six or seven fourth-class post offices in Catron County, a position she held until national politics decreed otherwise.

She agitated to have the county seat changed from Reserve tc Datil, and might have succeeded had it not again been for that long arm of national politics. As it was, her dream of Datil's becoming a metropolis, in spite of its advantageous position at the forks where the Reserve road branched off from the main highway, was doomed. She did sell a little of her land for business enterprises, and she and Tom conduct one themselves — catering to tourists, of course.

I had never used my own homestead right, for the reason that Jack Howard had beaten me to the spot I wanted. Although only eleven years old when I first saw it, I never coveted any other spot on this green earth. But ultimately Jack Howard died; twice, as a matter of fact. I am not sure just how he managed it, but there was a public announcement of his demise and his wife, whom he had married late in life, together with his friends, mourned him as dead. Years later, an old-timer who had known him told me that he had seen Jack recently and that Jack had sent me his regards and explained that he had taken the easiest way he knew to get away from his wife. He was past ninety when his departure from this earth was made final.

It was about the time of his first death that he told Fred Baldwin to sell his Datil property for him. His flat was his pre-emption claim. Newton and I bought it in 1903. Followed thirty-three years of what Tom Reynolds always referred to as the 'wind-work' on the place; thirty-three years during which Newton paid taxes and I hugged to my breast, as a little girl hugs her best-beloved doll, the knowledge that Jack Howard's flat was actually mine. Finally the 'wind-work,' the talk era, ended and logs, rock, and sheet-iron supplanted it.

'You must think up some nice romantic name for your little ranch,' friends advised. Sacrilege! The name is Jack Howard Flat. It lies in the heart of the Datils three miles from where the White House stood, at a spot where the main cañon bulges a bit and three lateral lesser cañons lead from it.

During the war, Ray took down the White House and moved it to what Lora calls the 'village.' On some of the logs were faint traces of the whitewash of Schlatter's cross put there twenty years earlier. In its new setting in Datil it still seems self-conscious and ill at ease. Ray named it 'Navajo Lodge,' built a flock of Navajo hogans around it to give authenticity to the name, and brought over a number of Navajo families from the lower end of the Alamosa Creek, Indians who were ethnologically Navajos but called themselves Alamos as well. One of the old Indians told me the story of their Big Walk.

When in the sixties the government was compelled to exert severe discipline upon the unruly Navajos who had committed a series of outrages against their peaceful neighbors, the Pueblo tribes, the Mexican settlers, as well as the pioneers from the East, and had delegated to Kit Carson the task of rounding them up and bringing them into old Fort Wingate, pending discussion of their ultimate fate, a small band, possibly two hundred men, women, and children, eluded capture.

This little band walked from some point in the vicinity of what is now Fort Defiance to their present home, near the mouth of the Alamosa Creek, a distance of possibly one hundred miles. What makes the adventure notable is the fact that they were fugitives and must draw subsistence from a country which offered little water, and a scanty supply of food. Considering they had no firearms nor pack-animals, and must carry on their backs the minimum of necessary equipment, along with the younger children, the Big Walk is an heroic contribution to the annals of people who have preferred death to loss of liberty.

That the passion for freedom still persists in them is attested by the fact that within this generation, when their case was brought to the official attention of the Indian Bureau, and that body decided they should be removed to the Reservation, the Alamosa Indians held a solemn conclave and swore to drink poison to the last man, woman, and child, before submitting, even though their purely physical well-being promised to be enhanced by the move. Uncle Sam had to give in.

When, after incredible hardship and much loss of life, the little half-starved remnant arrived at the Alamosa Creek, with its presumably steady flow of water (not very steady, it turned out to be), they must have felt that they had reached a Garden of Eden. Their arrival at the Alamosa antedated ours in Datil by about twenty years, so, of course, only the younger Indians had no memory of the trek when I first knew them.

They intermarried with the Jicarrila Apaches, ethnologically related, to keep the stock from too serious interbreeding. For several generations they managed to exist somehow, clinging to their age-old traditions in spite of a necessarily more intimate association with the Mexicans of the region than with their own kind.

The men spoke Spanish with reasonable fluency before the younger ones began going away to school to learn to speak the language of their fellow Americans.

So much of what I learned from them checks with tales of other friends who have intimately known 'reservation' Indians, that I feel sure that our Alamo Indians had lost little genuine Navajo culture.

Just a story or two.

Trinkalino, one of Ray's best hands, left his young bride in one of the hogans in Datil while he was off on his work. The young woman died in premature childbirth, although the infant miraculously survived.

Now, the Navajo attitude toward death is the outgrowth of their basic belief in spirit dominance, in literal form. They hold that misfortunes are the acts of evil spirits who hover for at least three days around the scene of the disaster they have wrought, lying in wait for other victims. So the living remain as far away as possible from the dead or dying. Our little hogan community immediately withdrew (dogs included) indoors, and stillness settled down over the once bustling settlement.

We whites felt uneasy and baffled. We didn't know just what to do, so many wrong moves were possible. Of course we did send

for Trinkalino. I shall **never** forget his arrival, his horse dripping
sweat despite the cold day, nor the way he flung himself from the
saddle into the blanketed doorway of the hogan in which he had
left his wife.

Ray shook his head ominously. 'I wonder,' he said, for in the
hogan still lay the body of the young woman.

An hour later, we noticed a small campfire several hundred
yards from the Indian settlement and a blanketed figure crouched
beside it.

'It looks like Trinkalino,' **we** said uneasily. 'Isn't there something ——'

Ray again shook his head. 'Better let them make the overtures.
They know we stand ready to help. Besides,' he went on, trying
to reassure himself, I thought, 'they're Indians and they know
how to take care of themselves. There's plenty of wood.' But he,
too, looked unhappily at the lonely figure by the little campfire.

I did not sleep well that night and as a consequence overslept
next morning — mercifully, for the white men on the place had
already brought Trinkalino's frozen corpse from beside the tiny
pile of ashes which bespoke a dead campfire, a fire he had not once
replenished after we saw it, and had laid his body beside that of
his young wife. Later we buried both, after one of the old Indians
had emerged from the still hogans and requested it. But he gave
no explanation of what had happened. Was it deliberate suicide
from grief, or was it the execution of sentence passed by the tribe
for his having gone into the presence of death and himself thereby
become accursed? We could not know. Trinkalino's hogan was
immediately torn down.

To the view that it may have been execution of sentence the
story of Frances gives some support. She was an educated reservation Indian who had spent her childhood largely in Albuquerque,
where her mother wove blankets for the tourist trade. I was sight-
seeing in the Reservation that summer, and at a big 'sing' and

squaw dance met Frances. She was strangely dispirited, and only after many overtures could she be prevailed upon to talk.

'I'm very nervous,' she said in idiomatic English. 'I don't know what's going to happen to me.' A little more encouragement and she went on: 'You know I was raised like a white child, but now I'm grown I must come back to the Reservation to find a husband. I don't know all of my people's customs very well and sometimes I make mistakes.' More encouragement. 'Well, I made one yesterday, an awful one.' She was standing before us in her full Indian costume, with downcast eyes, the picture of despair.

'A man was thrown from a horse and badly hurt,' she went on with her halting tale, 'and he was lying on the ground groaning. Well, I didn't know that it's Navajo custom not to go near an injured person for three days. You see, I was raised in Albuquerque.' Was she apologizing? 'The hurt man kept calling for water and I couldn't stand it. So I took him a drink and he drank it — and died.'

We gave her our poor consolation. It was like trying to touch hands across the ages. We never heard the sequel.

When someone has died in a hogan, the lintel of the door is broken and the hogan forever abandoned. Even today, there are such accursed dwellings on the Navajo reservation. But let no Indian see you enter one if you would not yourself thereafter be shunned as one with plague. When death is believed to be inevitable, the dying Navajo is carried as far from his hogan as time permits: he meets death alone.

An Indian agent's wife told it thus:

A Navajo boy lay stricken with tuberculosis in the Agency hospital. His mother came to see him. The boy, with all the passion of a dying request, begged to be taken away. As gently as possible, it was pointed out to the mother how much kinder it would be to allow him to remain where he was for the few days left to him. But mother and son were both inflexible. Forebod-

ingly, the hospital staff watched the rickety wagon drawn by two
scrawny ponies drive away, the boy lying on a sheepskin on the
floor of the wagon bed. Over the rutted dirt road the mother drove
the team, not toward the family hogan, but toward the mouth of
a cavernous shadow-filled cañon, whose overhanging walls barred
the sun for most of the daylight hours.

In halting words, the Indian woman later told the trader's wife
what had happened, just the facts, without comment. The trader's
wife drew the picture for me:

The only thing that had broken the silence of the ride was the
Indian mother's clucking to the apathetic horses and the creak of
the wagon wheels. She did not glance behind her to see how it
fared with the boy. That the evil spirits rode with him in the wagon
she knew, as she knew that they had been in the white man's
hospital.

Into the cañon's mouth she drove. The boy had hunted rabbits
there, had told her how beautiful it was, had said that his own
hogan would some day stand beside the great boulder which had
fallen from the face of the cliff above.

Around this boulder and close to it the woman drove, until her
team was headed back along the road over which they had come.
Then she tightened the reins. The horses stopped willingly
enough. But even now she did not look back. She felt but did
not see the slow movement in the wagon bed behind her. Very
slow it was, but she didn't turn her head, to see how the evil ones
were having their way with the boy. His alone to deal with them
now, hers but to hope that there might be good ones to come to
his aid. The place was so beautiful and he had loved it so, there
must be good ones!

Then she felt, rather than heard, the soft thud of the boy's body
on the sand at the wagon tail. She clucked to the horses and,
with eyes steadfastly fixed on the horizon, where the glow of the
sunset bathed the world in golden glory, drove back to her hogan

and to her duties as mother to the children who waited her coming.

But it was not always pathos when an Indian was carried away to die alone. Among the Indians of our little hogan settlement was an elderly squaw whom we knew only as Pah. Pah, it seems, is the Navajo word for 'woman,' and because Pah had no status other than an unwanted wife inherited from a dead brother, she was not accorded the dignity of an individual name but was called, disrespectfully, Pah.

But Pah was an excellent weaver and managed to shift pretty well for herself. She was not reticent about making her wants known. In fact, she was a shameless old beggar.

One day Pah seemed ailing and a young Indian asked me to prescribe a remedy. Inquiry as to the nature of the disorder brought forth the reply that her heart had fallen down into her stomach and wouldn't go back where it belonged.

This seemed a serious state of affairs, so I decided to make Pah a visit. I found her lying on a dirty blanket moaning and writhing, but knowing Pah I wasn't altogether convinced that her heart had slipped its moorings nor that she was otherwise critically ill. She, however, implored for something to alleviate her seeming distress.

Suspecting that she had tired of a monotonous diet I made her an eggnog, flavored with vanilla extract. She drank it with gusto. I made a succession of eggnogs, until I decided that either her wandering heart had gone back home or that she had had enough to eat. At any rate, she seemed greatly improved, and returned to her weaving, for which I knew that she had received a little ready cash.

But again came the young Indian. Pah had had a relapse. Her heart had again slipped. She wanted some more of the medicine which had proved so efficacious before.

'Tell Pah I've no more eggs,' which happened to be true, but

I could see disbelief in the messenger's eye. The request for eggnog came several times that day, each time with the report that Pah was growing worse. I wasn't impressed. I thought I knew Pah too well.

But toward dusk I was treated to a profound shock. They were carrying Pah out of the hogan in a blanket — to die under a tree in our cow-pasture. Remorse seized me. Possibly I could have eased Pah's last hours instead of turning a cold shoulder to her dying requests. Perhaps a little more human sympathy ——

Then I saw Pah, striding back under full steam to her hogan. Blazing mad, she was berating her premature pallbearers in the most effective words in the Navajo language. It was repeated to me afterward by one of the chagrined young men.

'She acted like she was dying. She wiggled so hard in the blanket we had a hard time carrying her. We thought her heart was going on down, but when we put her on the ground she jumped up and ran home. She says we just wanted her money and thought we could scare her to death. You know Pah's got a lot of money.'

Of course, 'lot' is a relative term, but Pah wasn't starving. That she had sought to make a stomachache serve her well is more than probable.

The last time I saw Pah, a number of years later, she sold me a blanket for a little more than the market price.

One more Indian story: a trader's wife, well versed in Navajo modes of thought, sat behind the counter of her trading-post in the remotest part of the Reservation, and knitted, waiting for any chance customer.

The door opens and a silent figure slips in and stands motionless. Versed in the Indian code of manners, she takes no notice of his presence but knits on in silence until he is ready to speak. Ultimately he does so.

'Big trouble,' he says.

She waits an appropriate length of time before she replies, 'Can I help?'

No sound but the click of knitting needles until finally he speaks again.

'My aunt kill her husband with axe. Chop his head.'

Again no sound but of knitting needles.

Finally: 'What do you want me to do?'

This time the pause is longer. Then: 'I want you to tell me if I must tell white police?'

The trader's wife had known the dead husband well.

'He needed killing, didn't he?'

The young brave nods violent assent.

'No tell white police,' comes the voice of judgment to the accompaniment of clicking needles.

A moment later she is alone, still knitting.

From cattle TO TOURISTS

ALTHOUGH Ray was over draft age when America entered the first World War, he tried to enlist, even going to Washington in an effort to get accepted; but he was told that his best service to his country would be to raise beef and do it on a grand scale. He obeyed, and stocked the ranch as never before; but the official order became increasingly difficult to carry out as, in his capacity of chairman of the local draft board, he certified for army service one after another of his cowhands.

In the end, his entire outfit went to war, and he had to recruit a new one. It consisted of Indians who were ineligible for the army, and boys who were too young for it. The Indians did the roustabout ranch work and sheepherding; the boys the cowpunching. They came to be known as 'Morley's kindergarten outfit.'

Cattlemen everywhere overstocked their ranges — an irresistible temptation since the government had designated the cattle business an 'essential war industry' and extended large credits to them, while three-year-old steers brought sixty to eighty dollars a head, as against twenty-five and thirty dollars only a short time before.

Then, without warning, soon after the armistice, the government withdrew its credit, and the cattle boom collapsed. This disaster was followed by a protracted drought, and everybody's ranges became a very tragic spectacle.

Mass starvation is not pleasant to contemplate, and I will not dwell upon it. We tried to save old cows who 'got on the lift,' meaning that they must be helped to their feet when down. A cow brute gets very easily discouraged and refuses to help herself even before her waning strength gives out. Unlike a horse, a cow gets up on her hind feet first, so a stout pull on her tail may be just the little help she needs; but if she cannot be 'tailed up,' a sling around her middle and some sort of block-and-tackle may have to be rigged up. I helped at the forward station — the head-end of the cow, where agility rather than strength was required. I could steady the cow by her horns while someone else heaved on her tail. As she unfolded and before she was quite balanced, there would be time to leap aside out of range of her vision, for nine out of ten times she would use her slight strength to charge you and fall down again.

One old cow to whom I was helping to play Good Samaritan seemed to be an exception. Once on her feet, she stood perfectly quiet, apparently a trifle dazed, and I started to walk in a leisurely way back to my horse twenty yards away. Before I reached him I was startled by the crack of a six-shooter. I whirled about. The cow was sinking to the ground almost at my feet.

'Don't you know enough not to turn your back on 'em?' my companion said irritably. 'She mighty near got yuh that time. Had to kill 'er. A bullet could git to her quicker'n I could.'

Then, as if making the best of a bad situation: 'It don't matter, I guess. She'd hev died anyway.'

He put his six-shooter back in his holster and I thanked him meekly. Neither of us placed a great deal of importance on the affair: irritation with me was unquestionably his chief emotion, and humiliation mine. I confess that I cannot even recall the name of my rescuer. He was just another of the succession of employees who came and went during those tragic days. If he is still alive, he is probably saying that a woman's place is in the home, and proving it by relating how he had to sacrifice a cow to save one woman who wasn't where she belonged. But at the time he appeared willing enough to take me along on his rounds of inspection of the watering-places where of course the poorest cattle were apt to be found.

Tailing up a few old cows, however, was a trifling gesture in face of the widespread tragedy. The New Mexico Cattle and Horse Growers Association, of which Ray was then president, decided on a drastic move. They sent Ray to Washington, to negotiate for an agreement to be made between this country and Mexico, whereby the starving herds of the Southwest could be sent over the border into Chihuahua, where grass was knee-high and scarcely an animal left to eat it. Francisco Villa had cleaned the country of its livestock to feed his rebel armies. Furthermore, northern Mexico had enjoyed a succession of good seasons in contrast to the bad ones north of the border.

Successful in Washington, Ray went to Mexico to complete the negotiations with that government. During this critical time, he had allowed himself to be forced into the presidency of the Magdalena Bank, although thoroughly alive to the fact that in so doing he was getting entirely out of his own proper theater of operations. But the bank's assets consisted almost exclusively of 'cattle paper,' and it was imperative that its management be in the hands of an experienced stockman, an unnatural union of qualifications. In Ray's case, it could have been called a shotgun wedding, for only a sense of duty to his community drove him reluctantly to take the risk. I well recall the weariness in his voice on one occasion:

'I wish to God lightning had struck me instead of a bank presidency.'

But when a financial institution's assets are lying down and dying of 'poverty' by the thousands, the management undoubtedly feels pretty helpless, and Ray went to the rescue.

When he left for Mexico I told him that I would stay and keep an eye on the Lodge. That, at least, was paying. It was properly staffed and my duties would be, so we both fancied, purely supervisory.

Ray grinned as he turned over the safe's combination to me. 'You know,' he said, 'you'll make a bang-up good hotel-keeper.'

Recognizing a well-known little gleam in his eye, I demanded defensively, 'Just why?'

'Because,' he chuckled, 'you are good at distracting guests' attentions from the deficiencies'; a talent, I may add, that was strained to its limits in the time that I functioned as an amateur Boniface and Ray struggled with a far more desperate problem of getting one hundred thousand head of dying American livestock onto the lush ranges of northern Mexico.

It was an epic hegira — those slow-moving skeleton-like herds that were prodded along to the railroad-shipping points and loaded into cattle cars for a destination that too many of them were never to reach. Carcasses were hauled from the cars whenever the train stopped.

The night the last trainload of Ray's cattle left Magdalena I was there, running errands in a chugging Model T, hauling saddles and bedrolls from stockyards to railroad station, hauling cowboys from stockyards to town, or the other way around.

It had been a trying day, this hour after hour of loading the bewildered cattle into the long train of empty cars. The air was heavy with dust and our spirits heavy with a foreboding that this was the closing chapter of the cattle business as we had known it. We told one another that the cattle were only going out under bond, that they would be brought back next year fat and sleek, that our ranges would be helped by rest and would reseed themselves, and that once more we would see our hillsides dotted with whitefaces. But deep in our hearts, I think, we really didn't believe it, and we were right.

Jesse Simpson was boss in charge of Ray's outfit, and I was taking orders from Jesse without resentment on my part or apology on his. At last he checked over the loads I had hauled from the chuck-wagon to the caboose, all the equipment for the several men who were going with the cattle, staying with them in Mexico, and believing themselves to be bringing them back a year later.

'Got everything now?' I asked finally. The train conductor was walking up and down beside the cars, growling over the lateness of the start. Jesse was apparently making a mental inventory. Suddenly he uttered an exclamation. 'Need two more prod poles — got to have 'em.' He yelled to the conductor, 'Back in a minute!' and vaulted into the car beside me. 'Uptown,' he ordered. We put Lizzie to her best performance.

'Where to?' I asked.

'Just along the main street,' Jesse told me, 'and slow down.'

In front of Jerry Wheeler's drugstore stood another Ford, with two slender ten-foot prod poles lying along the fenders. Obeying Jesse's signal, I stepped on the brake. He leaped from the car, gathered up the prod poles, and leaped back, holding the poles erect outside of the door. 'Back to the depot,' he commanded.

I turned Lizzie around. The conductor was yelling 'All aboard!' in an exasperated tone. The train moved slowly. Jesse swung onto the iron ladder on one side of a cattle car. I watched the train as it slowly gathered speed in the dusk. Then I saw Jesse silhouetted against the starlit sky, steadying himself with the prod poles in one hand and waving good-bye with the other. I waved back weakly.

I never found out to whom the prod poles belonged. Several

outfits were in town, waiting their turn to ship their herds. They had time to get extra prod poles. Jesse hadn't.

From now on it was not to cattle but to tourists that we looked for business in Datil. Distracting guests' attentions from the deficiencies of a twelve-room hotel, thirty-seven miles from the nearest source of supplies, including help, and operated by a novice whose heart wasn't in the business anyway, proved to be a harder job than Ray had so lightly suggested. Instead of supervising as I had innocently supposed, I found myself substituting for one after another of the decamping employees until a new one could be found from Heaven knew where. 'Why should I subject myself to this?' I asked myself in some bitterness of spirit, as I filled orders for 'straight up' or 'lookin' at ya' eggs, because no one else would, or could, cook, or as I swung Pendleton blankets on or off beds, raging at the Mexican girl who wanted to go to town and went.

The water supply was from a windmill and the wind didn't always blow, although mostly it did. When a guest couldn't have water, his attention was apt to be hard to distract from that particular deficiency, even by a tale of how Ray *said* he had killed the lobo wolf whose hide was nailed to the log wall of the lobby.

Why *did* I subject myself to it? Because, shortly after the last cattle train left Magdalena, the bank had folded its tired arms and quit. I had stared at the fateful slip of paper on the front door, 'This bank is in the hands of a receiver,' and had then gone quietly around to the rear door.

The drawn-looking vice-president let me in. 'The lightning struck,' he said wearily. 'It's lucky you're here in the country. Looks better to have a member of the family still around, with Ray in Mexico. He has to stay in Mexico until the business with the authorities down there is settled, and that's slow work with Mexican authorities. But people talk. It'll help for a member of the family to be right here.'

So I went back to my job of distracting attention from the deficiencies. After all, it was a good excuse if not a legitimate reason for staying on in New Mexico, and I cannot deny that in spite of the anxieties, I enjoyed myself on the whole.

Tourists are a funny lot, and I am sure that they in turn thought me a funny hotel-keeper. Highway 60 had but recently been designated a transcontinental highway, and the average tourist of the day who stopped with us appeared to look upon himself as an adventurer of high courage for daring to get so far off the beaten path.

Two women from Kansas who came into the lobby looking frightened and almost hysterical explained that their car had broken down ten miles from the lodge and that they had had to come in with a passing motorist, and 'leave Father out there alone in that awful place.'

I spoke brightly: 'We'll send a tow-car right down — just make yourselves comfortable.'

'Oh, but you don't understand,' they told me. 'Father's out

there *all alone.* You can't imagine what a desolate place it is. Anything might happen to him.'

My mind swept back to the times I'd been on those plains all alone, but it seemed futile to say anything other than that I'd tell the tow-car to hurry.

The most serious menace to the traveling public of that day came from the mechanical imperfections of their own automobiles. A considerable portion of our revenues were from the hotel bills of people compelled to stay with us while waiting for new automobile parts from El Paso or Albuquerque or even from Detroit, or wherever the home factory might be.

It was a period when I played a sort of mental hopscotch, back and forth over that line between my life as a lady and the other one. The line became considerably blurred the evening the two young oil prospectors, fresh from college, welcomed a pretty young tourist girl into the dining-room. Ray had brought the big Lazy Susan table down from the Drag-A Ranch, and after varnishing it up a bit and polishing its brass hub-cap had installed it in the Lodge. A big sign outside the dining-table invited the public to 'Eat at the Whirling Table.' A considerable number did. On this particular evening the two recently graduated college chaps sat at the table facing the dining-room entrance. With his back to the door sat Slim, a cowpuncher, a little self-conscious and constrained in the presence of the easy-mannered young men opposite him. A young woman entered the dining-room. There was instant commotion.

The two young men sprang to their feet at the approach of a lady to their table. Slim, seeing their action, also sprang to his feet — ready for trouble. He grabbed his chair and whirled to meet whatever might be confronting him. The young woman, seeing Slim's chair apparently ready to crash down on her head, gasped and stopped in her tracks. Everybody looked at everybody else in dumfounded amazement. Of all the people in that room I alone could interpret what was happening! and I added to the confusion by bolting into the kitchen to conceal my impending hysteria.

Slim bolted in after me. 'What did them fellers break t' run fer?' he demanded. 'Did they think that girl was a holdup?'

With superhuman effort I brought myself under control. 'Tenderfeet are easy scared,' I told Slim solemnly.

'They shore are,' he agreed, and returned to his seat at the table with restored self-confidence. It would never have occurred to him, he knew, to 'make a break to run' when it was only a girl who had come unexpectedly into the room.

After Slim had mounted his horse and left, I set the minds of the others at rest. They hadn't yet been able to figure out what had happened. Slim's respect for tenderfeet received a permanent setback. Years later he mentioned it as an example of the softening influence of city life. Again I agreed with him. I had become quite adept at keeping those two lives each in its own hemisphere.

Ray ultimately returned from Mexico. His protracted negotiations with the particular Mexican government which was enjoying an uneasy tenure of office at the moment had been less than reassuring. He foresaw insurmountable difficulties in getting those American cattle back over the border: and few in fact ever did get back.

He restocked in a modest way, and dishonored the holiest convention of cattlemen — that sheep and cattle cannot be run on the same range, and that enmity is the natural relationship between them — and had experimented with raising caraculs, an enterprise whose net profit to him was education in the ways of those rugged individualists.

I returned to California, taking with me nearly all documents of family interest, my father's and mother's diaries, a partially finished life of Father which Mother had begun and laid aside when she began to write the life of Francis Schlatter, business papers, old family letters, letters from personages with whom she had corresponded. We had agreed among ourselves, Ray, Lora, and I, that I was the logical custodian for most of these things. My life was less subject to unexpected interruptions, we said. I should have time to separate the important from the unimportant In this mass of yellowing papers.

I had been in Berkeley but a few weeks when our home burned. It took it exactly four minutes to do so, as calculated by the Berkeley Fire Department on the basis of sixty city blocks reduced to ashes in four hours' time. Possibly I should have let the May-nard Dixon picture go and tried to save the locked chest in which these irreplaceable records were kept. Well, I didn't. I have spent countless sleepless nights living over the two minutes given me to get out and stay out of my home after it was certain that it would burn. In those wakeful hours, I decided that the fire was a portent. I had no further business in Datil. The cattle were largely gone, although there is always a remnant in the rough country that cannot be gathered for years. Nobody needed me out there any 'onger. I was getting too advanced in years to play hopscotch, anyhow. I'd stay, I told myself, on the lady side of the line. This resolution held for almost two years.

Barbed wire SUPPLANTS HORSEFLESH

I DOUBT if many ever knew the exact boundaries of their properties in the early days, a condition which still exists to a lesser degree in this section. My cabin on Jack Howard's flat lies below a spring that bursts from a hillside six hundred feet above the house on the original Johnny Thompson homestead. Neither I nor anybody else *knows* exactly on whose patented land the spring lies. By a freak, the spring bubbles from the mountain-side at almost the exact point where four quarter-sections meet. In the course of years it has been claimed by four separate owners, each of whom has striven to substantiate his claim by various cornerstones, always in a different place from those of the other claimants. The ambulatory cornerstone has long been a well-known phenomenon in these parts. Within my memory there has been a veritable ring of them around Thompson Spring. Our cornerstones are not lengths of brass pipe embedded in cement, but a small mound of rocks with markings chiseled into the rough surface of one of them.

Why isn't the location of Thompson Spring, for example, established once and for all by an authoritative survey? For the
very good reason that a really accurate survey is almost a physical
impossibility. The base line lies six miles to the north, over
tumbled, up-ended, thickly wooded country, and the spring is
so close to the exact center of the four intersecting quarter section
lines that an error of a yard in those six miles of unbelievably
rough country would put the spring where three people would
contest it.

The interested parties have settled the matter more easily.
Except for a reservoir for house use, the spring flows into a stock
tank 'on the outside' that is unfenced and available to the range
stock of the other possible owners. Overflow from this tank then
takes its natural downhill course and supplies our playhouse garden.

All quite simple and satisfactory. But not always is this matter
of the restless cornerstone so easily disposed of. There was the
case of the senior Hubble, of the honorable Hubble clan, who still
own large portions of Catron and Valencia Counties and are
superior people even if they do run sheep.

After Ray's return from college with his civil engineering degree,
Señor Frank Hubble asked him to make a survey of one of his
ranches, whose cornerstones likewise seemed afflicted with wander-
lust. When Ray arrived at the ranch, host Hubble announced
that he had already sent one of his Mexican sheepherders to locate
a certain cornerstone which he felt sure must be approximately
in its appointed place while he and Ray ate dinner. At the finish
of the leisurely meal, they began wondering why the scout had
not returned. And then they saw him approaching, driving a
plodding burro, on whose pack-saddle was laced the cornerstone
in question.

'Aqui 'sta,' announced the sheepherder proudly.

It was with extreme difficulty and a final resort to authority
on the part of his employer that the man could be persuaded to

lead the surveying party back to where he had found the marker —
if, indeed, he actually did. Ray always doubted it. The man's
attitude was that he had brought them their old cornerstone at
considerable pains to himself and it served their unreasonableness
danged well right if he didn't take them to the exact spot from
which he had lifted it. That particular survey is still questionable.
It probably doesn't matter. The Hubbles own it all, anyway.

Some of this nonchalance toward 'established' corners was as
innocent as that of the old Hubble sheepherder, and some of it
was characteristic of men accustomed to thinking themselves the
law, with nobody ready to dispute them — unless their assumption
bore too directly upon another who likewise considered himself
the law, as we all did, more or less.

In general, however, we did not bother very much about where
our properties ended; there was plenty of land for all. Our only
fences were the fluctuating and impermanent barriers of horseflesh
with which we controlled our cattle.

It was barbed wire that dealt the first blow to the open range.
Even before the war produced its shortage of cowhands, barbed
wire began to supplant horseflesh in the business of keeping
cattle within bounds. Everybody fenced in as much territory
as he could afford barbed wire to stretch around. Naturally
our fencing had nothing to do with our property lines; what
we fenced was the water hole which belonged to us and adjoining
lands which did not, though by custom we used them.

There was of course rivalry between the fencers, and it reached
dangerous proportions. Many a dispute over whose 'right' it was
to encircle a few townships with barbed wire was settled with six-
shooters. Cutting one another's fences was common practice.
The victim having no very secure standing in the eyes of Uncle
Sam's law was compelled, perforce, to resort to Colt's law.

When Uncle Sam decided, none too soon, to conserve his natural
resources and established the National Forests, the Morley Ranch

was just the sort of place he had in mind. Of course there was no confiscation of legally owned lands, but the government laid a proprietory hand on all of that in-between land we cattle people had come to regard as our own range. Thereafter we used it on a permit basis.

The National Forest boundary lines had been established with regard not only to stands of commercial timber but to watersheds; therefore much of the original Datil Forest — its name has been changed to Cibola Forest — was composed of piñon and juniper thickets as well as pine forests.

To our discomfiture, uniformed young officials now notified us that we must take down any fences that did not mark our own boundaries. The shock was terrific. What, we wanted to know, was the world coming to when natural rights were thus invaded! Ray's bouts with the Forest Service became legendary, nor was he *always* wrong. A little authority can warp a man's judgment as effectually as a feeling of proprietorship over what you may not actually own. Typical was Ray's threat to take his grievance to the Board of Health when an overofficious young Ranger was slow in marking logs for a new bathroom.

In the end, however, Ray capitulated and many of our fences came down. Oh, the miles of barbed wire I have helped roll into great prickly hoops! He paid his forest fees, put out the stipulated amount of stock salt, kept his watering places in repair, and, most oppressive of all, rendered written reports. In short, he took program — bucking every step of the way, it must be allowed.

'The Old People'

W<small>E LED</small> the life of pioneers in a new country. And yet we were constantly being confronted with the evidence that people have lived in New Mexico since long before the beginning of history.

I think of the time the roundup was camped on the San Augustine Plains, close beside a peculiar earth crack that seemed not to have been caused by erosion. Somebody jumped down into it to explore, and came back lugging an object about the size of a ten-pound lard pail. Ultimately it turned out to be a fossil mastodon molar. When camp was moved every man in the outfit carried away some fragment of the huge skeleton. The molar served as the doorstep for a Magdalena saloon for years.

Then there was the ever-present possibility of discovering for one's self a cliff-dwelling or ruined pueblo whose owners had vanished a thousand years ago. There were areas on our range where almost every hilltop was strewn with shards of broken pottery and where we looked twice at every patch of loose rock to see if it was part of a ruined wall (better than even chances it was) and at every smooth-faced sandstone bluff to see if there was 'Injun writing' on it (and, again, better than even chances there was).

Almost every ranch house had specimens of prehistoric handiwork which somebody had picked up, sometimes marvelous specimens that should have been in museums. Tales of finding cliff-dwellings with intact mummies in them were familiar.

One man told me that he and a companion saw a cave high up on a mountain-side and succeeded in climbing to the top of the bluff above the cave. They were unable to approach it from below. My informant let himself down to the cave's mouth on a rope, leaving the other man on top.

In the cave was a mummy, a shriveled human form from which most, but not all, of the wrappings had fallen away. However, it gave promise of remaining intact with reasonably careful handling. My friend tied the rope around it and gave the signal to hoist. Up over the edge of the cliff went the grinning apparition. There was a yelp and the man above let go the rope. And that, of course, was the end of the mummy.

Such tales turned our local archaeologists into bitter cynics. Rightly they called it vandalism. But we who figured in such experiences were merely taking what came.

'Found an Injun pot' was local small-talk. One neighbor, a little ranchwoman, had a roomful of pottery, stone axes, arrowheads, and so forth, all of which she had dug herself, in larger part from ancient burial places on her own ranch. A half-teacupful of black obsidian arrowheads, none longer than a pin and some half that length, jewel-like little things of exquisite workmanship, she had scooped from a spring on top of Eagle Peak.

Another neighbor showed me a human jawbone and proved that there were giants in those days. This jawbone, with teeth twice the size of any I had ever seen, my host slipped over his own lower jaw to show its relative size.

Were there also pygmies? I will not expose my ignorance further than to say that it seems to me that a surprising number of 'children's relics' have been found.

But more exciting, of course, was that ever-present fabulously rich lost gold mine. Ours was 'Adams' Diggin's.' When we went to Datil, the tale was young. Adams had made his find, so ran the story, only a few years before. His party had been massacred by Indians. He alone escaped. The experience temporarily unhinged his reason, and it was years before he became sane enough to lead a party back into the country in search of 'the box cañon where I left a Dutch oven full of nuggets.'

More than a few Western writers have elaborated the tale, factually or in fiction form. I have known two men, Langford Johnson and Bob Lewis, who accompanied Adams on one or more of his several trips when he was an old man still trying to return to his gold. Bob Lewis will occasionally talk about it if one pushes the right button to loosen his tongue.

'I kept Adams from bein' lynched once,' Bob told me as we sat by a campfire. 'The men he brought out from Los Angeles with him decided he had never found any mine and was just makin' a livin' by gettin' up expeditions. So they was goin' to lynch the old geezer. I was just the kid horse-wrangler but I helped him escape.'

'Do you yourself believe there was ever any such mine?' I asked him.

'Well — uh ——' said Bob, scratching his head. 'Mebbe.'

Whatever Bob may believe in his heart, there are plenty who

explicitly do believe the tale. Year after year after year, they still come, looking for the Dutch oven full of gold nuggets.

Datil itself is not a mineralized country. Not an ounce of valuable ore has ever been dug from its igneous mountains. But isn't gold where you find it? So the hopeful still rig up their camp outfits and prowl among those, I wish I might say amused mountains. New maps, new data, are always the excuse. And then once in a blue moon something genuinely mysterious does happen to rekindle the embers of the imagination.

Two unusually large pine trees grew side by side in Datil Cañon, just far enough apart to make it possible to ride a horse between them. The first time I rode down that cañon in 1886 I rode between those trees — as wouldn't any child? — and ever afterward I did likewise. It would be bad luck to fail. How many times I have risked scraping the hide from my knees for the sake of preserving my luck!

Late one night not so many years ago a passerby reported that he had seen men with lanterns who seemed to be digging at the foot of those trees. But discretion being ever the better part of valor, especially in our country, this passerby did not investigate.

You may be sure, however, that bright and early next morning I did. Brother-in-law Tom Reynolds who went with me will vouch for what we found. First, on those trees were two very old blazes. The bark had so grown over them that I did not detect them until Tom's expert eyes had found them and pointed them out to me. 'If they are genuine,' he said, 'there ought to be a couple of witness trees about. Wait till I look.'

The witness trees were found, their blazes pointing to the big pines. What had the diggers found? Well, they had found a chest with handles to it. The mold of that chest in the hard-packed earth was beyond all possibility of mistake. The track of the handles as they scraped along the sides of the pit when the chest was hauled up was there. It had been a chest about 2 × 2 × 3 feet in dimension.

And I had ridden over it for forty years! So much for preserving one's luck.

Months later one vague but maddening clue came to light. A Mexican neighbor displayed an ancient and battered chest and talked of an old map from 'Mexico Viejo.'

What had the chest contained? He smiled, but his eyes were veiled. 'Oh, wheeskey, I guess.'

'Old maps from Mexico!' These were our romantic interest stock in trade. For ours was the area over which Coronado led his expedition in search of the fabulous Seven Cities of Cibola. And it was as though the spirit of those early thrill-seekers still hovered over the land and passed something of itself on to us. Occasionally a cowboy would find a bridle bit or a spur with rowels three or four inches in diameter. Up near Kid Spring Corky Wallace found a bayonet made of solid silver and, most interesting of all, in 1935 a pony's iron shoe struck fire against a bit of metal on the ground. When the rider dismounted to investigate, he picked up the iron sole of a human being's shoe — a human being with an incredibly small foot. It is hard to envision a child on this expedition of the Conquistadores. There were holes along the edge of the sole where leather uppers had undoubtedly been laced. Unless it had been an instrument of torture, it is hard to imagine its adequacy as a shoe sole, but such it most certainly was.

Naturally, every incident of this kind whetted imagination. Those early treasure seekers might possibly have missed the Seven Cities. Why not? These cities might still be waiting for oneself to stumble upon them. A map from 'Old Mexico' might unlock the secret.

But, without a map, I know where one of them is. My city has more reality than those which lured the Spaniard of the Middle Ages into our dreamland. Although those adventurers didn't find Cibola, they did stumble on the Grand Cañon.

My discovery of my own Cibola, though Lilliputian by contrast, was no less dramatic. I was with Ray. 'There's a big ruin up on that mesa,' he said, pointing. 'Want to take time out to climb up to it?'

He turned the Model T off the vague parallel tracks which he had been following, seemingly under the illusion that he was on a road, and began chugging straight across country over imbedded boulders and hummocks of bunch grass to the foot of the mesa he had indicated.

It rose abruptly from the edge of Poverty Pool Flat. Its upper rim was a mile-long white sandstone wall, against which stood tall pines, tall, but so short by comparison to the wall behind them they seemed but a feathery fringe to the top of the talus. This talus at its base was a mass of huge boulders, among which a scrubby growth spread its variegated greens — wild hop vines, pala verde bushes, scraggly clumps of small oak. Above it all, on the white walls of the mesa rested the turquoise sky.

Indeed, the 'old people,' as the Indians call them, 'walked in beauty.'

We skirted the foot of the mesa and came to the farther side where ascent was possible. A large two-storied house, with only a window or two, stood on the lower slope. It had been built of sandstone blocks torn from the ancient walls of the old pueblo on top. A Mexican family occupied it.

'Have they carted *all* the walls away?' I asked apprehensively.

'No,' Ray said, a little evasively. 'There were *some* left last time I was up there.'

We began to scramble up the precipitous mountain-side. Suddenly I stopped. 'Aren't we on the ruins of a stairway?'

Ray too stopped and looked about. 'Never saw it before!' he exclaimed.

We struggled, badly winded, to the top. And there stood my wonder city of Cibola. For an instant I seemed actually to see the place as undoubtedly it was a thousand years ago — a proud city, with people swarming in and out of its courts and into its terraced houses. Then Ray's voice broke the spell.

'Told you they hadn't hauled all the stones away.'

A thousand tons lay scattered about! Some were in crudely ordered formations, outlining hundreds of cell-like rooms; others were still in walls, five to six feet in height. Over it all grew a sparse forest of piñon and juniper trees.

But not yet had I seen the real glory of the place.

Scrambling over the rock piles and across the grass-grown plots between them, we came to the mesa's edge, the top of those sandstone cliffs which form its western face. Hundreds of feet below us spread a great plain, bounded on the remoter horizons by mauve and purple mountains, some so far away they seemed but opalescent shadings into the bright clear blue of the sky they pierced. Between our mesa and these mountains spread a lava-flow as it had issued from numerous volcanic cones which rose hive-shaped on its rim. Forty or fifty miles in cross-diameter this tumbled, glassy hardened lava spread out over the plain, sometimes smoothly wave-like, sometimes in huge sharp-edged fragments, reddish-brown as though still smouldering with heat, or green-black shading to obsidian. A colossal broken opal refracting light from a myriad facets! But there were flaws in the gem, for great zones of pine forest crisscrossed it, a deep-pile green nap springing from the brittle surface.

When the lava flow was hot and liquid, it had lapped the feet of the mesa. As successive outpourings cooled, a final black viscid tidal wave stopped, at its crest, before it broke against the barrier of the mesa. It stands today a sheer overhanging wall, as though struggling still to push itself forward. The passage between this lava wall and the mesa the Mexicans call 'La Angostura,' 'the narrow place.' (Mexicans do scale the heights of inspiration when they think up names!)

To our left stretched the clear hard brilliance of a cloudless sky.

To our right boiled a great bank of billowing clouds silver-rimmed on top, blue-black beneath. From it a dark shaft with straight sharp edges stretched from sky to earth. 'Cloudburst' is not a mere figure of speech! And, over all, silence.

Did those early Spaniards find this city and pass it by because there was no gold and turquoise to load upon their galleons?

Even for New Mexico's ruins, however, the old and unregulated days are over. To the passing of this era, as of many others, Inscription Rock bears witness. It stands beyond the western limits of the Malpais. More than three hundred years ago, a company of Spanish soldiers camped at the base of its sheer sandstone walls and with their sword-points carved on those walls notice of their passing. Throughout the years since that first autograph was etched on the enduring rock, other wayfarers added their names.

'Done carved my name on that big rock along with them old Spanish hombres,' more than one cowpuncher has reported when he returned from hunting strays to the north of us. 'Lots of room left. Why don't you go over and put your name there, too?'

But it was long before I made my first journey to Inscription Rock. The rock had just been declared a national monument although not yet was there an official custodian on the premises. Our party camped, as did the Spaniards, at its base.

Late summer rains had turned the country to a lush green. Little pools of surface water dotted the flats and sparkled in the late afternoon sunlight.

'I'll come back and help with the supper,' I salved my conscience. 'I want just one look from the top first.'

The climb to the top is a stiff demand upon lungs and leg muscles. The sun sat poised on the western horizon when I finally reached the topmost level of the peninsula-mesa. For an instant I looked squarely into its red-gold face, then turned away to rest my eyes.

Were those eyes playing me tricks? On the eastern horizon was another ball, twin in size, differing only in color, for this one was shimmering silver. Each stood lightly on the rims of opposite horizons, face to face, with Inscription Rock between them!

It was a moment before I recalled that on certain days of the year the sun sets exactly as the full moon rises. The kindly gods had placed me on top of Inscription Rock at one such instant.

A long piercing half-human cry broke against the sheer walls of the graven Rock, and the echoes went trailing off from it into the vast silence that finally swallowed them. A mountain lion had served notice that he resented intrusion into his world.

'You're right, old chap, you're right,' I assured him. 'But we're all caught in forces that are stronger than we are. We might as well bow gracefully to them.'

The next morning the newly appointed ranger appeared. 'The Department,' he told us, had taken over the care of Inscription Rock.

'The day is past,' he said, 'when Tom, Dick, and Harry can come along and carve their names. We've chiseled off all the names without historical significance.'

'Of course,' I philosophized, 'one never knows at the time what name may ultimately have historical significance.'

'True enough,' he agreed, 'and the man we set to do the chiseling didn't recognize one name that had it. The dumb bunny chiseled off the name of Kit Carson.'

On to Pie Town

IT WAS the homesteaders who, more crushing than the drought or the failure of the wartime market, dealt the final blow to the open range and the Morley enterprises.

In 1916 Congress had passed what was known as the Stock Raising Homestead law under whose terms six hundred and forty acres of unwatered, semi-desert land could be taken up on the same conditions that had obtained in the earlier homestead laws. Six hundred and forty acres of land to be had for the asking! The 'land-starved' moistened their lips and with hope in their eyes, began pouring in through Datil towards the non-Forest lands lying just to the west of us. I watched them come past while I was managing the Lodge. New pioneers, I thought; different from ourselves, of course, but to be encouraged, for I had become imbued with what had been presented to me as a 'social conscience' during some of those intervals in which I masqueraded as a lady.

Ray, on the scene day in and day out, had been less propagandized and was able to take stock of the actual facts. I reproached him for his seeming lack of 'social conscience.'

'Use your bean,' he snorted. 'Take this ranch country as it *is* and not as it ought to be. It's arid. Rainfall, including snow, averages about thirteen inches a year, and the moisture and the heat don't come together. When it's hot, it's dry; when it's wet, it's cold. We're lucky if we get two months' growing weather in a year. The forage which nature has finally adapted to these conditions will support one cow on fifty acres of land, one sheep on five. It's not a country for the small farmer. Even if a homesteader with his six hundred and forty acres of dry land can get water at three or four hundred feet depth, he can't stand the expense of maintaining a deep well. Do you know what it costs in time and money to pull a four-hundred-foot sucker rod and maybe the casing, too? But suppose he does keep his well up. His six hundred and forty acres will not support over sixteen head of cattle. How many people will sixteen head of cattle support? It just naturally can't be done.

'Every six hundred and forty acres he fences is that much taken out of production, because unwatered land might as well be one large rock pile, so long as the animal kingdom has to have water as well as food. Some day we're going to wake up and realize that facts are more important than laudable theories.' He lit his pipe in cold resignation.

I don't think people talked of submarginal lands at that time. Our vocabulary of social welfare was deplorably limited, so Ray didn't convince me — then. But that he was a prophet later events proved. If I could talk with Ray again, I should treat him to the shock of his life; I should acknowledge that for once he had been right and I wrong. Just for once, of course. Even the government admits it today. Of the fifty million acres taken under this so-called Stock Raising Act, over half have been abandoned and the act itself pronounced a failure.

That summer passed. I watched the homesteaders as they trekked by. They came in family groups, in any sort of conveyance that would roll, their household furnishings piled high and the overflow — washtubs, baby buggies, chickencoops — wired to any anchorage that would hold. In trucks, in automobiles, dragging heavy trailers, the rare exception in horsedrawn wagons, they came, and with them a new order.

'On to Pie Town,' Ray would say as the slow caravans passed through Datil. No, Pie Town is not our symbolic Promised Land; Pie Town is a very literal place. The man who first set up a roadside eating-place, when there was promise that Highway 60 would be a popular transcontinental route, had named his shack 'Pie Town' and had given authenticity to the name by serving pies of his own manufacture. It had struck a chord of popular fancy, and Pie Town it remained as it grew into a trading center for the homesteaders who settled to the north, east, south, and west of it. It lies fourteen miles beyond the Continental Divide and twenty-four miles from Datil Post-Office. Another twenty separate it from Quemado, still further west, and all these miles are dotted with homesteads. Their clearings may be seen with the stumps of the piñons still showing, or the dust of their plowed fields blowing across the face of the sky. A windmill is a rare exception, but 'dirt tanks' for restraining flood water during the rainy season are adjuncts of many of them.

The first wave of these invaders into our 'open-range' kingdom suffered a sordid hardship such as the pioneer ranchman never knew. The homesteader did not ride far and fast. He walked, he grubbed, he starved. Soon he had to face the hard fact that his six hundred and forty acres could not support his family. His bean crop failed far too frequently, his little patch of corn wilted with too great regularity under prolonged drought.

Beaten, he gave up and moved on, or back to where he had started from. That is to say, some did. 'Back from Pie Town,' we said, and felt compassionate as we watched the sad little parade retracing its steps.

Yet still other homesteaders came. At last, I could stand the sight no longer.

'Why doesn't somebody tell them?' I wanted to know. 'Why do *we* sit here and watch them go to this bleak and bitter disappointment? Why can't they be warned before they've used up what little capital they may have?'

'You tell them,' Ray said, and I wasn't sure whether it was irony that colored his voice.

An intelligent-appearing man came into the Lodge asking directions, as so many did. Through a window I could see his family in their battered car with its trailerload of home equipment. There were half a dozen bright-looking children, a wife for whom he need not apologize.

'Do you know anything of the conditions you are facing?' I asked after I had paved the way by a few banalities. A perceptible hardness replaced the friendly light in his eyes. Undeterred, I hurried on. I mentioned the seasonal rainfall, the distance from market, the acreage per cow support. I told him the simple truth. He let me finish my say and then he had his. He knew me and my kind! He knew my type of pampered female who had lived on the fruits of other people's labors and had now stationed herself at the gateway of a new Eden to prevent the honest toiler from entering and sharing its opportunities! It was time, he told me with blazing eyes, and an almost hysterical ring in his voice, that we 'cattle barons' were brought to our knees, and it afforded him no end of satisfaction to tell this Jezebel of the species just what a she-devil she was! Then he slammed the door behind him.

Ray stuck his head in through another door. 'Did you tell him?' he grinned. 'I tried it once myself.'

Maybe they weren't all like that. I made no further effort to find out!

Though the weaker and perhaps more civilized of the homesteaders gave up in defeat, others remained. A few, a very few, of the hordes who came turned out to be accomplished cattle-rustlers, good riders, and good ropers, and proficient in the art of reading brands. Not only did they benefit by Ray's reluctant compliance with Forest Service rules, which demanded sacrifices of the large established ranch owner but not of the newcomers; they proceeded to run their cattle on Ray's range, to cut his fences, to eat his beef, and in general to deport themselves in accordance with the precept, 'To him that hath shall it be given to support him who hath not.'

When finally he had reason to believe that his foreman had been murdered, although even this had not been a subject for investigation officially (it was a bad piece of road where the Model T went over the bank and maybe the foreman was drunk), Ray roused himself to action.

He had various and sundry of his neighbors indicted for trespass. Great was the excitement in Catron County. Threats and counter-threats swept like a hurricane over the community. Men went about armed, after a long period of outer conformity to more civilized usages. Even one or two physical encounters took place before the case came to court. When at last it did, the town of Reserve, our county seat, filled up with muttering suspicious-eyed men who rode in with their bedrolls on packhorses. Hotel accommodations in Reserve were practically nil. Six-shooters were worn openly in the street. At the courtroom door two deputies searched every man who entered for concealed weapons.

'I don't think more'n half a dozen guns got by,' one man later told me. 'I had mine stuck in my bootleg.'

Then Ray appeared. He wore a cartridge belt and his six-shooter in full view (this after the advent of the Model T!). He strode past the deputies with the manner of a grandee passing a couple of subservient flunkies.

The judge on the bench swallowed hard. 'I — I've ordered all weapons to be — uh — removed from this court,' he said, a trifle unsteadily.

'When I am convinced that I can expect any protection from this court, I'll disarm,' Ray replied dispassionately. 'Until then, I shall rely upon the first law of nature.'

His attorney jumped to his feet and asked for a continuance It was granted. No better example could be found of the fine distinction between legalism and justice, a distinction with which we were perpetually confronted.

Social progress went on, however, and Ray continued to oppose it. I was dismayed to learn that he was against local bond issues for new roads and new schools, on the ground that cattle took themselves to the shipping-point and didn't need highways to travel on, and that children had no business in the country, anyway. Trucking cattle to market was beyond anyone's vision.

The burden of supporting the homesteader continued to fall in no small measure upon him and upon the other few established cattlemen who, never considering the possibility of outside aid, had weathered a good many depressions by tightening their own belts and putting in longer hours in the saddle. It was their wells which supplied the homesteaders with water (barrels and barrels hauled away by the wagonload for household use and maybe a milch cow or two); it was their beef, butchered surreptitiously, which supplied meat; it was their taxes which maintained the schools.

Eighteen taxpayers, no one of whom himself had children of school age were maintaining three schools in one district in 1924 when Ray threw up his hands in defeat and sold the ranches.

'It was a good life while it lasted,' he said. 'But one can't buck the government. If the government encourages people to attempt the impossible, what is the poor sucker to do who clings to the idea that cause is somewhat related to effect?'

A half-dozen doctors had shaken ominous heads over the condition of his heart. His wife, Nan, and his daughter, Faith, had long been only occasional visitors at the ranch, for summer vacations. Their lives were definitely cast on the side of the tracks where ladies lived.

The day that Faith came to the roundup during the gathering of the cattle for shipment established that fact without shadow of a doubt. She came riding a high-stepping horse and followed by a pedigreed dog. Dogs are not welcome at roundups. The cattle mistake them for coyotes. Faith didn't know that. When she found it out, she obligingly took her dog and went back to where the chuck-wagon was camped. Dismounting, she tied her horse to the rear wheel of the wagon, which is to say she rode right into the kitchen and tied her horse in the very center of the cook's operations. The dog wandered about, sniffing at the pots and kettles that stood on the ground. The cook was an old-time round-up cook, a martinet of the tribe of martinets. An expression of utter incredulity spread over his weatherbeaten face, to be quickly replaced by one far more ominous. Without a word, he put his big fork down on the extended leaf of the chuckbox, walked over to Faith's horse, and untied him. The remuda was within sight and, of course, the horse set out to join it, walking with his head to one side to avoid stepping on his dragging bridle reins.

Faith, busy with getting her dog a drink from the water-keg on the opposite side of the wagon, realized what had happened only when she saw her horse a couple of hundred yards from camp and still going.

'Who turned my horse loose?' she wanted to know. There were two or three of us sitting about on bedrolls, and she swept us all with an accusing look, but our innocence could not be doubted. It was established beyond question by the cook.

'I done turned him loose,' he said briefly, lifting the Dutch oven off its bed of coals with a long iron pothook, and Faith said, 'If you didn't want him there, you could have asked me to move him.' She was reasonable even in her anger.

The cook made no reply. Faith's anger mounted. 'Well, you

can just go and bring him back.' The cook stirred the frying potatoes with a big spoon. 'Did you hear me?' Faith's voice was unsteady. 'I said *you could bring my horse back.*'

The cook spoke softly. 'I ain't the horse-wrangler — I'm the cook.' He turned his back on her.

'You bring that horse back or you'll get fired.' Faith was blazing now. 'This is my father's outfit and I'm ordering you to bring that horse back!'

'I ain't the horse-wrangler — I'm the cook.' It was repeated patiently, as one speaks to a child who is slow to comprehend.

'Better go get your own horse, Faith,' I cut in. 'You should know it isn't considered good form in the best cow-country circles to tie your horse to the rear wheel of the chuck-wagon.' And because Faith was fundamentally fair-minded, and had something of her father's sense of humor, she broke down and laughed and set off after her horse herself, followed by her frisking dog.

When told the story, Ray laughed too, but there was not real mirth in it. He seemed to realize more than ever that he could not bring his own ladies wholly into his life. Perhaps he should step over into theirs.

Soon after he sold the ranches I saw him. He was leaning back in a down-stuffed chair in a Southern California hotel. Over-stuffed chairs after the hard leather of a saddle were to him as insufferable as air to a fish.

'Bogging down in luxury is a horrible death,' he said prophetically.

Ray's appearance in court was the last occasion on which he figured as a personal power in Catron County. In 1933 he died, as he had foreseen, 'bogged down in luxury,' of a heart overstrained — or was it broken? — at seeing the dissolution of his life-work written upon the wall. But his presence is still there. Ask any oldtimer. Ask the Alamo Indians. Ask many a returning tourist who has driven back through Datil because he did not know that Ray had gone!

At the top of the divide which separates the Datils from the Alamosa Creek region is a simple little granite monument, which marks the place where his ashes were scattered. Scattering ashes was a new idea in our country, and it was long before some of his cattle-rustling neighbors would use the trail beside which the monument stands.

Ray had achieved in death something he could not achieve in life — keeping those neighbors on their own side of the mountain. I sometimes think as I stand beside his monument that I hear his quiet chuckle, at having had the last word in the contest.

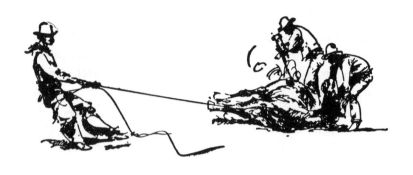

Streak 'COLD-JAWED'

It was almost the last summer of Ray's ranching. This day the 'work' was being held in that famous rough country on the north side of the Datils. Six or eight of us 'cowhands' were to make a drive through the head reaches of all the side cañons leading into Alamosa Creek.

It was arranged that we should hold the smaller bunches as they were driven in, on Woods Spring Flat, and then drive the entire herd over the divide and down Datil Cañon to the head-quarters ranch.

The best horse of the remuda had fallen to my lot, wise old Poker, who knew more about the cattle business than most of his riders.

Jesse Simpson, the range boss, rode Streak, a young animal whose cow education had not yet been completed. His sire had been a race-horse, and Streak seemed to have inherited more of that temperament than he had of 'cow sense.' In fact, Streak was beginning to 'cold-jaw' when he started after a cow brute, a trick which if not checked would of course ruin him for range work.

The first small bunch of cattle were brought to the flat and Jesse delegated me to 'hold them up.' They were fairly gentle and showed no disposition to break away, so I rode quietly around them enjoying myself hugely, with a feeling of recapturing my youth. Then Jesse came in with a few more. I saw he was having trouble with Streak. A third time he appeared, with still more cattle.

'I'm going to need help,' I told him. 'There's a snaky one or two among these last you brought in.'

'All right. Next feller that comes in, tell him to help you,' Jesse called back. 'A couple of steers broke out of my last drive and I want to git 'em before they're plumb gone,' and he was off at a run.

In a few moments he was back. Leaping to the ground beside me, he panted: 'Got to trade horses with you. Just had to knock Streak down with a wallop of my branding iron between his ears. He was fixin' to go over a high rimrock with me. He's plumb subdued now, but I can't handle wild cattle on him; but you can ride herd on this gentle bunch without him runnin' away with *you*.'

I was slightly dubious, particularly since I could not reach the stirrups of Jesse's saddle, and of course there was no time to change saddles. He was off on mine. If one goes along with a cow outfit engaged in serious business, one takes orders! A second later Jesse was out of sight. Dependable old Poker, responsive to every thought in his rider's mind, was under him; and I was aboard Streak!

Cautiously, I began to circle the bunch of cattle in my charge. Streak was as aware of my uneasiness as I was aware of his awareness of it. I knew he was debating just how far he dared make capital of it. I could read it in the way he mouthed that bit.

Then one of the snaky ones, a rangy two-year-old, broke from the bunch on the flat and began trotting toward the densely wooded ridge, on the far side of which stretched the rimrock of Jesse's latest adventure. I put Streak to a gallop to head off the animal, for if he went, the whole bunch went, an entire day's labor lost.

The two-year-old broke into a run as Streak and I came alongside — and I couldn't turn Streak: his race-horse heritage had come out.

I might have done better had my feet been in the stirrups. I like to think so, anyway. As it was, I realized that the horse had again 'cold-jawed.' I recall saying to myself, 'I won't go till I have to.' My regret is that no human eye saw some darned good horsemanship in the next few minutes. You'll have to take my word for it. We went over one rimrock, not so high as where Jesse had not dared risk it; we went under branches of trees and over fallen logs. How I stayed on is a mystery, for without stirrups it reduced itself to a matter of balance and what support there was to be had from the straining bridle reins.

Finally, after a mile or more of it, Streak, exhausted, stopped, and forty years rolled off my age. I was still a cowhand! I rode back exulting.

Jesse was just coming out of the timber on the other side of the flat in close escort of his two big steers, and, of course, there were no rounded-up cattle into which to throw them. The whole bunch had followed the lead of that two-year-old I had been unable to head off, and by now were well lost.

Jesse loped over to me. 'Fine cowhand *you* turned out to be,' he said with frank disgust. 'Couldn't even hold a gentle bunch in an open flat.'

My inflated ego collapsed. I remembered that excuses had no place in cowpuncher economy.

'You might let me have my own saddle,' I murmured, nearest approach to an excuse. We changed saddles, but not horses, in heavy silence. Jesse was too exasperated to trust himself to speak, and I was nursing a deep sense of injury. Hadn't I risked my life on his crazy horse, and what thanks was I getting?

None, gentle reader, none.

But that night in camp, after he had had his supper, and the characteristic reaction in mood of the well-fed male had begun to set in, he spoke a little more gently.

'You must have had some ride,' he acknowledged. Then, as if fearing he had gone too far: 'But you hadn't orter lost them cattle. See you do better tomorrow when we gather them again.'

Meekly, I promised to try.

I knew I had been paid the highest compliment within Jesse's power to bestow when he gave me another chance to make good on a job I once muffed. Of course, critical analysis would seem to show that part of the blame for my muffing it rested upon his own shoulders, but — well, men are men.

Anyhow, I hadn't had to knock Streak down with a branding iron, even though there was one at hand, thrust under the stirrup shield and through one of the latigo straps. Maybe I have it on Jesse after all.

The ox-chain

It was with mixed emotions that I came back to Datil after Ray sold his ranches. If they were no longer to be the Morley Ranches, it seemed important to me that the new owners should be people who would carry on with the understanding of the mind and heart of a cow that had been the especial virtue of the oldtime ranchman. No other kind of person, I was sure, belonged in the Datils. Since I have never considered the highway any part of the real Datils, catering to the tourist trade belongs, in my stubborn opinion, to another world. So I waited a little anxiously to discover just what kind of people the Jeffers tribe, Ray's successors, might prove to be.

At first that turned out to be not so easy as I had hoped — there were so many of them! Headed by 'Uncle Jim' and 'Aunt Ell,' it was a clan of sons, brothers, cousins, nephews. 'Kick a bush and Jefferses will come runnin' out like a bunch of quail,' one of them told me when I asked him to clear my mind about the relationship to one another of these big men who looked all right, but who, nevertheless, seemed not exactly like the cowboys with whom I had grown up.

On my first ride with Bill Jeffers I began to brag how I had 'come foggin' off of this ridge before you were born' when we ran on to a bunch of Jeffers PX cattle grazing in the draw. They raised their heads in the startled fashion I recognized and sniffed the air apprehensively. Now, I told myself, I would see how this latter-day cowboy, who hadn't been born when I raced across that same draw after VV cattle, would handle himself. I waited for Bill to lean forward in his saddle, giving silent direction to his horse, and take out after those PX's at a dead run, to intercept them before they could reach the thick brush of the opposite ridge toward which they had begun to trot.

But that is not what Bill did. He stopped his horse in its tracks and gave a long ingratiating whistle. The cattle also stopped and again sniffed the air. Neither Bill nor I moved and presently the cattle returned to their grazing. Then we rode quietly among them while Bill read brands and made whatever identification he needed for future use. I murmured something about changed methods of cowpunching. Bill sighed, 'This way isn't as much fun, but wild cattle don't make profits.'

Did it make expert cowboys, I wondered, or were all the experts in the movies or following the rodeo circuits? So many of the sons of fathers who had ridden the range for a livelihood had turned their inherited skill to the ends of professional showmanship that I wondered if there were any left in the cow business itself. Could this new generation of cowboys, those who had not gone into the movies, handle a lariat, ride a bronc, throw a diamond hitch with the skill of their fathers? Watching the men of the Jeffers tribe convinced me that they could, especially in that detail of handling a lariat!

One day Bill came to me with the request that I take an eagle for him to the Albuquerque Zoo. 'Bring on your eagle,' I jeered, sure that he was joking. 'Shall I wait for you to rope it?'

'Done roped it,' Bill assured me, 'over by Horse Mountain. Caught him just as he left the ground with a rabbit.'

He came back in a moment with a slatted crate. In it was a large golden eagle. We lashed the crate to the running board of my car. At Belen I looked to see how the eagle fared. He lay limp and gasping on the floor of his cage. I decided it was the heat and sprinkled water over him from the service-station hose. But the eagle was on my mind. It seemed symbolic and I didn't like my own rôle in the symbolism. I stopped the car and again inspected the eagle. He appeared to be a trifle revived and looked me squarely in the eye! I ripped the slats from the top of the crate and stood aside. When he was a speck in the blue — I felt better.

Reassured about the new cowboy, I pondered the question of the new Indian. Is he less himself because he has chosen Levi Straus for his tailor? I think not. He may make his moccasin soles of discarded tire casings and his drums of empty powder kegs with sections of heavy inner tubes for drumheads, but his moccasins wear longer and he chants his age-old chants to the accompaniment of drums whose tone is not inferior to those made of sheep hide stretched over sections of hollowed-out cottonwood log.

And the new homesteader: What of him? Here, certainly, is a different breed from the men who first settled in the Datils. Better or worse? I dare render no judgment. I confine myself to recording the difference.

In 1937 angry men muttered darkly in the streets of Quemado. On many a previous occasion in Quemado the muttering had given place to the spit of gunfire and men lying dead. But these angry men carried no six-shooters and they did not wear high-heeled

boots and broadbrimmed hats. No saddled ponies stood at
hitching-racks. These men had come to town in rickety automobiles over roads that had been surveyed and graded, even if
not surfaced, roads which were 'maintained' and upon which
they would not have long to wait before help reached them should
the unforeseen mishap befall.

Many had come from their little homesteads in western Catron
County, in the midst of piñon and juniper forests. We used to
call that the 'round country' where you met yourself coming back,
so alike were all the contours, so impossible, because of the bush-
like trees, to see distant landmarks by which to take bearings.
Cattle who strayed into the 'round country' were difficult to find
and more difficult to drive out. 'No good for anything' we pronounced it. But many of these men on the streets of Quemado
had come from it: and from the plains to the north and from the
Trechado district and from the Pie Town district and from the
Mangas district, and they had gathered in defense of their homes!
They hinted of 'tar and feathers,' but not of hanging or shooting.
They were a different breed!

They had survived when their less tenacious brethren had left;
they had survived when Ray and others of his kind went under;
they had, thus far, survived the Depression. We of the 'baronial'
class had had much to lose and had lost it. These had very little
and they had gained. Seventy per cent of Catron County had
gone on relief. Like unto the seagulls, who brought salvation to
the early Mormons relief workers had come to their rescue.

To eat was the major economic problem of this new homesteader. In his piñon thicket he need not fear cold. A trip every
few days to a central windmill, with a couple of steel barrels
solved his water problem. He 'owned' his six hundred and forty
acres, but was required to pay no taxes until after that distant
day of 'proving up.' He dressed as well as his neighbors. He suffered no social ostracism. He had but to eat to find life good,

better than any he had heretofore known and now the Government fed him!

Then a black shadow crept across this vale of contentment. Over their dry-cell radios the homesteaders listened to talk of 'resettlement.' With consternation they heard that plans were afoot to move them from their homes and establish them in better farming districts, but upon a third of the number of acres they now claimed. The grapevine that carries news in sparsely settled places buzzed with rumors. The Government which had sent seagulls was now about to send vultures! It was a plot on the part of the predatory 'cattle barons' to get the land back. Over the grapevine went forth the call to resist.

Lora had been appointed a member of the official Planning Board whose duty it would be to acquaint the homesteaders with the advantages of the Government's resettlement program, tell them of the better lands that would be given them in exchange, lands where they could raise their own food and where their children could have easier access to schools. She accompanied the young man who would speak for Uncle Sam at the scheduled mass meeting in Quemado. He was loaded to his fingertips with statistics; the average yearly rainfall, the number of acres required to support a cow, the market price for farm products and the distances these must be hauled to those markets only to compete with more easily, and certainly more copiously produced, commodities. He would explain what a mistake it had been to invite settlement of these 'submarginal lands' in the first place, and tell them that at last a Government with a new sense of social responsibility would rectify the mistakes of a predecessor and give them a fair opportunity to make a living.

He did not deliver his carefully prepared address. When he and Lora drove into town, they were met by the deputy sheriff, who promptly hustled the Government's spokesman off to jail — not as a malefactor, but for safe-keeping lest Quemado suffer the dis-

grace of a tar-and-feather episode. Quemado had been less sensitive to gunplay in the past!

Lora, in spite of her 'baronial' past, went freely among the
mob. Even they, she knew, were not without a sense of the
ridiculous if it could be touched off. She began snapping her
kodak, and announced that she was preparing an article for the
New York Times upon the Wild West of the moment, a Wild West
which asked for relief and then tried to tar and feather the Government's representative for proposing relief in a form that was
unacceptable. In the end the crowd laughed, got into their
jitneys — those without licenses dodging the sheriff — and headed
back toward their homesteads. The official Planning Board held
its meeting in the jail, where it confined its business to checking
the list of relief applicants, leaving the issue of resettlement to
be dealt with by a higher authority.

When Lora told me the story, I felt that it was the final act of
a drama that had opened with my trying to tell some of these
same people some of these same things years earlier. But mine
not to condemn them. These men were defending their homes
according to their own interpretation of inalienable rights. Judgment of one's fellowman is a dangerous sea upon which to em-
bark, no matter what the appearances, so I leave that hazard to
a hardier soul.

Perhaps after one's fellowman is dead, a safer judgment can
be rendered. As this record was going to press, some of his old
friends gathered at Gene Rhodes's grave, high in New Mexico's
San Andreas Mountains, to pay homage to his memory. We sat
on the ground and listened to one another telling simple tales of
his great human kindness, of his quizzical humor, of his prowess
as a cowhand. Not much was said of his literary ability. We felt
less at home in that field. We were swapping yarns with one another, with Alan, his son, with 'Mary and Martha,' serene with
her years and her honors; yarns about the Gene we knew. Cole

Railston, who had been foreman of the Bar X Ranch when Gene worked there, opened his remarks with the statement that he 'wasn't used to speakin' to more'n one feller at a time.' Former Governor Curry, Will Robinson, Watt Gilmore, Bob Martin, Hick Haines, Charley Hardin, and other oldtimers, each in turn spoke in simple tribute to a man they had loved.

When it was over, Cole Railston, slightly deaf, spoke to me judicially, 'I couldn't hear a word you said, but you seemed to be actin' all right.' Then, carrying his critical judgment farther, 'Gene was all we said he was — except that he could never water a trail herd right,' meaning as Cole watered one. Honesty came first with Cole. For that reason, Gene had loved him! I think he would have chuckled delightedly over that remark of Cole's could he have heard it!

We were a weather-beaten little crew, who still defied life to lick us. We carry our little chips on our shoulders jauntily. My own chip is the old ox-chain.

Bill Jeffers is responsible for my having the chain — supreme magnanimity after my turning his eagle loose! He not only forgave me for that, but went so far as to invite me to head a party to stay in his remotest camp on the Alamosa — the old Bob McCord place, not far from where, forty years earlier, two overawed little girls had gazed at the scene of an Indian massacre. As we drove up to the little log cabin, which was never left locked, my eyes bulged. 'That's sure Billy Swingle's chain,' I cried. It was stretched between two huge juniper posts set deep in the ground. Bob McCord had made his hitching-rack secure, so secure, in fact, that he had left it when he leased the place.

'Want it?' asked Bill. 'It's yours.'

But it was not to be that easy. While Bill's generosity was beyond question, his title to the chain was not. There was Bob McCord to be reckoned with — and others. They were duly reckoned with, in traditional fashion. By the time we had reck-

oned with them, someone else had possessed himself of the chain.
I got it, as he got it, completely illegally. Now is my turn to
own it — if I can keep it! My immediate predecessor in claiming
it has threatened to tack my scalp to his fencepost in reprisal for
my having come by it without his knowledge and very much
without his consent. I take his threat as familiar ritual; and I
hereby serve notice that I too have a large undecorated fencepost.

Because I see in its rusty links an unbroken tie with that past
wherein we held that 'a six-shooter makes all men equal,' but used
that six-shooter less frequently than we talked of doing, I love the
ox-chain. It is a souvenir; but not a souvenir at rest: its iron soul
still stirs within it.

The figger-4 roan

A FENDERLESS model T crunched to a stop in the loose gravel in front of the Lodge. Over its wired-up door stepped its driver, grinning broadly, his grizzled whiskers tobacco-stained, his pale eyes alight with friendliness. He held out a scaly hand. 'Howdy,' he greeted me; 'heered you was here and come over to tell you I ain't never forgot the favor you done me the first day I hit this here country. Seems good to see a oldtimer, what with all these newcomers takin' the country! Bet yo're glad to be back here yoreself.'

I assured him that I was, but hadn't the heart to add that I couldn't recall any favor I had done for him, nor even his name. He spared me the confession. 'Remember the day I rode up to the old Swinging W's and asked the way to the JL's? You tried to tell me about the trail through Swingle Cañon, but I was just from the Staked Plains over in Texas and these here mountains had me buffaloed, so, when you seen I wasn't sure what you meant, you saddled up yore horse and rode with me to the top of Swingle Cañon divide and pointed out the JL windmill. You was ridin' a little roan branded figger 4; had a runnin' walk and flung his head. You remember him, don't you?'

Yes, I remembered the 'figger-4 roan' and from that cue the embers of long-forgotten memories began to glow. My caller was rambling on: 'Them was the good old days. Can't ride no-wheres now 'thout runnin' into a bob-wire fence and meetin' up with some feller drivin' a Jersey cow.'

I was listening with only half my mind. With the other half I was trying to span the gap between this me and the young girl who had ridden three hours with an anything but handsome youth who offered no slightest romantic recompense, merely because he was a stranger needing a guide. It was then that this record began to formulate itself; that I began to want to put into some semblance of permanent form the story of the girl who had vanished, and her life, the life that was not for what the world calls a lady.

THE END